Simon Stafford
Nikon D200

P9-CPX-437

Magic Lantern Guides

Nikon D200

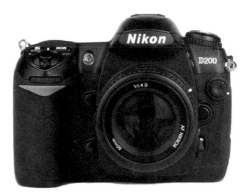

Simon Stafford

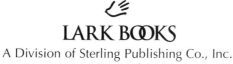

LARK BOOKS
A Division of Sterling Publishing Co., Inc.
New York

Editor: Danielle Andes
Book Design and Layout: Michael Robertson
Cover Designer: Thom Gaines
Editorial Assistance: Delores Gosnell and Dawn Dillingham

Library of Congress Cataloging-in-Publication Data

Stafford, Simon.
  Nikon D200 / Simon James Stafford. -- 1st ed.
     p. cm. -- (Magic lantern guides)
  Includes index.
  ISBN 1-57990-886-1 (pbk.)
  1. Nikon camera--Handbooks, manuals, etc. 2. Digital cameras--Handbooks,
manuals, etc. I. Title.
  TR263.N5S7328 2006
  771.3'3--dc22
                             2006020567

10 9 8 7 6 5 4 3 2

First Edition

Published by Lark Books, A Division of
Sterling Publishing Co., Inc.
387 Park Avenue South, New York, N.Y. 10016

Text © 2007, Simon Stafford
Photography © 2007, Simon Stafford unless otherwise specified

Distributed in Canada by Sterling Publishing,
c/o Canadian Manda Group, 165 Dufferin Street
Toronto, Ontario, Canada M6K 3H6

Distributed in the United Kingdom by GMC Distribution Services,
Castle Place, 166 High Street, Lewes, East Sussex, England BN7 1XU

Distributed in Australia by Capricorn Link (Australia) Pty Ltd.,
P.O. Box 704, Windsor, NSW 2756 Australia

The written instructions, photographs, designs, patterns, and projects in this volume are intended for
the personal use of the reader and may be reproduced for that purpose only. Any other use, especially
commercial use, is forbidden under law without written permission of the copyright holder.

Every effort has been made to ensure that all the information in this book is accurate. However, due to
differing conditions, tools, and individual skills, the publisher cannot be responsible for any injuries,
losses, and other damages that may result from the use of the information in this book. Because specifications may be changed by manufacturers without notice, the contents of this book may not necessarily agree with software and equipment changes made after publication.

If you have questions or comments about this book, please contact:
Lark Books
67 Broadway
Asheville, NC 28801
(828) 253-0467

Manufactured in the U.S.A.

All rights reserved

ISBN 13: 978-1-57990-886-7
ISBN 10: 1-57990-886-1

For information about custom editions, special sales, premium and corporate purchases, please contact Sterling Special Sales Department at 800-805-5489 or specialsales@sterlingpub.com.

Contents

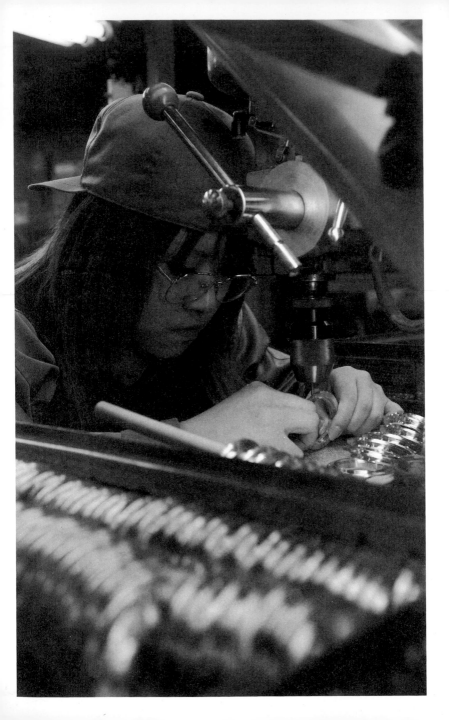

Introduction

The announcement from Nikon in early 2006 that production of all film cameras, with the exception of the F6, was to cease by mid 2006 is a clear and unequivocal message that the future of mainstream photography, regardless of whether it is performed at an enthusiast or professional level, is going to be digital. I am sure it is no coincidence that this message followed closely on the heels of Nikon's launch of the D200, a mid-range digital SLR intended to fill the yawning gap between the company's entry-level cameras, such as the D50 and D70s, and its flagship D2Xs model.

The Nikon Corporation has accrued many years of experience building digital cameras. Their first and second generation digital SLR (D-SLR) cameras, the D1, followed by the D1X and D1H, broke new ground technically and made high quality digital photography financially viable for many professional photographers. Subsequently, with advances in sensor technology, their third generation camera, the D100, pushed resolution beyond that of their earlier models. Its good technical specifications coupled with the fact that it was about half the price of a D1X tempted many keen enthusiasts to take the digital plunge! Building on these solid foundations, the company went on to introduce several more cameras, including those in the professionally specified D2-series, the D50 entry-level camera, and the phenomenally successful D70-series camera models. It is from this heritage that Nikon has introduced the D200.

The D200 is assembled at Nikon's production facility in Thailand.

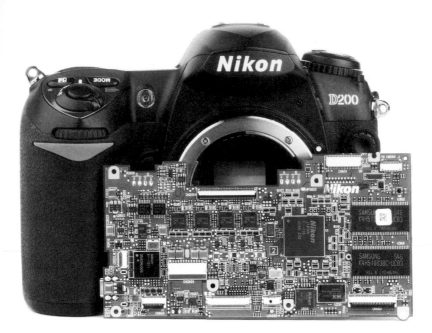

The D200's main circuit board is produced at the Nikon factory in Sendai, Japan.

The Nikon Corporation is hardly renowned for introducing new camera models at a frequency to match some of its well-known rivals, but as the replacement for its aging D100 camera launched during mid-2002, the protracted gestation of the D200 tried the patience of even the most ardent Nikon devotees. In the interim, many of them turned to the newer D70-series cameras as an alternative. So, has the wait been worth it? The short the answer is a categorical yes!

Nikon's accomplishment with the D200 is remarkable; by combining features inherited from the evolutionary line of the D100, D70, and D50 cameras, and incorporating the latest digital imaging technologies seen in the D2Xs, the D200 camera has moved up market by leaps and bounds, making any further comparison to the D100 meaningless. It is a photographic tool that has the flexibility to be used either in a simple, fully automatic point-and-shoot style, or with total user control of all its features and functions. Consequently, it is capable of meeting the requirements of a very broad band of photographers, from the dedicated enthusiast to the full-time professional.

Production of the Nikon D200

The D200 is assembled at Nikon's wholly owned production facility in Thailand, about 50 miles (80 km) north of Bangkok, Thailand's present day capital. (I say "assembled" because a number of the D200's core parts are manufactured elsewhere, such as the camera's main circuit board and its associated electronic components, which are produced at the Nikon factory in Sendai, Japan.) The Nikon Thailand plant has nearly fifteen years experience in precision manufacturing, including production of the Nikon F80, F65, F75, and F55 cameras along with a wide range of modern autofocus lenses.

About This Book

To get the most from your D200, it is important that you understand its features so you can make informed choices about how to use them in conjunction with your style of photography. This book is designed to help you achieve such an understanding. Besides explaining how all the basic functions work, this book also provides you with useful tips on operating the D200 and maximizing its performance. You do not necessarily need to read it from cover to cover; you can move from section to section as required, study a complete chapter, or just absorb the key features of functions you want to use.

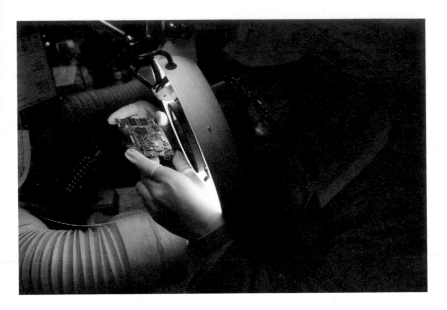

The key to success, regardless of your level of experience, is to practice with your camera. You do not waste money on film and processing costs with a digital camera; once you have invested in a memory card, it can be used over and over again. Therefore, you can shoot as many pictures as you like, review your results almost immediately, and then delete your near misses and save your successes. This trial and error method is a very effective way to learn!

Conventions Used In This Book
Unless otherwise stated, when the terms "left" and "right" are used to describe the location of a camera control, it is assumed that the camera is being held in the shooting position. In describing the functionality of lenses and external flash units, it is assumed that the appropriate Nikkor lenses (generally D- or G-type) and Nikon Speedlight units are

being used. Note that lenses and flash units made by independent manufacturers may not necessarily function properly with the D200. If you use such products, refer to that product manufacturer's instruction manual to check for compatibility and operational details. When referring to applicable Nikon software, it is assumed that the most recent versions of each application are used. At the very least, the D200 requires Nikon PictureProject version 1.6.1 or newer, Nikon View version 6.2.7 or newer, or the optional Nikon Capture version 4.4.0 or newer to ensure compatibility with D200 image files.

Simon Stafford
Wiltshire, England

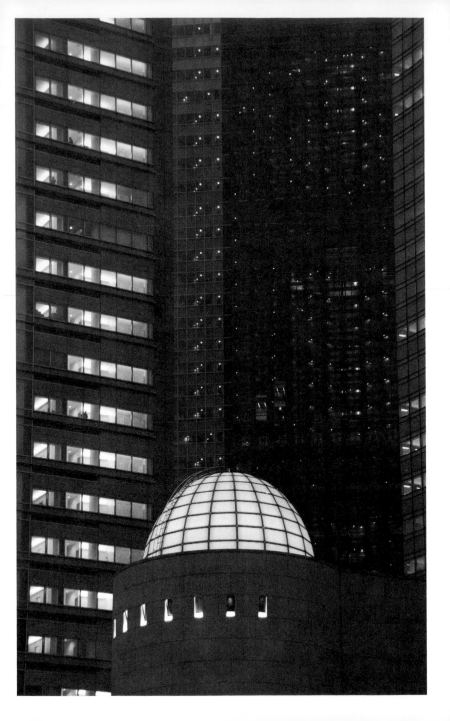

Introducing the Nikon D200

Design

In designing the D200, Nikon adopted an approach aimed at integrating the ease of operation of their popular D-SLR (digital single-lens reflex) models, such as the D100 and D70-series, with the professional specifications and performance of their "flagship" D2-series cameras. Through this melding of qualities, they have produced a camera that can be used by people at any level of experience, from the relatively inexperienced hobby photographer who seeks nothing more than point-and-shoot convenience all the way up to meeting the demands of professional photographers.

Externally, the D200 appears somewhat similar to its predecessor, the D100. This is due in large part to its compact size, but in truth, that is as far as the similarity goes. The D200 has an all-metal frame with extensive sealing to prevent moisture and dust from getting inside. It also has an entirely new 10.2-megapixel CCD sensor that supports four-channel processing (first seen in the original D2X camera) to speed up the movement of data from the sensor to the memory card. This fast data transfer combined with a completely new mechanical shutter design permits a maximum five frame-per-second (5 fps) frame rate. Another new aspect of the D200 camera is its autofocus system, which has not been seen in any previous Nikon camera. Add to this a set of features, control layout, and a comprehensive menu system that closely mirrors those of the D2Xs and you will soon realize the D200's incredible potential.

The flexibility of options on the Nikon D200 cater to any photographic situation, whether you are shooting quick snapshots at a family picnic or long exposures at night.

The D200 is an interchangeable lens D-SLR camera that offers complete automation of exposure and focusing, as well as full manual control of all its features and functions. The camera body is built around a very sturdy magnesium alloy frame that gives a solid, rugged feel to the camera. Its approximate dimensions are 5.8 x 4.4 x 2.9 inches (147 x 113 x 74 mm), and it weighs about 29 ounces (830 g) without battery or memory card. Data storage is to either a CompactFlash card (Type I or II) or a Microdrive.

The D200 has a Nikon F lens mount with an automatic focusing (AF) coupling and electrical contacts. The origins of this lens mount design can be traced back to the Nikon F 35mm SLR introduced back in 1959; many early Nikkor lenses can be used with the D200. The greatest level of compatibility, however, is achieved with either AF-D or AF-G type Nikkor lenses. Other lenses can be used but they provide a variable level of compatibility; AF and Ai-P type Nikkor lenses offer a slightly reduced functionality in terms of the camera's TTL metering system, but even manual focus Ai, Ai-s, Ai converted, and E-series Nikkor lenses can be used with the D200.

Note: When the terms "left" and "right" are used to describe the locations of camera components, it is assumed that the camera is being held in the shooting position.

Nikon D200 – Front View

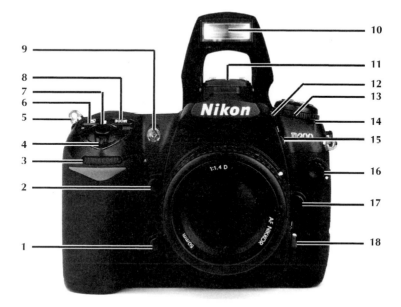

1. FUNC. button
2. Depth-of-Field Preview button
3. Sub-command dial
4. Power/Illuminator switch
5. Eyelet for camera strap
6. Exposure Compensation ⊞ /Reset button ●
7. Shutter release button
8. Exposure Mode/Format button 🗚
9. AF-assist illuminator/Self-timer and red-eye reduction lamp

10. Built-in flash
11. Accessory shoe
12. Flash pop-up button
13. Mode dial
14. Mode dial lock release
15. Flash Sync Mode ● / Flash Compensation button 🗲
16. 10-pin remote terminal
17. Lens release button
18. Focus mode selector

Nikon D200 – Back View

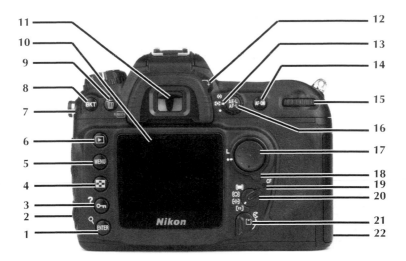

1. Enter ⊕ /Playback
   Zoom button ♀
2. Connectors cover
3. Protect ⊕ /Help button
4. Thumbnail button ⊕
5. MENU button ⊕
6. Playback button ⊕
7. Flash sync terminal
8. Bracketing button ⊕
9. Delete ⊕ /Format
   button [FORMAT]
10. LCD Monitor

11. Viewfinder
12. Diopter adjustment control
13. Metering selector
14. AF-ON button ⊕
15. Main command dial
16. AE/AF Lock button ⊕
17. Multi Selector
18. Focus selector lock
19. Memory card access lamp
20. AF-area mode selector
21. Card slot cover latch
22. Memory card slot cover

Nikon D200 – Top View

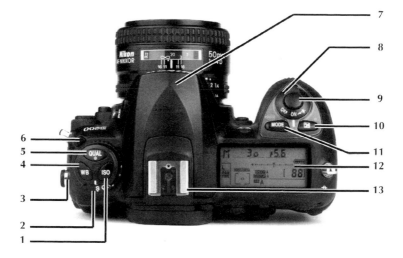

1. ISO sensitivity button ISO
2. Mode dial
3. Flash sync terminal
4. White Balance button WB
5. Image Quality/Size QUAL /
   Reset button ●
6. Mode dial lock release
7. Built-in flash

8. Power/Illuminator switch
9. Shutter release button
10. Exposure Compensation
    ● / Reset button ●
11. Exposure Mode ● /
    Format button FORMAT
12. Control panel
13. Accessory shoe

Power

A single Nikon EN-EL3e (7.4V, 1500mAh) rechargeable Lithium-ion battery that weighs approximately 2.8 ounces (80 g) powers the D200; it is distinguished from other types of EN-EL3 batteries by its light grey casing. There is no alternative power source for the D200 that can be fitted internally; no other type of non-rechargeable or rechargeable battery can be used. Battery performance is dependent on a number of factors, including the condition of the battery, the camera functions and features being used, and the air temperature. At a normal room temperature of 68°F (20°C) the power-up time of the camera is just 0.15 seconds, and it is quite possible to make many hundreds of exposures on a single fully charged EN-EL3e. The Nikon EH-6 AC adapter can also support the D200 for extended periods of use.

Note: The D200 is not compatible with the earlier EN-EL3 (7.4V, 1400mAh) or EN-EL3a (7.4V, 1500mAh) batteries used with the Nikon D70-series and D50 cameras, although these camera models are compatible with the D200's EN-EL3e battery.

MB-D200 Battery Pack

The MB-D200 is a battery pack/grip that attaches to the base of the standard D200 body via the tripod socket. It can accept either one or two EN-EL3e batteries, or six AA-sized batteries that must be fitted in the MS-D200 battery holder. In addition to providing extra battery capacity, the MB-D200 has a shutter release button, Main and Sub-command dials, and an AF-ON button to improve handling when the camera is held in the vertical (portrait) orientation.

Hint: Fitting the MB-D200 requires the battery chamber door of the D200 camera to be removed. To prevent its loss, stow the battery chamber door in the slot set in to the shaft of the MB-D200 that enters the camera's battery chamber.

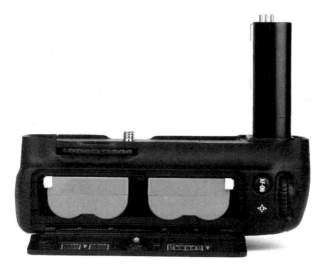

The MB-D200 battery pack can be fitted with one or two EN-EL3e batteries.

Note: All electronically controlled cameras very occasionally exhibit some strange behavior with unexpected icons or characters appearing in the LCD displays, or the camera simply ceases to function properly. This is usually due an external electrostatic charge. To remedy the situation, try turning the camera off, remove and replace the battery (or disconnect then reconnect the AC adapter if you're using that as your power source), then turn the camera on again.

The Sensor

The CCD (Charge Coupled Device) sensor used in the D200 is unique to the camera. Produced by Sony (a fact not officially acknowledged by Nikon), it has a total of 10.92 million pixels, of which 10.2 million are effective image forming areas. Each pixel is 5.9 microns (mm) square. This gives the camera a maximum resolution of 3872 x 2592 pixels, sufficient to produce 11 x 16 inch (27.5 x 40 cm) prints at 240 ppi without interpolation (resizing).

The sensor dimensions are .66 x 1 inch (15.6 x 23.7 mm), which is smaller than a 35mm film frame of 1 x 1.5 in (24 x 36 mm), though it does retain the same 2:3 aspect ratio. Nikon calls this their DX-format (elsewhere it is often referred to as the APS-C format) and they use the same DX designation to identify those lenses that have been optimized for use with their D-SLR cameras. Due to the smaller size of the DX-format digital sensor, the angle-of-view offered by any focal length is reduced when compared with a lens of the same focal length used on a 35mm film camera. This effect is commonly referred to as the magnification factor. Given the size difference between the D200's sensor and a 35mm frame of film, the focal length of a lens used on the D200 should be multiplied by a magnification factor of 1.5x to provide you with the effective focal length (see pages 261-263 for a full explanation).

In front of the CCD sensor is an array of filters/layers with four specific purposes. There is the Bayer pattern filter, the micro-lens layer, the low-pass anti-aliasing filter, and the infrared coating layer. The following sections describe the functions of these various components in detail.

Bayer Pattern Filter
The pixels on the CCD sensor do not see in color; they can only detect brightness levels. To impart color to the image, a series of minute red, green, and blue filters are arranged over the pixels in a Bayer pattern (named after the Kodak engineer who invented it). These filters are arranged in an alternating pattern of red/green on the odd numbered rows and green/blue on the even numbered rows. The final image—made up of 50% green, 25% red, and 25% blue—is reconstructed when the camera's microprocessor interpolates the values at each pixel site.

Micro-Lens Layer

A CCD sensor is most efficient when the light striking it is perpendicular to its surface. To help realign the light rays projected by the camera lens onto the sensor pixels, the filter array contains a layer of micro-lenses. These help to achieve more efficient image capture by adjusting the angle of the light to ensure that the sensor is functioning at its ideal capacity.

Low-Pass Anti-Aliasing Filter

When you take a picture of a scene that contains very fine detail (i.e., the weave pattern in a piece of material) it is possible that the frequency of this detail matches, or is close to, that of the pixel sites on the sensor. This can lead to color fringes appearing between two areas of different color or tone on either side of a distinct edge. The low-pass anti-aliasing filter softens the image formed on the sensor to reduce the risk of this occurring.

Infrared Coating Layer

Although infrared (IR) light is not visible to the human eye, a CCD sensor can detect it. This is a problem in digital cameras because IR light can cause a perceived loss of image sharpness, reduced contrast, and other unwanted effects such as color shifts. Therefore, the newly developed optical low-pass filter used in the D200 has an anti-reflective IR coating that virtually eliminates the transmission of IR light to the sensor. Consequently, the D200 cannot be used for digital IR photography in the way that some earlier Nikon D-SLR cameras (such as the D1 and D100) can.

The Shutter

The electronically timed all-new mechanical shutter used in the D200 is impressive; the release lag time is just 50 milliseconds, with a viewfinder (mirror) blackout time of only 105 milliseconds and a maximum flash sync speed of 1/250 second (assuming Auto FP High-Speed Sync mode is not active – see page 250 for details). Apparently, a mechanical shutter was chosen in preference to an electro-mechanical shutter type, in which, above a certain point, a faster shutter speed is emulated by switching the sensor on and off for the appropriate duration in order to maintain image quality with a sensor that has so many pixels.

The D200's shutter speed range runs from 30 seconds all the way up to 1/8000 second and can be set in increments of 1/3,1/2, and 1 EV. There is a Bulb option for long exposures beyond 30 seconds. The D200 has a noise reduction option that can be set to operate at shutter speeds of 8 seconds or longer, however, the recording time is extended by 50 - 100% (see pages 181-182 for details).

The Viewfinder

The D200 has a fixed optical pentaprism eye-level viewfinder that shows approximately 95% (vertical and horizontal) of what the sensor actually sees. It has an eye-point of 19.5 mm, which should provide a reasonably good view of the focusing screen and viewfinder information for users who wear eyeglasses. There is also a built-in diopter adjustment that can be set from −2.0 to +1.0m-1. To set the diopter to suit your eye, mount a lens on the camera and leave it set to infinity. Then, point the camera at a plain surface that fills the frame and rotate the diopter adjustment control (on the right side of the viewfinder eyepiece) until the AF sensor brackets appear sharp. It is essential to do this to ensure you see the sharpest view of the focusing screen. Since the built-in correction is not particularly strong, optional viewfinder eyepiece correction lenses are available for between −5 to +3m^{-1}. These correction lenses are attached by slotting them onto the eyepiece frame. (The rubber eyecup must be removed first.)

The viewfinder eyepiece does not have an internal shutter to prevent light from entering when the D200 is used remotely. For this reason, the camera is supplied with the DK-5 eyepiece cap. This cap is fitted to the camera using the same method as the eyepiece correction lenses (described above).

The focusing screen is fixed and the viewfinder provides a very useful magnification of approximately .94x (much better than the D70-series and D50 cameras). The viewfinder display includes all the essential information about exposure and focus, including shutter speed, lens aperture, exposure compensation factor, ISO value, metering pattern, focus confirmation, battery status indicator, and flash ready signal. The focusing screen is marked with four arcs to define a central reference circle, 8 mm in diameter, and eleven small squares to indicate the center point of each autofocus area. The D200 employs holographic illumination in place of the more conventional LED type illumination for its focusing screen, so the screen only shows the bracket markings for the active focus area, which makes the rest of the viewfinder image far less cluttered and easier to see. There is a user selectable reference grid pattern that can also be displayed, which is very useful for aligning critical compositions and keeping horizons level.

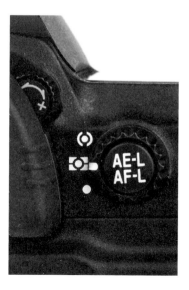

The diopter adjustment control is located on the right side of the viewfinder eyepiece on the camera back.

Viewfinder

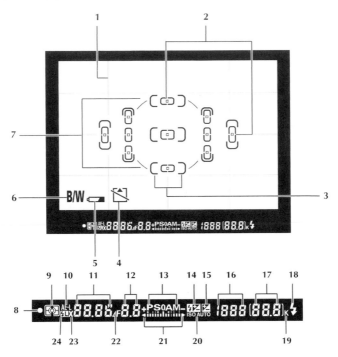

1. Framing grid (displayed when ON is selected for Custom Setting d2 (Grid Display)
2. Normal-frame focus brackets (focus areas)
3. Wide-frame focus brackets (focus areas)
4. "No memory card" warning
5. Battery indicator
6. Black-and-white indicator
7. 8-mm (0.31-inch) reference circle for center-weighted metering
8. Focus indicator
9. Metering
10. Autoexposure (AE) lock
11. Shutter speed
12. Aperture (f/number) & number of stops
13. Exposure mode

14. Flash compensation indicator
15. Exposure compensation indicator
16. ISO sensitivity
17. Number of exposures/shots remaining before buffer fills/ Preset white balance recording indicator/Exposure & flash compensation values/ PC connection indicator
18. Flash-ready indicator
19. "K" (appears when memory remains for over 1000 exposures)
20. Auto sensitivity indicator
21. Electronic analog exposure display
22. Aperture stop indicator
23. Flash sync indicator
24. Flash value (FV) lock

Control Panel

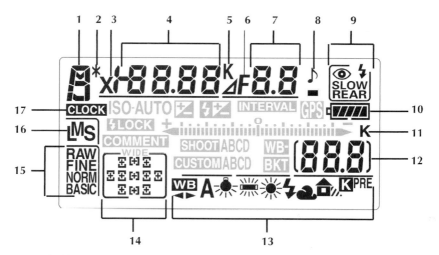

1. Exposure mode
2. Flexible program indicator
3. Flash sync indicator
4. Shutter speed/Exposure & Flash compensation values/ISO/White balance fine-tuning, color temperature, & preset number/ Number of shots in bracketing sequence
5. Color temperature indicator
6. Aperture stop indicator
7. Aperture (f/number) & number of stops/Bracketing increment/ Number of shots per interval/ Maximum aperture/ PC connection indicator

8. "Beep" indicator
9. Flash sync mode
10. Battery indicator
11. "K" (appears when memory remains for over 1000 exposures)
12. Number of shots remaining/Shots remaining before buffer fills/PC mode indicator/Preset white balance recording indicator
13. White balance mode
14. Focus area/AF-area mode
15. Image quality
16. Image size
17. "Clock not set" indicator

The Control Panel

This large monochrome LCD display on the top of the D200 is called the control panel, not to be confused with the color LCD monitor on the camera back. If the power is switched off, the only information shown in the control panel will be the number of remaining frames available on the memory card; if no card is inserted, the control panel will display (**-E-**) . As soon as the camera is turned on, the

31

Control Panel

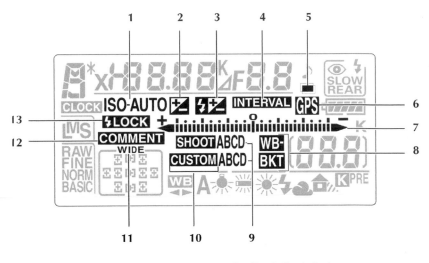

1. ISO sensitivity indicator
2. Exposure compensation indicator
3. Flash compensation indicator
4. Interval time indicator
5. Multiple exposure indicator
6. GPS connection indicator
7. Electronic analog exposure display/Exposure compensation/Bracketing progress indicator/PC connection indicator
8. Bracketing indicator
9. Shooting menu bank
10. Custom menu bank
11. Wide-frame focus area indicator
12. Image comment indicator
13. Flash value (FV) lock

control panel will display a wide range of camera settings, including battery status, shutter speed, aperture, shooting mode, active focus sensor and focus mode, white balance, audible warning, and image quality and size. Other controls will be also be indicated on the control panel if and when they are activated.

The LCD Monitor

On the rear of the D200 is a 2.5-inch (6.35 cm), 230,000-pixel color LCD monitor that offers a viewing angle of 170° which, unlike the viewfinder display, shows virtually 100% of the image file during image review. Pictures can be reviewed either as a single image or in multiples. When used to display a single image, the review function has a zoom capability that enables you to enlarge the image by up to 25 times.

Using the Multi Selector, you can scroll through a range of seven pages (or eight if a GPS unit was attached to the camera when an image was recorded) containing shooting information. These info pages are superimposed on images reviewed in single-image playback. There is a page of basic information, a page of file information, two pages of shooting data, a single page showing individual histograms for each color channel (red, green, and blue) plus a histogram for the composite channel, a page with a single composite channel histogram, and a page that displays a highlight warning option that causes potentially overexposed areas to blink. The eighth page displays Global Positioning System (GPS) data if it was recorded at the same time as the image.

You can also edit your pictures in-camera by reviewing them on the LCD monitor. You will have the option to delete them one at a time or erase the entire memory card worth of shots, or you can protect images from being deleted unintentionally (see page 109 for more details). In addition, the LCD monitor is used to display the various camera menus, from which you can activate or deactivate a wide range of camera features and functions. The brightness of the LCD monitor screen can be adjusted via the Setup Menu.

Menus

Although most of the principal controls of the D200 can be easily accessed and operated by buttons or dials located on the camera body, there are some core functions that must be set via the camera's four menus: Playback ▶ , Shooting ◻ , Custom Settings ✐ , and Setup ⛾ . To facilitate access to items in the Shooting and Custom Setting menus, the D200 has a fifth menu known as the Recent Settings menu ▤ . It displays the fourteen items used most recently from the two former menus, and can be customized to save you the time of having to open and navigate through the Shooting and Custom Settings menus to make a change.

To access the menus, press the Menu button ● on the camera back to the left of the LCD monitor. Select the appropriate menu by using the Multi Selector. The various options and sub-options are color coded to facilitate navigation and selection of the required setting. The D200 supports menus in no less than thirteen different languages (selectable via the Setup menu).

The Autofocus System

The D200's autofocus system is based on the new CAM1000 AF module (i.e., the system has 1000 individual points that are assessed in the process of focus acquisition). It features seven individual sensing areas arranged in a diamond pattern. The central sensor area is a cross-type, whereas the other six (top, bottom, inner left, outer left, inner right, and outer right) are single line sensor areas. The inner left and inner right sensors can be configured to act as three separate focus sensing areas; this provides the D200 with the ability to be used with either an 11-area AF or 7 wide-area AF system. The latter helps to improve the camera's ability to acquire focus with a moving subject.

The detection range of the AF system is –1 to +19 EV at ISO 100. In low light, there is an AF assist lamp that has an effective range from 1ft. 8 inches – 9ft. 10 inches (0.5m - 3m). The system has three focusing modes: single-servo focus, continuous-servo focus, and manual focus. There are four focus area modes: Single-area AF, Dynamic-area AF, Group-Dynamic-area AF, and Dynamic-area AF with Closest Subject Priority. In the continuous-servo focus mode the camera will activate predictive focus tracking automatically if it detects subject movement at any point while the autofocus system is operating. The camera will attempt to predict the position of the subject at the moment the shutter is released. In single-servo focus mode, focus tracking will only operate if the AF system detected subject movement at the time autofocus was activated. The D200 also has Nikon's proprietary Lock-On system that controls whether the camera re-focuses if the subject-to-camera distance changes significantly in an abrupt manner (see pages 146-163 for full details of the focusing system).

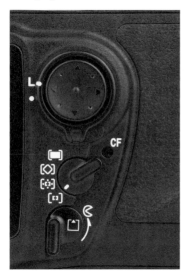

The AF-area mode selector is located on the camera back to the right of the LCD monitor. Use it to select single-area AF [ ] , dynamic-area AF [ ] , group-dynamic-area AF [ ] , or dynamic-area AF with closest subject priority [ ] .

Exposure Modes

The D200 offers four exposure modes that determine how the lens aperture and shutter speed values are set when the exposure is adjusted: Programmed Auto (P), Aperture-Priority Auto (A), Shutter-Priority Auto (S), and Manual (M). The following is a short break-down of each mode:

P – Programmed Auto selects a combination of shutter speed and aperture automatically, but the photographer can override this using the flexible program feature (see pages 86-87).

A – Aperture-Priority Auto mode allows the photographer to select the lens aperture while the camera assigns an appropriate shutter speed.

S – Shutter-Priority Auto mode allows the photographer to select the shutter speed while the camera assigns an appropriate lens aperture.

M – Manual mode places selection of both the shutter speed and lens aperture in the hands of the photographer.

Exposure compensation can be set within a range of –5 to +5 stops in increments of 1/3, 1/2, or 1 EV. Exposure bracketing and/or flash exposure bracketing are both available for either 2 or 3 frame sequences in increments of 1/3, 1/2, 2/3, or 1 EV. In the automatic exposure modes (P, S, and A), the exposure settings can be locked using the AE/AF lock button located on the camera back to the right of the viewfinder eyepiece.

The AE/AF lock button is in the center of the metering selector on the camera back, just right of the viewfinder eyepiece.

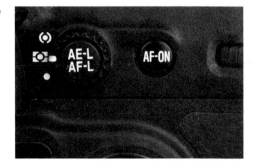

The D200 has a sensitivity range (ISO equivalent) between ISO 100 and ISO 1600 that can be set in steps of 1/3 EV. Additionally, the sensitivity can be increased by up to 1 EV above ISO 1600, again in steps of 1/3 EV, to an equivalent ISO rating of 3200. The camera also has a noise reduction function that can be activated for use with ISO 400 or above (see page 182 for details).

Exposure Control

The D200 offers three options within its TTL metering system, enabling the camera to respond to a variety of different lighting situations.

3D Color Matrix Metering II 🔲

The D200 uses a 1005-pixel RGB sensor within the camera's viewfinder to assess the brightness, color and contrast of light with this metering method. Additional information from compatible lenses (D-type or G-type Nikkor lenses) and the autofocus system is also taken in to account; based on the focused distance and which focus sensor is active, the camera makes an assumption as to the likely position of the subject within the frame area. The D200 then uses a reference of over thirty thousand examples of photographed scenes and compares these with the information from the metering system to provide a final exposure value.

Note: Standard Color Matrix Metering is performed if other CPU type lenses or certain non-CPU lenses (i.e., Ai, Ai-modified, Ai-s, and E-series lenses) are mounted.

Center-Weighted Metering 🔲

The camera meters using the entire frame area, but it assigns a bias to the central 8 mm (.31 inch) circle at a ratio of 75:25. (The diameter of the metered area can be altered from within the Custom Settings menu—see pages 206-207.)

Spot Metering 🔲

The camera meters a 3 mm (0.1 inch) diameter circle, which represents approximately 2% of the full frame area, and is centered on the selected (active) focus area brackets. This occurs regardless of whether the 11-area or 7 wide-area AF mode is selected (see pages 158-159).

White Balance

The D200 offers several choices for white balance control, including a fully automatic option **A** that uses the same 1005-pixel RGB sensor in the viewfinder as the metering system. Then there are six user-selectable manual modes for specific lighting conditions: Tungsten ☀ for incandescent lighting, Fluorescent ⚏ for fluorescent lighting, Direct Sunlight ☀ for sunny days outdoors, Flash ⚡ for lighting from the built-in flash or external flash units, Cloudy ☁ for daylight under an overcast sky, and Shade ☗ for daylight in deep shade. Each of these settings can be fine-tuned to impart a slightly warmer (redder) or cooler (bluer) tone.

In addition, the D200 has an option that allows you to set the white balance control to a specific color temperature, choosing from 31 different values expressed in degrees Kelvin **K** . Or, you can use the white balance preset option **PRE** that allows you to use the camera to assess the color temperature of the prevailing light as reflected from an appropriate test target (see pages 119-121 for instructions). Up to five preset white balance values can be stored in the camera and recalled as needed.

Shooting Modes

The shooting mode determines when the camera makes an exposure. In single frame mode the camera takes a single photograph each time the shutter release button is fully depressed. In continuous low-speed mode the camera shutter cycles up to a maximum rate of 4 fps (frames per second); in high-speed continuous mode the maximum is 5 fps. However, the effective frame rate will be limited by a number of factors, including the camera functions that are active, the selected shutter speed, and the capacity of the remaining memory buffer.

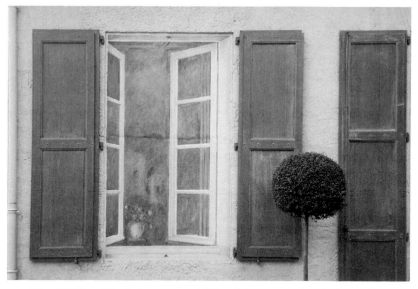

The D200's white balance capabilities take you a step further, offering fine-tuning for all of the preset white balance settings to ensure you achieve exactly the look you are aiming for.

Self-Timer Mode

The self-timer mode is useful for self-portraits or reducing loss of sharpness caused by camera vibrations (although in this respect it is not as effective as using the mirror lock-up feature—see below) or hand shake at slow shutter speeds. The delay of the self-timer can be set to 2, 5, 10, or 20 seconds.

Mirror Lock-Up

The D200 can be set so that its reflex mirror is raised and locked in the up position before the shutter is released to eliminate the risk of internal camera vibrations, caused by the movement of the mirror, that may affect the sharpness of an image. This is a two-stage feature during which the first press of the shutter release causes the reflex mirror to be raised and locked in place, then the second press of the shutter release operates the shutter mechanism.

Note: This feature should not be confused with the lock-up feature for the reflex mirror used to facilitate cleaning the surface of the filter array in front of the camera's sensor (see page 186).

Both the self-timer ☉ and Mirror-Up Mᵤₚ can be selected from the Mode dial on the left top of the camera.

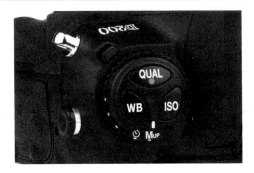

File Formats

The D200 records images using two file types: those compressed using the JPEG standard, and those saved in Nikon's proprietary Nikon Electronic File (NEF) RAW format. The NEF files can be saved in either an uncompressed or compressed form. The files recorded using the JPEG standard can be saved at three different sizes, Fine (low compression 1:4), Normal (medium compression 1:8), and Low (high compression 1:16). As the level of compression increases, more image detail is lost. Furthermore, all JPEG files are saved to an 8-bit (as opposed to a 12-bit) format, which can affect the tonal range of the image.

The highest quality results come from the NEF files, as these contain the data direct from the sensor with virtually no other in camera processing. Nikon states that the compression applied to the 12-bit NEF files is "visually loss-less." This claim is due to the method of compression used by the camera during the minimal processing of NEF files. It averages out the highlight data to reduce the file size for saving, but when this data is converted back to a 12-bit form, the human eye is unlikely to resolve any change in the highlight tones. To get the most out of NEF files, you will need additional software, such as Nikon Capture NX or a good third party RAW file converter like Adobe Camera RAW.

Image Processing

In P, S, A, and M modes, image attributes including sharpening, contrast, color mode, saturation, and hue can be assigned through the *Optimize Image* selection in the Shooting menu. The purpose of the *Optimize Image* options is to allow you to instruct the camera to process an image a certain way according to how you intend to use that image (or on the particular subject or scene being photographed). You can choose *Normal* (the default setting), *Softer, Vivid, More Vivid, Portrait, Custom,* or *B&W*. Once you make your selection, the camera sets values automatically, with the exception of the *Custom* option, which allows you to define your own values. (Refer to pages 124-133 for more detailed information.)

Additional Shooting Features

Multiple Exposure: The camera supports a multiple exposure mode. Up to ten separate exposures (using either NEF or JPEG standard files, but not a combination of the two) can be combined in a single image. The user can select an automatic gain control within this feature to adjust the density of the final image to compensate for the total number of exposures made (see pages 76-77).

Image Overlay: It is possible for the D200 to create a single composite image using two NEF format files shot on the camera and saved on the same memory card. The composite image can be saved in either the NEF or JPEG format; the two original NEF files are unaffected by this process, as the new image is saved separately. (See pages 75-76 for more information.)

Interval Timer: Using the interval timer function, it is possible to perform time-lapse photography with the D200. The user can determine the start and finish time for photography, the duration between each exposure or set of exposures, the number of intervals between each exposure or set of exposures, and the number of exposures taken at each interval. (See pages 77-79 for a detailed explanation.)

The Built-In Speedlight

Nikon always refers to their flash units, built-in or external, as Speedlights. The D200 has a pop-up Speedlight housed above the viewfinder. Unlike the Nikon D70-series and D50 cameras, the D200's built-in Speedlight will not activate automatically if the camera determines the light level is sufficiently low to require additional illumination from the flash. The flash can activated manually in any of the exposure modes by pressing the flash pop-up button ⚡ on the camera top just left of the built-in flash.

At full output, the built-in Speedlight has a GN (guide number) of 39 feet (12 meters) at ISO 100 in automatic flash mode and a GN of 42 feet (13 meters) at ISO 100 in manual flash mode. The built-in flash is fully compatible with Nikon's Creative Light System, including the latest i-TTL flash exposure control system for balanced fill-flash, but it defaults to standard i-TTL flash when spot metering is selected. It also supports the Advanced Wireless Lighting system, whereby the built-in flash can be used to control a number of remote flash units (SB-800, SB-600, or SB-R200).

The built-in flash can be used with any CPU-type lens with a focal length between 18 – 300mm. The minimum distance at which it can be used is two feet (.6 meters). With

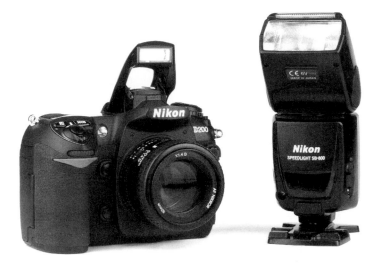

The D200 has a built-in Speedlight, shown in the active position on the camera at left. You may also elect to use an external flash, such as the SB-800 shown at right.

certain lenses, however, the minimum distance must be greater due to the proximity of the flash tube to the central axis of the lens, otherwise light from the flash is prevented from illuminating the entire frame area. (See pages 224-259 for full details on using the D200 for flash photography.)

External Ports

On the left side of the D200 there are a pair of rubber port covers. Under the larger of the two is one port for connecting the EH-6 main AC adapter, and another for connecting the camera to a TV set for image playback. Under the smaller cover is the port for connecting the camera to a computer or printer; the D200 supports High-speed USB (2.0) for data transfer.

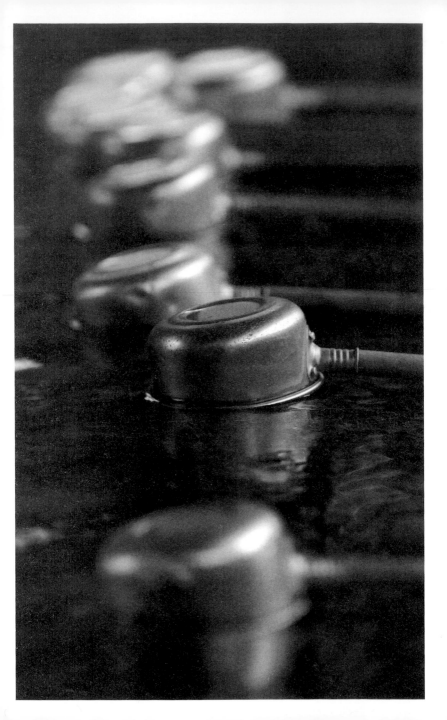

Quick Start Guide

Getting Ready To Shoot

As you lift your new D200 camera from its box you will no doubt be eager to take some pictures. However, before doing so, there are a few basic steps that you need to take to prepare the camera. It is also well worth spending a little time to acquaint yourself with the D200's principle controls and functions.

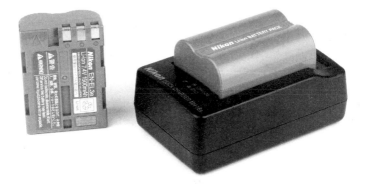

This photo shows two EN-EL3e batteries, one of which is placed on the MH-18a charger.

Charging/Inserting the Battery

The D200 is entirely dependent on electrical power so, at the risk of stating the obvious, it is essential the EN-EL3e battery is fully charged and inserted before you can use your camera. There is no need to pre-condition the battery, but

The D200 offers a variety of shooting modes, giving the photographer as much, or as little, control as preferred. The many custom settings available create even more opportunity and make the D200 a highly versatile D-SLR.

45

the first time you charge it, leave it connected to the MH-18a charger until it is cool to the touch. Do not be tempted to remove it as soon as the charge indicator lamp on the MH-18a has stopped flashing.

When the battery is cool and you are getting ready to insert it into the D200, make sure the camera power switch is set to OFF. Then, turn the camera over and slide the battery-chamber cover lock toward the center of the camera. Open the cover and insert the battery, making sure its three contacts enter first. Lower the battery into place and press the chamber cover down until it locks; you should hear it click into place. Now turn the camera power switch to ON and check the battery-status indicator in the control panel on the camera top to confirm that the battery is fully charged; ▐▀▀▀▌ should be displayed. You can also monitor battery status via the *Battery info* option in the Setup menu (see page 193).

The battery chamber can be accessed from the right side of the camera bottom.

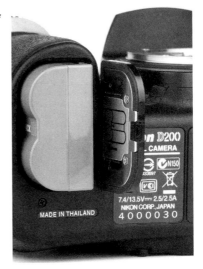

Attaching the Camera Strap

While you're waiting for the battery to charge, you can attach the camera strap. The strap is not only useful for securing the camera when carrying it to prevent it from being dropped accidentally, but it is also useful for bracing the camera to help reduce the risk of camera shake blurring your pictures if you adjust the strap to a length where when it is wound around your arm it is taught and aids the support of the camera.

Starting with the left camera strap eyelet, thread one end of the strap through it and feed it back through the keeper-loop that is attached to the strap itself. Then, pass it through the inside of the buckle before pulling it tight. Repeat these steps with the other end of the strap. Finally, adjust the strap to your preferred length.

Choosing a Language
Once you have inserted a fully charged battery it is time to turn the camera on by rotating the power switch to the ON position. To select the language to be used for the camera menu system, press the ⬤ button; when you do this after switching the camera on for the first time, the *Language* option from the Setup menu is automatically displayed. To access your options, press the Multi Selector to the right. Then Multi Select down until the required language is high-lighted and Multi Select right to confirm your selection. If you wish to change the language any time after that first power-up, just go to the Setup menu and highlight the *Language* option, then repeat the procedure just described.

Setting the Internal Clock
The D200 has an internal clock powered by an independent rechargeable battery. This battery is charged from the camera's main power source (either the EN-EL3e or the EH-6 AC adapter).

Note: The clock battery requires approximately 48 hours of charging by the camera's main battery (or the AC adapter) to power the clock for approximately three months. Should the clock battery become exhausted, **CLOCK** will flash in the control panel and the clock will reset to a date and time of 2005.01.01 00:00:00. (See page 187 for more information.)

To set the clock, go to the Setup menu and Multi Select down to highlight the *World Time* option. Multi Select right to display the menu options, then use the Multi Selector to highlight *Time Zone*; pressing the Multi Selector to the right displays a map of world time zones. Select the appropriate time zone and press ⏺ to confirm the selection and return to the *World Time* menu.

Now highlight *Date* and Multi Select right to display the date/time clock. Use the Multi Selector to select each item in turn, as well as to adjust them as required until the full date and time have been entered. Finally press ⏺ to confirm the settings and return to the *World Time* menu.

Next, highlight *Date Format* and Multi Select right to display the list of options. Highlight the date format you wish to use (i.e., the order in which the date/time are displayed), then Multi Select right to confirm the selection and return to the *World Time* menu. To exit this menu and return to the main Setup menu, press ⏺ .

Hint: The internal clock is not as accurate as many wrist-watches and domestic clocks, so it is important to check it regularly. If recording accurate time and date information with each image is essential, you may wish to consider connecting a GPS device to the D200 (see pages 308-309 for details).

Mounting a Lens

To access all the functions and features of the D200, you will require either a G-type, or D-type Nikkor lens. When-ever you attach or detach a lens from the D200, be sure that the camera is turned off. Identify the mounting index-mark (a white dot) on the lens and align it with the mounting index-mark (another white dot) next to the bayonet ring of the camera's lens mount on the camera front. Enter the lens bayonet into the camera and rotate the lens counter-clock-wise until it locks into place with a click. Then, in order for you to get an accurate meter reading from any lens with a CPU and a conventional aperture ring (does not apply to G-type lenses), before using such a lens it is necessary to set

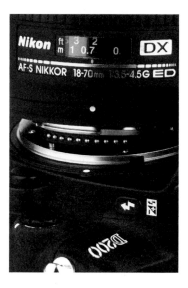

Match up the white dot on the lens with the white dot on the camera's lens mount before attempting to attach the lens to the camera body.

and lock the lens to its minimum aperture value (highest f/number).

Hint: If you turn the camera on after mounting a lens and **FE E** appears and blinks in the control panel and the viewfinder, the lens has not been set to its minimum aperture value. In this state, the shutter release is disabled and the camera will not operate.

To remove a lens from the camera, press and hold the lens release button on the camera front, then turn the lens clockwise until the mounting index-mark on the lens is once again aligned with the mounting index-mark next to the bayonet ring of the camera's lens mount. Then lift the lens clear of the camera body. If you do not intend to mount another lens right away, always place the BF-1A body cap back on to help prevent unwanted dust and debris from entering the camera.

Adjusting Viewfinder Focus
The viewfinder eyepiece lens of the D200 has a diopter adjustment so that the camera can be used regardless of whether you normally wear eyeglasses or not. To check and

set the viewfinder focus, attach a lens to the camera as described in the previous section, then turn the camera on and use the Multi Selector to select the central focus sensor area. Now look through the viewfinder and turn the diopter adjustment control (located on the right side of the viewfinder eyepiece on the camera back) until the focus area brackets appear sharp. If the viewfinder display turns off as you make adjustments, lightly press the shutter release button down halfway to reactivate the displays.

Note: It is usually easier to assess viewfinder focus if the camera is pointed at a plain, light-colored surface. To prevent the focusing system from "hunting" when pointed at a featureless subject such as this, switch to manual focus by rotating the focus mode selector (located on the camera front to the left of the lens) to M and set the lens to focus at infinity (set the ∞ mark on the lens distance scale against the focus index point).

Memory Cards

The D200 can accept either solid-state (no moving parts) CompactFlash Type I/II cards, or a Microdrive, which is a miniature hard disk drive that has moving parts. The only difference between a Type I and Type II CompactFlash card is their physical thickness; Type II is thicker. Microdrives are mounted inside a CompactFlash Type II card casing and can be inserted in the same corresponding memory card slot. The card port of the D200 can only accommodate one card at a time. (A list of memory cards tested and approved by Nikon is shown on page 284.)

Inserting and Removing the Memory Card
Regardless of whether you choose to use a CompactFlash card or a Microdrive to store your digital pictures, the procedure for using them is identical. First, ensure the camera is turned off. Open the card slot door by turning the card slot cover latch counterclockwise; the door will spring open and swing back to reveal the memory card slot.

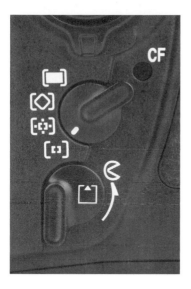

The card slot cover latch can be found just below the AF-area mode selector on the camera back.

Insert the card with its contacts pointing toward the camera and the side of the card that has the main label facing you. The card will slide in just so far before you feel a slight resistance. Keep pushing the card until it clicks in to place

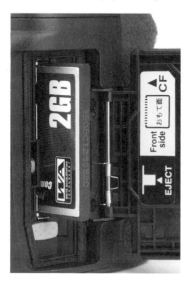

Insert the memory card into the slot with the label facing you.

(the green memory card access lamp illuminates briefly as confirmation that the card is installed properly) and the gray eject button pops up. Finally, close the card slot cover.

Hint: Pay attention to the orientation of the memory card when you insert it in the D200. The main label of the card must face you (i.e., face towards the back of the camera). This is important to note, as it is the reverse of previous Nikon D-SLR cameras where the memory card was inserted with the main label facing away from the user and towards the front of the camera.

Caution: *On a number of occasions while carrying the D200 over my shoulder by its strap, with the back of the camera facing toward my body, I have found that the card slot cover latch has snagged on my clothing and the card slot door has opened inadvertently. Generally, this has occurred when I had a longer, heavier lens attached to the camera, which caused the camera body to tilt so that the latch is more exposed.*

To remove a memory card, begin by making absolutely sure that the green memory card access lamp is not illuminated before you switch the camera off. Then open the card slot door and push the grey eject button towards the center of the camera. The memory card will be partially ejected and can then be pulled out by hand.

Note: You should be aware that memory cards can become warm during use; this is normal and is not an indication of a problem.

Note: If the D200 has no memory card inserted when a charged battery is installed (or when it is powered by the EH-6 AC adapter), [-E-] appears in the exposure counter brackets both in the viewfinder and in the control panel.

Formatting the Memory Card

All new memory cards must be formatted to before their first use. In addition, any card that was previously used with a different camera body should be formatted for use with each new camera body you introduce it to before using the two together. To format a card using the D200, insert a card as described in the previous section, then switch the camera on. Press and hold the 🔘 and 🔘 buttons for approximately two seconds until **For** flashes in the control panel together with a flashing frame count display. To proceed with the formatting process you must then release the 🔘 and 🔘 buttons momentarily and press them again.

Note: If you press any other button after **For** begins to flash, the format function is cancelled and the camera returns to its previous state.

During formatting, **For** appears continuously within the frame-count brackets of the control panel display. Once complete, the frame-count display shows the approximate number of photographs that can be recorded at the current size and quality settings. Alternatively, you can use the *Format* command in the Setup menu, but this method is slower to perform and involves using the LCD monitor, which increases power consumption during formatting and drains the battery faster.

Note: You should never switch the camera off or otherwise interrupt the power supply to the camera (i.e., don't unplug the AC adapter) during the formatting process.

Hint: It is good practice to format a card each time you insert it into the camera. If you do not get into the habit of doing this, there is an increased risk of problems occurring with the communication between the memory card and the camera, particularly if the memory card is used in different camera bodies.

Simple Photography

In line with the professional specifications of the D200, Nikon has, thankfully, dispensed with the subject/scene orientated point-and-shoot program mode options found on cameras such as the D70-series and D50 models. I have always considered these fully automated exposure modes a backward step in the process of encouraging users to experiment with their camera and thereby understand more about it in the process. However, the D200 can still be used in a fully automated way if that is what you require. This section is included for those less experienced users eager to take some pictures with their camera right away.

If you have followed the various steps set out in the previous sections of this chapter, the camera should be ready to use. However, it is worth checking the battery charge status by looking at the icon displayed in the control panel; if the battery is fully charged, ⟨▨▨⟩ will be displayed. You might also look for the exposure count display in the viewfinder and/or in the control panel. The number displayed within the brackets is the approximate number of exposures that can be made at the current settings for image size and quality, taking into account the amount of storage space available on the installed memory card.

Note: The exposure count display is only an approximation, as file size can vary depending on the camera settings you use from shot to shot. It is often possible to store slightly more images than the exposure counter initially suggests.

Shooting at Default Settings

Probably the easiest and quickest way to set up the camera for fully automated shooting is to use its default settings. These can be set or restored at any time by pressing and holding the **QUAL** and ⟨▨⟩ buttons down for three or more seconds (these two buttons have a bright green dot to indicate the dual button operation for the reset function). The default settings for the D200 are listed in the following table:

Note: Any selections made in the Custom Setting menu remain unaffected by the two-button reset option (see pages 100-101 for more information).

Camera Option	Default Setting
Image quality	NORM (JPEG Normal)
Image size	L (large – images are 3,872 x 2,592 pixels)
Sensitivity (ISO)	100 (equivalent to ISO 100)
White Balance	Automatic
Exposure mode	P (programmed auto)
Focus area	Center focus area

In addition to ensuring that the default values have been reset, a number of other camera controls should be set as follows to ensure easy and consistent operation:

• Press and hold the mode dial lock release button (just above the mode dial on the left top of the camera) to release the mode dial. Then, rotate the mode dial to S (single frame shooting). At this setting, one exposure will be made each time the shutter release button is fully depressed.

• Turn the AF-area mode dial (on the camera back just below the Multi Selector) until the white index mark is set against 〔▫〕 (single-area AF). At this setting, the focus area selected by the user will be used; simply place the brackets for the selected focus area so that they cover a part of the subject and the camera will focus on this point.

• Rotate the focus mode selector (on the camera front below the lens release button) until the white index mark is set against S (single-servo AF). At this setting, autofocus is activated when the shutter release is pressed halfway. As soon as the camera has acquired focus, ● will appear in the viewfinder display. In this focus mode, the shutter release is disabled until focus has been acquired.

- Finally, select Matrix metering by turning the metering selector (on the camera back to the right of the viewfinder eyepiece) until the white index mark is set to ▣ . To confirm that Matrix metering has been selected, check that ▣ is also displayed in the viewfinder.

Holding the Camera

It may sound obvious, but how you hold your camera can have a significant influence on its ability to produce sharp pictures. Camera shake—the inadvertent movement of the camera when it is held in your hands—is probably the leading cause unwanted image blur. Proper handholding technique will reduce the risk of camera shake. Regardless of whether you want to shoot with the camera held horizontally or vertically, it should be grasped firmly but not with an overly tight grip. The finger of your right hand should wrap around the handgrip in such a way that your index finger is free to operate the shutter release button. Cup your left hand under the camera so it acts like a cradle to support the camera and lens; your left thumb and index finger can rotate either the focus or zoom ring of a lens. Keep you elbows tucked in towards your body while standing with your feet shoulder-width apart and one foot half a pace in front of the other. Following these simple tips will provide an extra measure of stability for your camera.

Composing and Shooting

Compose your shot so that the AF area brackets cover the main area of the subject. Press the shutter release lightly to activate the focusing system. If the camera can acquire focus, you will hear a "beep" sound, and the focus indicator ● will appear in the viewfinder. The focus will lock at the current camera-to-subject distance. If the subject moves closer to or further away from the camera before you release the shutter, you will need to repeat the focusing step again.

When shooting at slow shutter speeds, make sure your battery is ⇨ fully charged or have a backup battery close at hand.

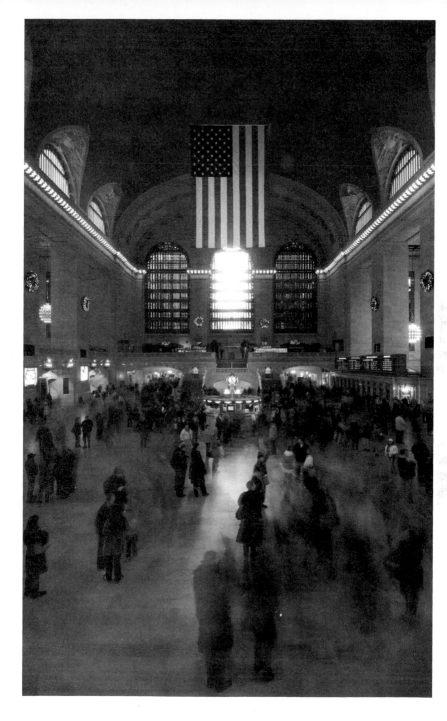

Note: If the focus indicator blinks, the camera cannot acquire sharp focus. In such a case, recompose the picture and try placing the AF area brackets over an alternative part of the subject before pressing the shutter release halfway again.

As the camera is set to P (Programmed Auto mode), it will select a combination of shutter speed and lens aperture for you. If the meter determines that the picture will be over- or under-exposed at the selected aperture and shutter speed settings, the camera will display ᕼᎥ or ᒪᗝ respectively. To prevent over-exposure, use a polarizing or neutral density (ND) filter; to prevent under-exposure, increase the ISO sensitivity setting. Assuming the camera is able to select an appropriate shutter speed and lens aperture value, you are ready to make an exposure.

The shutter button on the D200 is a two-stage release; pressed halfway, the camera activates the autofocus and TTL metering systems, while pressing the shutter release all the way down activates the shutter mechanism and takes a photograph. Avoid jamming your finger down on the shutter release button, as this will increase the risk of camera shake. Practice the good hand holding technique described in the previous section and then just roll you finger tip smoothly over the edge of the shutter release button when it comes time to take the picture. As soon as the exposure has been made, the green access lamp on the back of the camera will light up to indicate that the camera is recording the image.

Caution: Under no circumstances should you switch the power off or eject the memory card until the green memory card indicator lamp has extinguished.

Basic Image Review
To review the most recent picture recorded by the D200, press the ⬛ button; the picture will be displayed in the LCD monitor on the camera back. To review other previously recorded pictures, Multi Select left or right to scroll through the pictures stored on the memory card. If you want to delete the displayed picture press the ⬛ button. A message will be shown over the displayed picture asking for confirmation of the

delete action. Press the 🗑 button again to proceed with the deleting of the picture. To cancel the delete process press ▣ , or the press shutter release button halfway.

To protect an image from accidental deletion, display it on the monitor screen by pressing ▣ then press the 🔑 button. The key icon will appear in the top left corner of the displayed image to indicate its protected status. To un-protect the image, press the 🔑 button again while the image is displayed; the key icon will disappear.

Note: Never be in too much of a hurry to delete pictures unless they are obvious failures; I always recommend that it is better to leave the editing process to a later stage when you can get a better look at the image.

Note: Any image file marked as protected will maintain a read-only status even when the image file is transferred to the computer or other data storage device. For this reason, you should un-protect your images before transfer if you plan to perform any image processing on them.

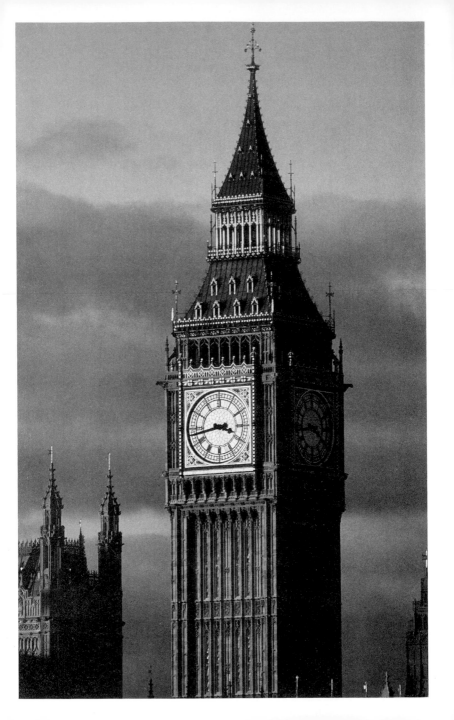

D200 Shooting Operations In Detail

Powering the D200

The D200 can be powered by a variety of choices. The main battery is the rechargeable lithium EN-EL3e (7.4V, 1500mAh) that weighs approximately 2.8 oz (80g). The profile of the battery ensures that it can only be inserted the correct way into the camera. It is charged with the dedicated MH-18a Quick Charger (supplied with the camera). Alternatively, the predecessor to the MH-18a, the MH-18, can also be used, as can the MH-19 Multi-Charger, which supports both AC and DC power supplies. A fully discharged EN-EL3e can be completely recharged in approximately 135 minutes using the MH-18a or MH-18. Unlike some other types of rechargeable batteries, the EN-EL3e does not require conditioning prior to its first use. However, it is advisable to ensure that the initial charge cycle for a new battery is continued until the battery cools down while still in the charger before removing it. Do not be tempted to remove it as soon as the indicator lamp stops flashing, as the battery is unlikely to have reached full charge.

Using the EN-EL3e Battery
To insert an EN-EL3e into the D200:

- Invert the camera and push the small button on the battery chamber cover toward the tripod socket. The battery chamber lid should swing open.
- Open the lid fully and slide the battery into the camera, observing the diagram on the inside of the chamber lid.

The D200 is powered by the proprietary, rechargeable lithium EN-EL3e battery. If you are on the road, it pays to take two or three extra batteries with you so you will never be without a fully charged spare.

Make sure the D200 is turned off before you remove or insert the battery.

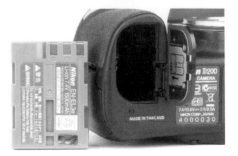

- Press the lid down (you will feel a slight resistance) until it locks. You will hear a click as the latch closes.

To remove an EN-EL3e from the D200:

- Repeat step 1 (above).
- Hold the lid open, turn the camera upright, and allow the battery to slide out into your hand, taking care that it does not drop.
- Close the battery chamber cover.

Before you insert or remove the battery, it is essential that you set the power switch of the D200 to the OFF position. If you are in the process of making any changes to the camera settings and the battery is removed while the power switch is still set to the ON position (or the power supply from the AC adapter is interrupted), the camera may not retain the new settings. Likewise, if the camera is still in the process of transferring data from the buffer memory to the storage media (CompactFlash card or Microdrive) when the battery is removed, image files are likely to be corrupted, or data could be lost.

To charge an EN-EL3e:

- Connect the MH-18a Quick Charger to an AC power supply.

Note: The MH-18a, MH-18, and MH-19 chargers can be used worldwide; they can be connected to any AC power supply at any voltage from 100V – 250V via an appropriate power socket adapter.

• Align the slots on the side of the battery with the four lugs (two each side) on the top of the MH-18a / MH-18 and lower the battery before sliding it toward the indicator lamp until it locks in place. The lamp should begin to flash immediately, indicating that charging has commenced. A full charge of a completely discharged battery will take approximately 135 minutes.

Hint: To ensure the battery has recharged fully, do not remove it from the charger as soon as the charge lamp stops flashing; leave the battery in place until it has cooled to the ambient room temperature.

Hint: Lithium batteries do no exhibit the "charge memory" effects associated with NiCd batteries. Therefore, a partially discharged EN-EL3e can be placed back on the charger for recharging without any adverse consequences to battery life or performance.

Hint: If you carry a spare EN-EL3e, always ensure that you keep the semi-opaque plastic terminal cover in place. Without it, there is a risk that the battery terminals may short and cause damage to the battery.

The EN-EL3e rechargeable battery has an electronic chip in its circuitry that allows it to communicate detailed information regarding the status of the battery to the D200 camera body. This is the reason that the EN-EL3e battery has three contact plates as opposed to the two its EN-EL3 and EN-EL3a predecessors had. To access this information, select *Battery Info* from the Setup menu and three parameters concerning the battery will be displayed on the LCD monitor (see the table on page 193).

Parameter	Description
Bat. Meter	Current level of battery charge expressed as a percentage.
Pic. Meter	Number of times the shutter has been released with the current battery since it was last charged. This number will include shutter release actions when no picture is recorded (e.g. to record an *Image Dust Off* reference frame or measure color temperature for a preset white balance value).
Charg. Life	Displays the condition of the battery as one of five levels from 0 -4). Level 0 indicates the battery is new, and level 4 indicates the battery has reached the end of its charging life and should be recharged.

Note: The EN-EL3 and EN-EL3a battery types are not compatible with the D200. If you attempt to enter either of these two battery types in to the battery chamber of the D200, they will not fit.

The MB-D200 can hold one or two EN-EL3e batteries or six AA batteries.

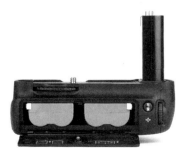

Note: The EN-EL3e battery supplied with the D200 can also be used in the D100, D70-series, and D50 camera models.

Using The MB-D200 Battery Pack

The MB-D200 is a battery pack/grip that attaches to the base of the standard D200 body via the tripod socket. It can accept either one or two EN-EL3e batteries, or six AA-sized batteries that must be fitted into the battery holder. In addition to providing extra battery capacity, the MB-D200 has a shutter release button, main and sub-command dials, and an AF-ON button to improve handling when the camera is held in the vertical (portrait) orientation.

Hint: Fitting the MB-D200 requires the battery chamber door of the D200 camera to be removed. To avoid losing it, stow the battery chamber door in the slot set into the shaft of the MB-D200 that enters the camera's battery chamber.

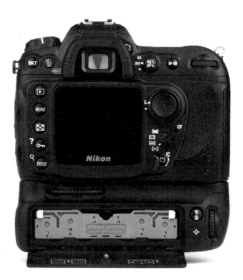

The MB-D200 accepts six rechargeable AA batteries, which must be inserted into its MS-D200 AA battery holder.

Note: If the MB-D200 battery pack is fitted to the D200 and has two EN-EL3e batteries inserted, the *Battery Info* display will show information for each battery separately; they will be listed as *L Slot* for the battery in the left hand chamber and *R Slot* for the battery in the right hand chamber. If AA sized batteries are inserted in the MS-D200 battery holder, no information about the batteries is available through the *Battery Info* display.

The EH-6 AC Adapter
The Nikon EH-6 AC adapter can also power the D200. This accessory is particularly useful for extended periods of shooting, such as time lapse photography, as well as for image playback and data transfer direct from the camera to a computer. Any interruption to the camera's power supply during recording or transfer of data to an external device may lead to files becoming corrupted or data being lost. The adapter connects to the D200's DC-In socket (the bottom socket underneath the larger of the rubber covers on the left side of the camera). The EH-6 is also useful for preventing the camera from powering off while the reflex mirror is raised using the mirror lock-up function for inspection or cleaning of the low-pass filter array.

Hint: Always ensure that the power switch is set to the OFF position before connecting/disconnecting the EH-6 to the DC-In socket. There is a risk that the camera's circuitry could be damaged if you plug/unplug the EH-6 while the power switch is set to the ON position.

Note: All electronically controlled cameras very occasionally exhibit some strange behavior with unexpected icons or characters appearing in the LCD monitor, or sometimes the camera simply ceases to function properly. This is usually due an electro-static charge. To remedy the situation try switching the camera off, removing and replacing the battery (or disconnecting and reconnecting the AC power supply) before switching the camera on again.

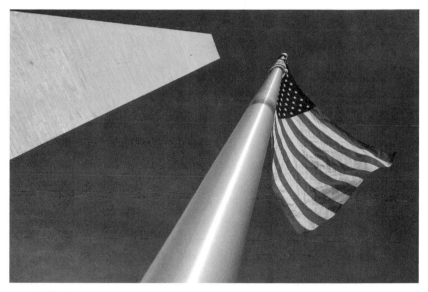

Digital cameras are perfect for documentary photography because their LCD monitor provides proof that you got the picture you needed. However, if you review your photos a lot, make sure you have packed plenty of battery power.

The Clock/Calendar Battery

The D200 has an clock/calendar that is powered by an internal rechargeable battery. Fully charged, it will power the clock/calendar for approximately three months. It requires charging for approximately 48 hours by the camera's main power supply. Should the clock battery become exhausted, **CLOCK** will flash in the control panel and the clock is reset to a date and time of 2005.01.01 00:00:00. If this occurs, the clock/calendar will need to be reset via the *World Time* option in the Setup menu.

Hint: Since the clock/calendar battery is not changeable by the user, if it reaches a point where it will no longer hold a charge, the camera must be returned to a Nikon service center in order for a replacement battery to be fitted.

Battery Performance

Obviously, the more functions the camera has to perform, the greater the demand for power. Reducing the number of functions and the duration for which they are active is fundamental to reducing power consumption. Since operation of the D200 is totally dependent on an adequate electrical power supply, here are a few suggestions as to how you can preserve battery power.

- A fully charged EN-EL3e battery, in good condition, will retain its full capacity over a short period of a few days. If the battery is left dormant for a month or more, expect it to suffer a substantial loss of charge, so ensure you recharge it fully before use.

- Using the camera's LCD monitor increases power consumption significantly. Unless you need it, turn the monitor off. Consider setting the *Image Review* option in the Playback menu to *OFF*; the default setting is *ON*.

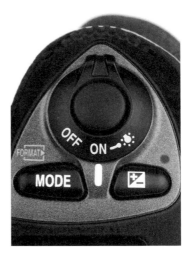

The D200's power switch is in the ON position.

Hint: If the *Image Review* feature is *ON*, as soon as you have had a quick glance, press the shutter release button lightly. This switches the LCD monitor off immediately.

• While the autofocus itself draws relatively little power, the Vibration Reduction (VR) feature on some Nikkor lenses reduces battery life by approximately 10% when active.

• A CompactFlash card requires significantly less power than a Microdrive; you will be able to record more images per battery charge with a CompactFlash card.

• Regardless of the battery type, low temperatures cause a change to the internal resistance of a battery that impairs performance. Lithium batteries are fairly resilient to cold conditions. However, to ensure you can keep shooting, you should have a spare battery in a warm place such as an inside pocket; if the battery in the camera begins to give out, exchange it for the warmer one. Allow the used battery time to warm-up again and keep rotating between the two batteries to maximize their shooting capacity.

Shutter Release

The D200's shutter release button is located right top of the camera. If the camera is switched on, a light pressure on the shutter release button (pressing it halfway down) will activate the metering system and initiate autofocus (assuming an autofocus mode has been selected). Once you release the button, the camera remains active for a fixed period, the duration of which depends on the selection made within Custom Setting c3 *(Auto Meter-off Delay)*; 6-seconds is the default setting.

If you continue to press the shutter release button all the way down, the shutter mechanism will operate and an exposure will be made. There is a short delay between pressing the button and the shutter opening; this is usually referred to as shutter lag. The shutter lag time of the D200 is approximately 50 milliseconds—about half the lag time of the D70-

series and D50 cameras, and only slightly longer than that of the D2Xs model. The mirror black out time (i.e., the amount of time that the viewfinder goes dark) is about 105 milliseconds. However, the release of the shutter can be delayed further, and in some cases prevented, if certain features and functions are in operation at the time the shutter release button is pressed. The following are some of the reasons for a delay in shutter operation:

• The capacity of the buffer memory is probably the most common cause of shutter delay. It does not matter whether you shoot in single frame mode or one of the continuous frame modes; once the buffer memory is full, the camera must write data to the memory card before any more exposures can be made. As soon as sufficient space is available in the buffer memory for another image, the shutter can be released. For this reason, using memory cards with a fast write speed is recommended.

• If the camera is set to single-servo autofocus mode, the shutter is disabled until the D200 has acquired focus. In low light or low contrast scenes, the autoocus system can often take longer to achieve focus, adding to the delay, though Custom Setting a2 (*AF-S Mode Priority*) allows focus priority to be overridden.

• In low light situations, the D200 will activate the AF-assist lamp provided it has been instructed to do so via Custom Setting a9, which introduces a short delay while the lamp illuminates and focus is acquired.

Note: The AF-assist lamp only operates in single-servo autofocus mode.

• The red-eye reduction feature introduces an additional and significant full second delay between pressing the shutter release button and the exposure being made. This is the time during which the lamp emits light that causes your subject's eye pupils to constrict before the shutter opens and the flash unit fires.

Shooting Modes

Unlike a film camera, the D200 does not have to transport film between each exposure, so in that sense, it does not have a motor drive, but the shutter mechanism still has to be cycled. The camera offers a range of shooting modes, single-frame, and two continuous-frame options, plus a self-timer and a remote shutter release feature.

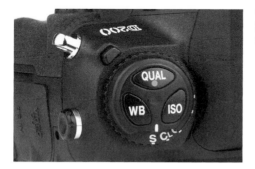

The mode dial is located on the left top of the camera.

To set a shooting mode, hold down the shooting mode dial lock button and rotate the dial to the required position: **S** single-frame, **CL** continuous low-speed, **CH** continuous high-speed, ☼ self-timer, or **MUP** mirror-up.

Single Frame S : In this shooting mode, a single image is recorded each time the shutter release button is pressed. To make another exposure, the button must be released and pressed again; as long there is room on your memory card, you can continue to do so until the buffer memory is full, in which case you must wait for data to be written to the card.

Hint: You do not have to remove your finger from the shutter release button completely between frames; by raising it slightly after each exposure and maintaining a slight downward pressure on the shutter release button you can keep the camera active and be ready for the next shot.

Hint: If you want to take a rapid sequence of pictures in single-frame mode, avoid "stabbing" your finger down on the shutter release button in quick succession. Keep a light pressure on it and roll your finger over the top of the button in a smooth, repetitive action. This will reduce the risk of camera shake spoiling your pictures.

Continuous Low-Speed Cʟ : In this mode, if you press and hold the shutter release button down the D200 will continue to record images up to a maximum rate of 4 fps (frames per second). Use Custom Setting d4 to select the frame rate.

Continuous High-Speed Cʜ : In this mode, if you press and hold the shutter release button down the D200 will continue to record images up to a maximum rate of 5 fps.

Note: Nikon quotes the frame rates for the D200 based on the camera being set to continuous-servo autofocus, manual, or Shutter-Priority exposure mode at a minimum shutter speed of 1/250. It is important to remember that buffer capacity, other autoexposure modes, and single-servo autofocus (particularly in low-light) can reduce the frame rate significantly.

Using the Self-Timer ↻

When set to the self-timer, the camera will not fire the shutter immediately when the shutter release button is pressed. Instead, it waits for a predetermined period of time and then makes the exposure. The default time delay for the self-timer is 10 seconds, but it can be adjusted to 2, 5, or 20 seconds through Custom Setting c4.

Traditionally, the self-timer has been used to enable the photographer to be included in the picture, but there is another very useful function for this feature. By using the self-timer to release the shutter, the photographer does not have to touch the camera to release the shutter, thus reducing the risk of camera shake. This is particularly useful for long exposures when the subject is static and precise timing of the shutter release is less critical. During use of the self-timer, the camera will normally be placed on an independent means of support such as a tripod. Compose the picture and ensure focus is confirmed before depressing the shutter release button (the shutter release will be disabled unless focus is acquired).

Hint: Make sure you do not pass in front of the lens after setting the self-timer, as this the point of focus may shift and may prevent the camera from operating. I recommend that the camera be set to manual focus mode when using the self-timer feature.

Note: If any of the automatic exposure modes (P, A, or S) are used in conjunction with the self-timer feature, it is essential to cover the viewfinder eyepiece with the supplied DK-5 eyepiece cap. In normal shooting, your eye is placed against the viewfinder eyepiece, blocking extraneous light from entering the viewfinder and influencing the camera's TTL metering sensor.

Hint: Fitting the DK-5 requires the user to remove the DK-21 rubber eyecup; this is a nuisance and increases the risk that the eyecup might be lost. I recommend keeping a small square of thick felt material in your camera bag; drape this over the viewfinder eyepiece when using the self-timer mode instead of using the eyepiece cap. It is far quicker and more convenient!

After the shutter release button is pressed, the AF-assist lamp will begin to blink (if the audible warning is active it will also beep) until approximately two seconds before the exposure is due to be taken, at which point the light stops blinking and remains on continuously (the frequency of the beep will increase) until the shutter releases. To cancel the self-timer operation during the countdown, simply turn the mode dial to an alternative shooting mode.

Mirror-Up Mᴜᴘ

The mirror-up shooting mode should not be confused with the *Mirror-Up* option available via the Setup menu, which is used to facilitate inspection and cleaning of the low-pass filter. This mode locks the reflex mirror into its raised position to eliminate the vibrations that can occur when the reflex mirror lifts up out of the way to let light hit the camera's sensor, particularly at shutter speeds between 1/2 second and 1/30 second. However, once the mirror is locked into the up position, it is not possible to see through the viewfinder. Therefore exposure, composition, and focus must be confirmed before initiating this mode.

Note: Once in the raised position, the reflex mirror prevents light from reaching the TTL meter sensor located in the viewfinder head. Likewise, autofocus detection is no longer possible. For this reason, when the camera in an autofocus mode, the focus distance is locked at the distance set prior to the mirror being raised.

The mirror lock-up feature has two distinct phases; the first press of the shutter release button will cause the mirror to lift and lock in the raised position. The shutter release button must be pressed a second time to operate the shutter and make the exposure. Once the exposure has been completed the mirror will return to its normal position. If you are using the mirror-up mode to avoid camera shake, you should also avoid pressing the shutter release button by hand. In such cases, a remote release is often the best option.

Using a Remote Release

Since the purpose of using the mirror lock-up feature is to eliminate camera vibrations it seems pointless to then press the camera's shutter release button with your finger to release the shutter. To reduce any other potential source of vibration, mount the camera on a tripod or other camera support and use a remote shutter release to operate the shutter. The D200 has a 10-pin terminal for connecting a variety of remote release accessories; probably the most useful of which is the MC-30 cord, which is 2 feet 7 inches (80 cm) long. (Refer to pages 274-276 for information on other accessories that are compatible with the D200.)

Image Overlay

Image Overlay is one of two features available on the D200 that enable the user to combine multiple images. In the case of this feature, it is limited to using a pair of NEF files and combining them to form a single, new image (the original image files are not affected by this process). The images do not have to be taken in consecutive order, but they both must have been recorded by a D200 and be stored on the same memory card.

Note: The new image is saved at the image quality and size currently set on the camera. Therefore, before using this feature, ensure that the image quality and size are set to appropriate values.

To use *Image Overlay*:

- Select *Image Overlay* from the Shooting menu. The *Image Overlay* page will open with *Image 1* highlighted.
- To select the first picture, press the ⊕ button and a thumbnail view of all NEF files stored on the memory card will be displayed. Scroll through the images using the Multi Selector to highlight the image you wish to select.
- Press the center of the Multi Selector and the selected image will appear in the *Image 1* box and the *Preview* box.
- Highlight the *Image 2* box using the Multi Selector and press the ⊕ button to select the second picture you wish to combine.
- Press the center of the Multi Selector to select the second image, which will appear in the *Image 2* box and in the *Preview* box, overlaying the first image.

- Adjust the gain value of *Image 1* and *Image 2* by scrolling up and down using the Multi Selector while the image you wish to adjust is highlighted. The effect of the gain control can be observed in the preview box (the default value is x1.0).
- Once you have adjusted the gain of both images to achieve the desired effect, highlight the Preview Box. To view a larger version of the preview image, press the ✪ button. To generate a preview of the new image, highlight *Overlay* and press the ⓔ button.
- To save the new image, press the ⓔ button. To return to the editing screen press the ✪ button. To save the image without a preview, highlight Save and press the ⓔ button.

The image will be saved on the memory card using the quality and size settings currently selected. Image attributes such as white balance, sharpening, color mode, saturation, and hue will be copied from the image selected as *Image 1*. Similarly, the shooting data is copied from the same image.

Multiple Exposure

The other method of combining images using the D200 is the *Multiple Exposure* feature. This enables you to combine multiple exposures (up to a maximum of 10) into a single image. However, the images must be shot in consecutive order, and they are not saved as individual files but as a single combined image.

To use *Multiple Exposure*:

- Select *Multiple Exposure* from the Shooting menu and scroll down to *Number of Shots*. Multi Select right to select this option.
- Select the number of images you wish to combine, between 2 – 10, and Multi Select right to confirm.
- Select *Auto Gain* and then choose either *On* or *Off* by highlighting the desired option and Multi Selecting right.

Hint: When *Auto Gain* is turned on, the camera will automatically make gain adjustments to each image recorded so the final exposure is correct (i.e., it obviates the need to make exposure calculations to compensate for the cumulative effect of combining the individual exposures).

- Highlight *Done* and Multi Select right to confirm.
- Begin shooting the images you intend to combine.

The will appear in the control panel while the exposures are being made. When the selected number of exposures has been completed the will disappear from the control panel and the multiple exposure feature is turned off automatically. To create another multiple exposure, repeat the steps outlined above.

Note: If you wish to maintain the same settings for *Number of Shots* and *Auto Gain* that you previously selected, simply go right to the *Done* option to begin another multiple exposure sequence.

Interval Timer Shooting

The interval timer shooting feature of the D200 enables you to tell the camera to take a set number of pictures of the same scene over a period of time at a predetermined interval—a technique often called time-lapse photography. It has applications for both scientific and pictorial purposes. Given a suitable subject or scene, this technique can produce some very interesting results, especially if you play the images sequentially in a slide show. For example, the opening and closing of a flower head during the course of a day or the changes that take place at a busy street corner every few minutes during rush-hour can be fascinating to observe. The D200 provides you with the ability to capture such changing conditions using the *Intvl Timer Shooting* option in the Shooting menu.

To configure the camera for interval timer shooting involves several steps, but the results can definitely be worth the effort. Due to the protracted duration required for some time-lapse sequences, it may be necessary to use the EH-6 AC adapter. If this is not an available option, make sure that the EN-EL3e battery is fully charged, or better still, use a pair of EN-EL3e batteries in the MB-D200 battery pack, as this will extend shooting time and battery power.

Note: Precise and consistent framing is often an important aspect of time-lapse photography, so I recommend the use of a tripod or other form of sturdy, rigid camera support.

To use interval timer shooting:

- Select *Intvl Timer Shooting* from the Shooting menu.
- The first option presented to you is the *Start time* selection. If you select *Now*, the camera will initiate the shooting sequence approximately 3 seconds after settings have been confirmed in the camera. If you select *Start time*, the camera will delay the beginning of the shooting sequence until the specified time. In this case, when you Multi Select right to select *Start time* a screen will open that allows you to tell the camera what time the first image should be taken. The maximum delay is 23 hours and 59 minutes.
- Next, select *Interval* and set the amount of time that will pass between each shot (the camera will power down between shots); the maximum duration is 23 hours and 59 minutes.
- Now go to *Select Intvl Shots*. Select the total number of intervals in which the camera is to operate and the number of exposures it should make at each interval. The first number in the equation is the number of intervals, and the second is the number of shots at each interval. The third number is the total number of shots that will be fired throughout the duration of the interval timer shooting process (the maximum number of intervals is 999 and the maximum number of shots at each interval is 9).
- Then go to the *Start On / Off* selection. Choose either *On*

to initiate the time-lapse sequence set or *No* to save the settings without initiating the interval timer shooting.

• Finally, press the ● button to confirm your selections.

Once *Intvl Timer Shooting* has been set correctly, and a delayed start time has been selected, a message stating TIMER ACTIVE will appear in the control panel momentarily, and the INTERVAL icon will remain displayed in the control panel, blinking until the full shooting sequence has been completed; immediately before each shooting interval commences, the number of intervals remaining will be displayed in the control panel where the shutter speed is normally displayed, and the number of exposures remaining in the current interval will be displayed where the aperture normally appears. At any other time, the number of intervals remaining and the number of exposures in each interval can be displayed by pressing the shutter release button halfway. To view other settings for the time-lapse sequence, select *Intvl Timer Shooting* from the Shooting menu.

Note: If any of the automatic exposure modes (P, A, or S) are used in conjunction with the interval timer feature, it is essential to cover the viewfinder eyepiece so that light does not leak in and influence the camera's TTL metering sensor.

ISO Sensitivity

Film requires you to choose which ISO rating to use in order to cope with the prevailing or expected lighting conditions. Once loaded into the camera, the entire roll must be exposed at the same ISO value. One of the great advantages of digital photography is that digital cameras generally allow you to adjust the sensitivity from picture-to-picture. The D200 is no exception, and offers ISO sensitivity options ranging from 100 to 1600, plus the option to increase sensitivity by a maximum of 1 EV above 1600, all in increments of 1/3 EV (one-third stop). There is a specific noise reduction feature for use with high ISO settings and, in addition to this, the camera has an *ISO Auto* feature that is intended to vary the ISO sensitivity value automatically according to the light conditions (see the following page for details).

Note: The term "ISO sensitivity" should be used advisedly in reference to digital cameras. Digital camera sensors actually have a fixed sensitivity; the D200's sensor sensitivity is equivalent to ISO 100. The higher ISO values are achieved by amplifying the signal from the sensor.

Setting the ISO

To set the ISO sensitivity value on the D200 you can take two different routes; either open the Shooting menu, scroll to *ISO*, Multi Select right to open the sub-menu of values, then scroll down to highlight the required value and Multi Select right again to set it. Alternatively, you can also adjust the ISO by pressing and holding the **ISO** button on the top of the camera and turning the main command dial. The selected ISO value will be displayed in the control panel.

You can set the D200's ISO value through the Shooting menu or by pressing the ISO button, found on the left top of the camera, and turning the main command dial.

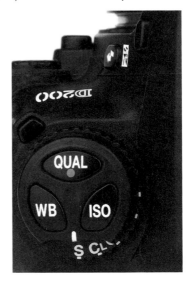

At higher ISO settings, you images will likely show increasing amounts of digital noise (i.e., colored artifacts or a general lack of smoothness). For optimum image quality in ideal light conditions, keep the D200 set to ISO 100. Image quality at the ISO 200 setting is virtually as good. At the ISO 400 setting, there is slight increase in graininess; at ISO 800, it is highly likely that you will see color shifts in your pictures, and a reduction in saturation and contrast; at 1600, digital noise is clearly perceptible, as is the affect on color saturation and contrast, but even at this high setting, the images the D200 produces are certainly usable. However, in my opinion, the settings above 1600 should be considered only when no other option (wider aperture, or slower shutter speed) would get the picture.

Hint: If the light level begins to drop as you shoot you can either raise the ISO setting, or using a longer shutter speed. Confronted with this situation I recommend putting the camera on a tripod, and selecting a longer exposure.

ISO Auto

I dislike this option so much that I will begin this section by suggesting you ignore it completely! Why? Well, it is important to understand that it does not work in quite the way I expect most users imagine. In P (Programmed Auto) and A (Aperture-Priority) modes, the ISO will not change until the exposure reaches the limits of the shutter speed range. The upper limit is always 1/8000 second, but the lower limit can be adjusted within Custom Setting b1 to be between 1/2 second and 1/250 second.

In S (Shutter-Priority) exposure mode, the ISO is shifted when the exposure reaches the limit of the available aperture range. Indeed, this is the only exposure mode with which *ISO Auto* might be useful because it will raise the ISO setting and thus maintain the pre-selected shutter speed which, in this mode, is probably critical to the success of the picture. In M (Manual) exposure mode, ISO is shifted if the selected shutter speed and aperture cannot attain a correct exposure (as indicated by the display in the viewfinder). It is also possible to select a maximum ISO setting for the *ISO Auto* control using the relevant option in Custom Setting b1.

The biggest problem with the *ISO Auto* mode is that you can never be quite sure of exactly what sensitivity value the D200 has set. Although ISO-AUTO appears in the control panel to indicate that this function is active, there is no indication of what ISO value has been set.

TTL Metering

The D200 has three metering options that will be familiar if you have used a Nikon AF camera before. To select a metering mode, rotate the metering mode dial (on the camera back to the right of the viewfinder eyepiece). The appropriate icon will be displayed in the control panel.

Matrix Metering

The metering pattern for this mode divides most of the image area into a series of segments and assesses the light seen through the lens to look for a number of attributes. The values for these attributes are then compared against a database of reference images stored in the camera's memory. From this comparison, the camera suggests a final exposure setting. The Matrix meter in the D200 is very sophisticated 1005-pixel RGB CCD-type sensor located in the viewfinder head that divides the frame area into 1005 different segments using an alternating pattern of red, green, and blue sensors to measure light values. In fact, it is a slightly modified version of the same system used in Nikon's flagship D2Xs D-SLR camera.

To get the most from the Matrix metering capabilities of the D200, use a D-type or G-type Nikkor lens, as these provide additional information from the autofocus system that assists the camera in estimating where in the frame the subject is likely to be. (The camera assumes the subject is in the plane of sharp focus and located in the region of the active focus area.) Nikon refer to the highest functionality of this system as 3D Color Matrix Metering II. If a Nikkor lens that does not communicate focus information to the camera is used, the system defaults to regular Color Matrix Metering II (i.e., the 3D assessment is not performed). By assessing color as well as brightness, this metering system helps to reduce the influence of overly bright or dark colors, thereby improving its overall accuracy. Earlier versions of Nikon's Matrix metering system are less capable.

Note: The very extreme edges of the frame are outside the area covered by the Matrix metering pattern.

Matrix metering uses four principle factors when calculating an exposure value:

• The overall brightness level of a scene

• The ratio of brightness between Matrix pattern segments

• The active focus area, which suggests the position of the subject in the frame

• Focus distance information provided by the lens (D-, or G-type only)

The D200 will endeavor to preserve highlight values over shadow values because, like transparency film, once the highlight detail is overexposed, data is lost and no amount of subsequent image manipulation will recover it. However, it is possible to recover shadow detail from underexposed areas (although the risk of digital noise increases). Therefore, if the scene you photograph has a wide contrast range (large variation in brightness), do not be surprised if it looks as though it has been very slightly underexposed. Fortunately, the D200 has two features that help you to evaluate an exposure: the histogram and the highlights displays (see pages 104-108 for details).

Center-Weighted Metering ⊙
The center-weighted metering pattern harks back to the very first TTL metering systems used by early Nikon SLR film cameras. In these cameras, the frame area was usually divided in a 60:40 ratio, with the bias being placed in the

central portion of the frame. The D200 uses a stronger ratio of 75:25, with 75% of the exposure reading based on the central area of the frame and the remaining 25% based on the outer area. Using Custom Setting b6, you can alter the diameter of the central metering area; at its default value of 0.31inches (8 mm), it corresponds to the circle defined by the four quadrant marks in the center of the camera's focusing screen.

Hint: Center-weighted metering is the least sophisticated of the three metering patterns available with the D200. Matrix metering will do an excellent job in most situations, and for particularly tricky lighting, spot metering is more useful than the center-weighted pattern.

Spot Metering [·]

Spot metering is extremely useful for measuring a highly specific area of a scene. For example, faced with a subject against a virtually black background (which might cause the Matrix metering system to overexpose the subject), spot metering allows you to take a reading from the subject without it being influenced by the background. The sensing area for the spot metering function of the D200 is a circle approximately 0.12 inches (3 mm) in diameter. The center of the metering area is aligned with the center of the selected (active) AF-sensor area, unless group dynamic AF is selected, in which case it is aligned to the center AF area of the currently selected group.

Note: If a non-CPU lens is used, or autofocus with closest subject priority is selected, the spot metering function is aligned with the center AF-sensor area only.

Hint: It is essential to remember that every TTL metering system measures reflected light and is calibrated to give a correct exposure for midtones. When using spot metering, you must make sure that the part of the scene you meter from represents a midtone. Otherwise, you will need to compensate the exposure value (see pages 89-91 for information about exposure compensation).

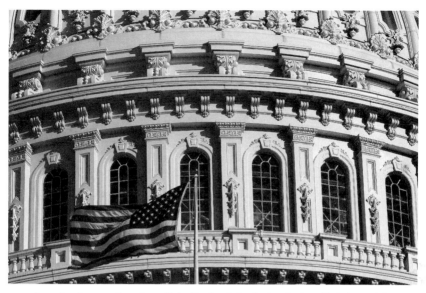

I prefer to use Aperture-Priority for telephoto shots when I want to make sure that depth of field is adequate to render everything sharply. For added stability, I recommend a monopod. It enhances sharpness but eliminates hassle of carrying and setting up a tripod.

Hint: In dynamic area AF, the D200 will attempt to follow a moving subject by shifting focus control between any of the AF-sensor areas. When this occurs, the spot metering also shifts to follow the active AF-sensor area. If in doubt, switch to manual focus, as the D200 will always use the selected AF-sensor area for spot metering in this focus mode.

Exposure Modes

The D200 offers four exposure modes: Programmed Auto (P), Aperture-Priority Auto (A), Shutter-Priority Auto (S), and Manual (M). To select an exposure mode, press and hold the 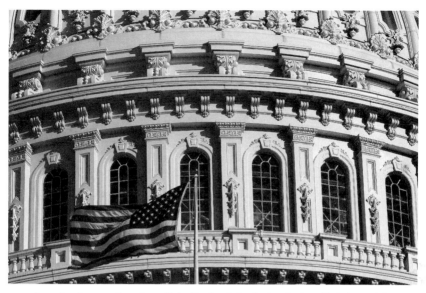 button on the camera top and rotate the main command dial until the required mode (P, A, S, or M) is displayed in the top left corner of the control panel.

Note: In order for P or S modes to operate, you must have a CPU lens attached to the camera. If you attach a non-CPU type lens, the exposure mode defaults to Aperture-Priority (A) and the icon for the selected mode (P or S) that is displayed in the control panel will blink.

Note: If you attach a non-CPU lens, A and M modes can be used but be sure lens data is entered via the Non-CPU Lens Data selection in the Shooting menu.

To select an exposure mode, press the ▣ button located on the right top of the camera behind the shutter release button, then turn the main command dial.

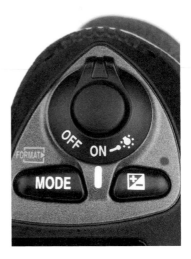

Programmed Auto Mode (P)

Program mode, as it is often referred to, automatically adjusts both the shutter speed and lens aperture to produce a correctly exposed image, as defined by the selected metering mode. If you decide that a particular combination chosen by the camera is not suitable, you can override the settings by turning the main command dial when the camera meter is activated. P * appears in the control panel (the camera is now in flexible program mode) and the viewfinder will display the altered shutter speed and aperture values you select. The two values change in tandem so the overall exposure remains the same (i.e. increasing the shutter speed will automatically decrease the aperture).

Hint: If you override the Program mode it will remain locked to its new settings for shutter speed and aperture even if the meter powers off. To cancel the override, you can do one of four things: rotate the main command dial until the indicator for flexible program P * is no longer displayed in the control panel, change the exposure mode, turn the camera off, or perform a camera reset.

Hint: In my opinion, Program mode is little better than the point-and-shoot options on many entry level cameras (i.e., the modes represented by icons, such as Portrait, Landscape, Sports, etc.). If you want to make informed decisions about shutter speed and aperture for creative photography, do not use Program mode!

Aperture-Priority Auto Mode (A)

In this mode the photographer selects an aperture value and the D200 will automatically choose a shutter speed to produce an appropriate exposure. The aperture is controlled by the sub-command dial and can be changed in increments of 1/3-stop at the default setting. The shutter speed the D200 selects will also change in increments of 1/3-stop by default. These EV step levels can be adjusted using Custom Setting b3 (see page 205).

Shutter-Priority Auto Mode (S)

In this mode, the photographer selects a shutter speed and the D200 will automatically choose an aperture value to produce an appropriate exposure. The shutter speed is controlled by the main command dial and is changed in increments of 1/3-stop at the default setting. The aperture value the D200 selects will also change in increments of 1/3-stop by default. These EV step levels can be adjusted using Custom Setting b3.

Note: In P, A, and S modes, if the subject or scene is too bright, the D200 will display a **Hi** warning in the viewfinder and the control panel. Likewise, if the subject or scene is too dark the D200 will display a **Lo** warning in the viewfinder and control panel.

Hint: If you use the D200 remotely, that is to say without having your eye to the viewfinder when you make an exposure (such as when taking a self-portrait using the self-timer or using the ML-3 IR Remote Control to release the shutter), you should cover the viewfinder eyepiece so that light does not leak into the exposure. The metering sensor of the D200 is located within the viewfinder head, therefore, light entering via the viewfinder eyepiece will affect exposures made in P, A, and S, modes. Nikon supplies the D200 with the DK-5 eyepiece cover specifically for these purposes, but to use it, the rubber eyecup fitted onto viewfinder eyepiece must be removed first. Personally, I find attaching the DK-5 a fuss, so I keep a small square of thick, black felt fabric in my camera bag and drape it over the camera to block light when I am shooting remotely.

Manual Mode (M)

This mode offers the photographer total control over exposure, and is probably the most useful if you want to learn more about the effect of shutter speed and aperture on the final appearance of your pictures. You choose and control both the shutter speed (via the main command dial by default) and the lens aperture (via the sub-command dial by default). An analogue display shown in the viewfinder indicates the level of exposure your settings would produce. If the camera determines the exposure values are set for a proper exposure, a single indent mark appears below the central 0. If the camera determines that the settings would produce an under-exposed result, the degree of under-exposure is indicated by the number of indent marks that appear to the right side of the central 0. Conversely, if the chosen settings would create an over-exposed result, the degree of over exposure is indicated by the number of indent marks to the left side of the central 0. The more indent marks that appear, the greater the degree of exposure "error."

Note: The priority of the two command dials can be changed via Custom Setting f5 (see page 222).

Autoexposure Lock (AE-L)

If you take a meter reading in any of the three autoexposure modes (P, A, or S) and recompose the picture after taking a reading, it is likely (particularly when using center-weighted or spot metering) that the metering mode sensing area will now fall on an alternative part of the scene and probably produce a different exposure value. To avoid this, the D200 allows you to lock the initial exposure reading so you can reframe the shot and take the picture. Start by positioning the part of the scene you want to meter within the appropriate metering area, press the shutter release button halfway down to acquire a reading, then press and hold the 🔘 button. You can now recompose and take the picture at the metered value. AE-L will appear in the viewfinder display while this function is active.

Hint: It is possible to use the shutter release button to perform the autoexposure lock function; just select +Release Button for AE-Lock in Custom Setting c1.

Hint: While AE-L works with all three metering modes, it is generally most effective with center-weighted and spot metering. These two metering modes are most useful in very difficult lighting conditions where they can take a more accurate exposure reading from a specific area of the scene. Difficult lighting conditions like these may "fool" the Matrix metering.

Exposure Compensation

As mentioned previously, the TTL metering system of the D200 works on the assumption that it is pointed at a scene with a reflectivity that averages out to the equivalent of a mid-tone. Nikon seems to have calibrated against a reference that has a reflectivity value of approximately 12 – 13%, so if you use a standard 18% grey card to estimate exposure, you will find your results will be a third to a half-stop underexposed.

Many scenes you encounter will not specifically reflect 12 – 13% of the light falling on them. For example, a landscape under a blanket of fresh snowfall is going to reflect far more light than a mountain covered with black volcanic rock. Unless you compensate your exposure, these more extreme scenes will both be reproduced as middle gray in your pictures.

To set exposure compensation, hold down the ⊠ button on the camera top behind the shutter release button, then turn the main command dial until the required value is shown in the control panel. The value is also displayed in the viewfinder while the ⊠ button is held down.

Note: The degree of compensation will change in steps of +/- 1/3, 1/2, or 1 EV depending on which step size is selected from Custom Setting b4.

In Manual mode (M), the exposure is set according to the value suggested by the camera's TTL meter if the analogue display shows no deviance on either side of the 0 midpoint. If an exposure compensation factor is applied, the display shifts either to the left (+ compensation) or right (- compensation) of the 0 midpoint by the amount of compensation you have dialed in and the 0 blinks.

As you dial in the compensation, you will see a small + or - icon displayed to the right of the analogue scale along the bottom of the viewfinder display (the ⊠ button must be depressed to see this; as soon as you release the ⊠ button, +/- appears in its place, and is also shown in the control panel on the camera top. To put the exposure compensation into effect, you must now adjust the shutter speed and/or aperture so the analogue scale display is shifted back so there is no deviance on either side of the 0 midpoint.

Note: Once you have made these adjustments and the analogue scale is centered on 0 again, if you press the 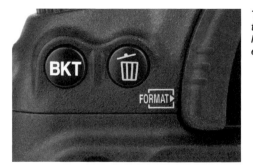 button, the analogue scale shifts to show the amount of compensation applied and the icon to the right of the scale indicates whether it is a + or - value. This is a useful and quick way to check how much compensation you have applied

The exposure compensation icon +/- remains visible in the viewfinder and control panel, regardless of the exposure mode in use, as a reminder that you have an exposure compensation value applied. Once you have set a compensation factor, it will remain locked until you hold down the button and reset the value to 0.0.

Bracketing Exposure

It is important when shooting digital pictures to expose as accurately as you can, since overexposure will lose highlight detail and underexposure tends to degrade image quality with digital noise. The TTL meter of the D200 is very effective, but not infallible. To increase the chances of getting a correct exposure, particularly when confronted with difficult lighting conditions, it is often wise to bracket exposures (i.e., take a series of pictures at slightly different settings).

The bracketing system in the D200 allows you to take a sequence of exposures varied by increments of 1/3, 1/2, or 1 EV, based on which you select from Custom Setting b3. The

The ● button is on the camera back to the left of the viewfinder eyepiece.

bracketing sequence can also be selected to affect the exposure (*AE Only*), flash output (*Flash Only*), or a combination of the two (*AE & Flash*) based on your selection from Custom Setting e5.

To set the bracketing function, press the 🔘 button and turn the main command dial to select the number of exposures to be made in the bracketing sequence. BKT will be displayed in the control panel and the exposure compensation icon +/- will be shown in the control panel and in the viewfinder. Press the 🔘 button and turn the sub-command dial to select the exposure increment to be applied.

Note: It is possible to set the main command dial and the sub-command dial to operate exposure bracketing by using the options found in Custom Setting e8.

Note: In M mode, there are further bracketing options available; access to these is via Custom Setting e6.

To cancel bracketing, press the 🔘 button and rotate the main command dial until the number of shots in the bracketing sequence is set to zero and BKT is no longer displayed in the control panel. The full range of bracketing values for the AE only, Flash only, and AE & Flash options is shown in the tables below:

Bracketing Considerations
- In single frame shooting mode, the shutter release button must be depressed to make each exposure in the bracketing sequence.

- When using exposure bracketing, if the D200 is set to continuous high-speed or continuous low-speed shooting mode and you press and hold the shutter release button down, the camera will only take the number of frames specified in the bracketing sequence. The camera stops regardless of whether or not the shutter release button continues to be depressed.

- If you turn the D200 off or have to change the memory card during a bracketing sequence, the camera remembers which exposure values are outstanding, so when you turn the camera back on or insert a new memory card, the sequence will resume from where it left off.

- You can combine a bracketing sequence with a fixed exposure compensation factor. For example, if you apply an exposure compensation of +1.0 EV to deal with a scene such as a snow covered landscape and then set a bracket sequence of three frames at an increment of 1 EV, the actual exposures you make will be at 0, +1 EV, and +2 EV.

EV Step of 1/3

Control panel display	No. of shots	Exposure increment	Bracketing order (EVs)
+ 3F 0.3+ ······₁₁P········ −	3	+1/3	+0.3, 0, +0.7
+ 3F 0.7+ ·····₁₁₁P········ −	3	+2/3	+0.7, 0, +1.3
+ 3F 1.0+ ···₁·₁·P········ −	3	+1	1.0, 0, 2.0
-- 3F 0.3+ ········Pᵢᵢ······ −	3	−1/3	−0.3, −0.7, 0
-- 3F 0.7+ ········P·ᵢᵢ····· −	3	−2/3	−0.7, −1.3, 0
-- 3F 1.0+ ········P·ᵢ·ᵢ···· −	3	−1	−1.0, −2.0, 0
+2F 0.3+ ·······₁P········ −	2	+1/3	0, +0.3
+2F 0.7+ ·····₁₁P········ −	2	+2/3	0, +0.7
+2F 1.0+ ···₁·P········ −	2	+1	0, +1
--2F 0.3+ ········Pᵢ······ −	2	−1/3	0, −0.3
--2F 0.7+ ········P·ᵢ····· −	2	−2/3	0, −0.7
--2F 1.0+ ········P·ᵢ···· −	2	−1	0, −1
3F 0.3+ ·····₁₁Pᵢ······ −	3	±1/3	0, −0.3, +0.3
3F 0.7+ ·····₁·P·ᵢ······ −	3	±2/3	0, −0.7, +0.7
3F 1.0+ ·····₁·P·ᵢ·ᵢ···· −	3	±1	0, −1, +1
5F 0.3+ ·····ᵢᵢPᵢᵢ······ −	5	±1/3	0, −0.7, −0.3, +0.3, +0.7
5F 0.7+ ····ᵢ·ᵢP·ᵢ·ᵢ···· −	5	±2/3	0, −1.3, −0.7, +0.7, +1.3
5F 1.0+ ·ᵢ·ᵢ·P·ᵢ·ᵢ· −	5	±1	0, −2.0, −1, +1, +2.0
7F 0.3+ ····ᵢᵢᵢPᵢᵢᵢ······ −	7	±1/3	0, −1.0, −0.7, −0.3, +0.3, +0.7, +1.0
7F 0.7+ ···ᵢ·ᵢ·P·ᵢ·ᵢᵢ··· −	7	±2/3	0, −2.0, −1.3, −0.7, +0.7, +1.3, +2.0
7F 1.0+ ᵢ·ᵢ·ᵢ·P·ᵢ·ᵢ·ᵢ −	7	±1	0, −3.0, −2.0, −1.0, +1.0, +2.0, +3.0
9F 0.3+ ····ᵢᵢᵢᵢPᵢᵢᵢᵢ···· −	9	±1/3	0, −1.3, −1.0, −0.7, −0.3, +0.3, +0.7, +1.0, +1.3
9F 0.7+ ·ᵢ·ᵢ·ᵢ·P·ᵢ·ᵢ·ᵢ· −	9	±2/3	0, −2.7, −2.0, −1.3, −0.7, +0.7, +1.3, +2.0, +2.7
9F 1.0▄ᵢ·ᵢ·ᵢ·P·ᵢ·ᵢ·ᵢ▶	9	±1	0, −4.0, −3.0, −2.0, −1.0, +1.0, +2.0, +3.0, +4.0

EV Step of 1/2

Control panel display	No. of shots	Exposure increment	Bracketing order (EVs)
+ 3F0.5 + ·········ᵢ·ᵧ̂·········–	3	+½	+0.5, 0, +1.0
+ 3F 1.0 + ·····ᵢ·ᵢ··ᵧ̂·········–	3	+1	1.0, 0, 2.0
-- 3F0.5 + ·········ᵧ̂·ᵢᵧ·······–	3	−½	−0.5, −1.0, 0
-- 3F 1.0 + ·········ᵧ̂·ᵢ··ᵢ····–	3	−1	−1.0, −2.0, 0
+ 2F0.5 + ·········ᵧᵧ̂·········–	2	+½	0, +0.5
+ 2F 1.0 + ·······ᵢ··ᵧ̂·········–	2	+1	0, +1
-- 2F0.5 + ·········ᵧ̂ᵧ·········–	2	−½	0, −0.5
-- 2F 1.0 + ·········ᵧ̂··ᵢ·······–	2	−1	0, −1
3F0.5 + ········ᵧᵧ̂ᵧ········–	3	±½	0, −0.5, +0.5
3F 1.0 + ·······ᵢ··ᵧ̂··ᵢ·······–	3	±1	0, −1, +1
5F0.5 + ······ᵢᵧᵧ̂ᵧᵢ······–	5	±½	0, −1.0, −0.5, +0.5, +1.0
5F 1.0 + ·····ᵢ··ᵢ··ᵧ̂··ᵢ··ᵢ·····–	5	±1	0, −2.0, −1, +1, +2.0
7F0.5 + ·····ᵧᵢᵧᵧ̂ᵧᵢᵧ·····–	7	±½	0, −1.5, −1.0, −0.5, +0.5, +1.0, +1.5
7F 1.0 + ᵢ··ᵢ··ᵢ··ᵧ̂··ᵢ··ᵢ··ᵢ–	7	±1	0, −3.0, −2.0, −1.0, +1.0, +2.0, +3.0
9F0.5 + ····ᵢᵧᵢᵧᵧ̂ᵧᵢᵧᵢ····–	9	±½	0, −2.0, −1.5, −1.0, −0.5, +0.5, +1.0, +1.5, +2.0
9F 1.0 ⬅ᵢ··ᵢ··ᵢ··ᵧ̂··ᵢ··ᵢ··ᵢ➡	9	±1	0, −4.0, −3.0, −2.0, −1.0, +1.0, +2.0, +3.0, +4.0

EV Step of 1

Control panel display	No. of shots	Exposure increment	Bracketing order (EVs)
+ 3F 1.0 + ·····ᵢ·ᵢ··ᵧ̂·········–	3	+1	1.0, 0, 2.0
-- 3F 1.0 + ·········ᵧ̂·ᵢ··ᵢ····–	3	−1	−1.0, −2.0, 0
+ 2F 1.0 + ·······ᵢ··ᵧ̂·········–	2	+1	0, +1
-- 2F 1.0 + ·········ᵧ̂··ᵢ·······–	2	−1	0, −1
3F 1.0 + ·······ᵢ··ᵧ̂··ᵢ·······–	3	±1	0, −1, +1
5F 1.0 + ·····ᵢ··ᵢ··ᵧ̂··ᵢ··ᵢ·····–	5	±1	0, −2.0, −1, +1, +2.0
7F 1.0 + ᵢ··ᵢ··ᵢ··ᵧ̂··ᵢ··ᵢ··ᵢ–	7	±1	0, −3.0, −2.0, −1.0, +1.0, +2.0, +3.0
9F 1.0 ⬅ᵢ··ᵢ··ᵢ··ᵧ̂··ᵢ··ᵢ··ᵢ➡	9	±1	0, −4.0, −3.0, −2.0, −1.0, +1.0, +2.0, +3.0, +4.0

Exposure Challenges

If the D200 is your first digital SLR camera and your previous photography has been done with a 35mm camera and color negative film, you may find controlling exposure with the D200 rather more demanding. Color negative (print) film is very tolerant to exposure errors, particularly overexposure, and the automated processing machines used to produce your prints are capable of correcting exposure errors over a range of −2 to +3 stops, plus they can adjust color balance at the same time. Chances are that you may never have noticed your exposure errors when looking at the finished prints!

Controlling exposure with a digital SLR is analogous to shooting on transparency (slide) film; there is virtually no margin for error. Even moderate overexposure will blow out highlight detail, leaving no usable image data in these areas. Underexposure isn't much better since, to correct for its affects, the sensor signal will require amplification (i.e., the camera has to boost the signal to fill in the gaps). The result of correcting an underexposed digital image is often the manifestation of digital noise, which will degrade image quality.

Digital Infrared Photography

Some digital cameras have the ability to record light beyond the limits of the spectrum visible to the human eye, such as infrared light. However, most camera designers work hard to keep infrared light out of digital cameras because it adversely affects apparent sharpness, reduces the contrast in skies, and can reveal unflattering skin features that would otherwise not be visible.

The low-pass filter array in front of the CCD sensor in the D200 includes a layer designed to reduce the transmission of infrared light (see page 27); it is this filter that produces the green tint when you look at the surface of the filter array when inspecting or cleaning it. This infrared blocking layer is very effective, therefore the D200 cannot be recommended for digital infrared photography.

Aperture and Depth of Field

When a lens brings light to focus on a camera's sensor, there is only ever one plane-of-focus that is critically sharp. However, in the two dimensional picture produced by the camera there is a zone in front of and behind the plane-of-focus that is perceived to be sharp. This area of apparent sharpness is often referred to as the depth of field, and its extent is influenced by the camera-to-subject distance together with the focal length and aperture of the lens in use.

If the focal length and camera-to-subject distance are constant, depth of field will be shallower with large apertures (low f/numbers) and deeper with small apertures (high f/numbers). If the aperture and camera-to-subject distance are constant, depth of field will also be shallower with long focal lengths (telephoto range) and deeper with shorter focal lengths (wide-angle range). And finally, if the focal length and aperture are constant, depth of field will be greater at longer camera-to-subject distances and shallower at closer camera-to-subject distances. Depth of field is an important consideration when deciding on a particular composition as it has a direct and fundamental effect on the final appearance of the picture.

Depth-of-Field Preview
In order that the viewfinder image is as bright as possible for composing, focusing, and metering, modern cameras such as the D200 operate with lenses automatically set to their maximum aperture. The iris in the lens does not close down to the shooting aperture until after the shutter release button has been pressed and the reflex mirror has lifted, just a fraction of a second before the shutter opens. However, this means that the image you see in the viewfinder is as it would appear if the photograph were to be taken at the lens' maximum aperture. To assess the depth of field visually, you

must close the lens iris down to the shooting aperture by using the depth-of-field preview feature.

Note: Remember, as the size of the lens aperture decreases (higher f/number), the depth of field increases.

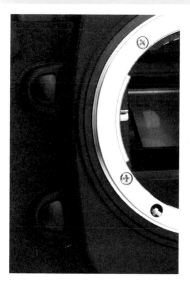

The Depth-of-Field Preview button is the top of two buttons found on the camera front to the right of the lens mount when then camera is held in the shooting position.

The D200 has a Depth-of-Field Preview button (the upper button of the two buttons on the front of the camera between the hand grip and the lens mount) that, when pressed, stops the lens down to the selected shooting aperture allowing you to see the effect the aperture has on depth of field. The viewfinder image will become darker, as less light passes through the lens when the aperture iris is closed down.

Hint: At apertures of f/11 or smaller (higher f/numbers), the viewfinder image will become very dark and difficult to see, even with brightly lit scenes. In these situations it is often better to make a general assessment of depth of field at f/8 and then change the aperture value to the one required for shooting.

Depth of Field Considerations

Probably the most important consideration concerning depth of field is that it is slightly less for images shot on a D200 than those shot on a film camera. This is due to the smaller size of the sensor in the D200 (23.7 x 15.6 mm) compared with a 35mm film frame (24 x 36 mm); the digital picture must be magnified by a greater amount compared with 35mm film to achieve any given print size. Therefore, at normal viewing distances, detail that appears to be sharp in a print made from a film-based image may no longer look sharp in a print of the same dimensions made from a digital file. If you use the depth of field values given in tables for 35mm lenses, you will find they do not correspond to images shot on the D200, assuming the same camera-to-subject distance and focal length apply. To guarantee that the depth of field in pictures taken on the D200 is sufficiently deep, use the values for the next larger lens aperture. For example, if set your lens to f/16 use the depth of field values for f/11 with the D200.

Apart from setting a small aperture (large f/number) to maximize depth of field in a landscape picture, it is worth remembering that, at mid to long focus distances, the zone of apparent sharpness will extend about 1/3 in front of the point of focus and 2/3 behind it. Therefore, by placing the point of focus about a third of the way into your scene you will maximize your depth of field.

In portrait photography, it is often preferable to render the background out-of-focus so it does not distract from the subject. The simplest way to achieve this effect is to use a longer focal length lens; a short telephoto of 70 – 105mm is ideal, in combination with a large aperture (low f/number). You can assess the effect using the camera's depth-of-field preview feature.

In close-up photography, depth of field is limited so convention suggests you set the lens to its minimum aperture value (largest f/number). However, I strongly recommend that you avoid doing this because the effects of diffraction at (or near) the minimum aperture of a lens cause a significant loss of image sharpness. Generally, you will achieve superior results at an aperture two-stops more (lower f/number) than the minimum value. It is likely that, even in good light, the shutter speed will be rather slow when shooting with a small lens aperture, so consider using a tripod or other camera support whenever possible.

Unlike the distribution of the depth of field zone for mid to long focus distances, at very short distances, the depth of field extends by an equal amount in front of and behind the plane of focus. By placing the plane of focus with care, you can use this fact to further maximize depth of field. The camera's Depth-of-Field Preview button will allow you to preview the depth of field in your composition.

Shutter Speed

If you handhold your camera, it is worth remembering a rule of thumb concerning the minimum shutter speed that is generally sufficient to prevent a loss of sharpness due to camera shake: Take the reciprocal value of the lens focal length and use this as the slowest shutter speed with that lens. For example, with a focal length of 200mm, set a minimum shutter speed of 1/200 second.

Note: Longer focal length lenses and higher subject magnification in close-up photography will amplify the effects of camera shake.

Shutter speed can be used for creative effect because it controls the way that motion is depicted in a photograph. Generally, fast shutter speeds are used if you wish to stop motion in sports or action photography. Slower shutter speeds (1/30th second or longer) can be used to introduce a degree of blur that will often evoke a greater sense of movement than a subject that is rendered pin-sharp. Alternatively, you can pan the camera with the subject so that it appears relatively sharp against an increased level of blur in the background.

If you are photographing a stationary subject and there are other elements moving in and out of the scene that you would prefer not be a part of the shot, a very long shutter speed of several minutes or more can often be very effective. This enables your static subject to be rendered properly while the moving elements do not record sufficient information in any part of the frame to be visible. Generally, this technique will require a strong neutral density filter to be effective in daylight conditions. So next time you want to take a picture of a famous building and exclude all the other visitors from cluttering up your composition you know how!

Two-Button Reset

If you want to restore the default settings on the D200, press and hold the **QUAL** and 🔲 buttons. The green dots beside each button are a reminder of their function for this feature. Here are the settings and menu options that are affected:

Option	Default
Focus area	Center 1
Exposure mode	Programmed Auto
Flexible program	Off
Exposure compensation	+/- 0
AE hold	Off 2
Bracketing	Off 3
Flash Sync mode	Front-curtain
Flash compensation	0
FV lock	Off
Image quality	JPEG Normal
Image size	Large
White balance	Auto4
ISO sensitivity	100

1. Mode is not reset in self-timer and remote control options.
2. Custom Setting c2 AE-L/AF-L is not affected.
3. Number of shots resets to zero, increment resets to 1 EV for exposure and 1 for white balance bracketing.
4. Fine tuning is reset to 0.

Note: Options selected in the Custom Settings menu are not affected by this action.

Image Playback

One of the most useful features of a digital camera is the ability to review your photographs as you shoot. Using the playback functions on the D200 will allow you to see not only the images you have taken but also a range of helpful and interesting information. When you review your images, however, keep in mind that the small image displayed on the screen is not represented with sufficient precision to make any critical analysis of color or exposure. Personally, I believe that the image displayed on the LCD monitor should only be considered for confirmation that an exposure has been recorded, noting whether the image appears sharp, and observing the success or otherwise of the composition.

Immediately after taking an exposure on the D200, the image review will provide a brief display of the photograph on the LCD monitor (assuming On is selected from the Image Review option in the Playback menu). A quick glance as to whether you have captured the image as intended is often all that is required. In single frame and self-timer shooting modes, the image is displayed almost immediately after the exposure is made. In either of the continuous shooting modes (high- or low-speed), the camera must write the image data from the buffer memory to the memory card for each image recorded, so there is a short delay. The camera then displays each image chronologically as soon as it has been saved.

Note: Select *Off* from the *Image Review* option in the Playback menu if you do not want the camera to display the image automatically after shooting.

Pressing the ⊡ button just to the left of the LCD monitor on the camera back will display the most recent image taken by the camera. If you wish to view other saved images, simply Multi Select left or right to scroll through them. To return to shooting mode, press the ⊡ button again, or just press the shutter release button halfway down.

Note: If you want images shot in an upright (vertical) composition to be display in the correct orientation select *On* for the *Auto Image Rotation* option in the Setup menu.

Information Pages

A very useful feature of the image playback function on the D200 is the host of information that can be accessed while viewing the image on the LCD monitor. This information can help you ensure that you have achieved a good exposure, as well as give you detailed information about how, when, and where the exposure was made. Depending on the selections made using the *Display Mode* option in the Playback menu as well as whether or not an image file contains data recorded from a GPS, there are up to eight different pages of information that can be displayed for each image.

To access these pages when an image is displayed, Multi Select down to scroll through each page in the following order: Histogram (composite), Basic Information, File Information, Shooting Data (1), Shooting Data (2), GPS Data, Histogram (RGB), and Highlights. If you Multi Select up, you will access these pages in the reverse order.

Note: The following five pages can be selected or deselected for display using the *Display Mode* option in the Playback menu: *Histogram (composite), Shooting Data (1), Shooting Data (2), Histogram (RGB),* and *Highlights.* The *Basic Information* and *File Information* pages are always displayed.

Note: The *GPS Data* page is only available if the displayed image file contains data recorded from a GPS.

The following is a breakdown of exactly what each information page contains:

Basic Information:
* Provides minimal information for simple, uncluttered viewing of the image.
* Displays: *Protect Status, Folder Number/File Number*

File Information:
* Shows an unobstructed view of the image while providing additional information.
* Displays: *Protect Status, Focus Brackets (set from Display Mode in the Playback menu), Frame Number/Total Number of Frames, Folder Name, File Name, Image Size, Image Quality, Date of Recording, Time of Recording, Folder Number/File Number*

Shooting Data (1):
* A block of information will be displayed superimposed over the center portion of the screen, obstructing the view of the image.
* Displays: *Protect Status, Camera Name, Metering Method, Shutter Speed, Aperture, Exposure Mode, Exposure Compensation, Focal Length, Flash Sync Mode, Folder Number/File Number*

Note: Shooting Data (1) can be particularly useful when trying to achieve similar results to those of another shot in a similar environment, learning about your shooting style, and learning what settings produce particular results.

Note: This page will only be displayed if *Data* is selected from the *Display Mode* option in the Playback menu.

Shooting Data (2):

- A block of information will be displayed superimposed over the center portion of the screen, obstructing the view of the image.
- Displays: *Protect Status, Image Optimization, ISO Sensitivity, White Balance/White Balance Adjustment, Tone Compensation, Sharpening, Color Mode/Hue Adjustment, Saturation, Image Comment, Folder Number/File Number*

Note: *Shooting Data (2)* can help you understand the effects of image settings and adjustments on the appearance of your picture.

Note: This page will only be displayed if *Data* is selected from the *Display Mode* option in the Playback menu.

GPS Data:

- A block of information will be displayed superimposed over the center portion of the screen, obstructing the view of the image.
- Displays: *Protect Status, Latitude, Longitude, Altitude, Coordinated Universal Time (UTC), Folder Number/File Number*

Note: The *GPS Data* page will only be displayed if the camera was connected to a compatible GPS unit at the time of exposure.

RGB Histogram:

- Provides an individual histogram for each of the red, green, and blue channels, together with an RGB composite histogram and a thumbnail of the image file.
- Displays: *Protect Status, Image Highlights, Folder Number/File Number, Histogram – RGB composite, Histogram – Red Channel, Histogram – Green Channel, Histogram – Blue Channel, Current Channel*

Note: This page will only be displayed if *RGB Histogram* is selected from the *Display Mode* option in the Playback menu.

Note: To show a highlight warning display, which indicates areas of the image that may be overexposed, press the Multi Selector while holding the ⊛ button down. To scroll through a highlight warning for each channel keep ⊛ pressed and Multi Select right or left to select the required channel; a yellow frame will surround the histogram of the selected channel.

Highlights:
- Shows an unobstructed view of the image.
- Displays: *Protect Status, Image Highlights, Current Channel RGB and individual channels, Folder Number/File Number*

Note: This page will only be displayed if *Highlight* is selected from the Display Mode option in the Playback menu.

Note: The *Highlights* page is very useful for checking to see if information may have been lost as a result of overexposure; a flashing border will mark any relevant areas. You can display the highlight areas for each separate color channel by Multi Selecting right or left.

Note: To scroll through a highlight warning for each channel (composite, red, green, and blue) press and hold the ⊛ button then Multi Select right or left to select the required channel. The selected channel is indicated at the bottom of the screen.

Histogram:
- A composite histogram will be displayed superimposed over the center portion of the screen, obstructing the view of the image.
- Displays: *Protect Status, Histogram, Folder Number/File Number*

Note: This page will only be displayed if *Histogram* is selected from the *Display Mode* option in the Playback menu.

Note: The *Histogram* page offers a graphical display of the tonal values recorded by the camera. The horizontal axis represents brightness, with dark tones shown to the left and bright tones to the right. No data (i.e., pure black) is shown at the extreme left end of the axis and total saturation (i.e., pure white) is shown at the extreme right end of the axis. The vertical axis represents the number of pixels that have that specific brightness value.

Understanding the Histogram

The shape and position of the histogram curve indicates the range of tones that have been captured in the picture. Dark tones will be distributed to the left of the histogram graph and light tones to the right. In a picture of a scene containing an average distribution of tones—from a few dark shadows, through a wide number of mid-tones, to a few bright highlights—the curve will start in the bottom left corner of the graph, slope upwards towards the middle, then curve down to the bottom right corner. This means a wide range of tones have been recorded. If the curve begins at a point some way up the left or right side of the histogram display, so the curve looks as though it has been cut off abruptly, the camera will not have recorded tones in either the shadows (left side) or highlights (right side). This is often an indication of under- or overexposure.

Generally, controlling exposure to ensure that highlight detail is retained is more important than exposing for shadow areas. If the histogram curve is weighted heavily toward the right side of the graph and cuts off at a point along the right-hand vertical axis, highlight data has likely been compromised or lost. In this case, reduce the exposure until the right-hand end of the curve touches the bottom horizontal axis of the graph before it reaches the vertical one. Conversely, if shadow detail is important, make sure the curve stops along the bottom horizontal axis before it reaches the left-hand vertical axis.

Obviously, not all scenes contain an even distribution of tones; many will have a natural predominance of light or

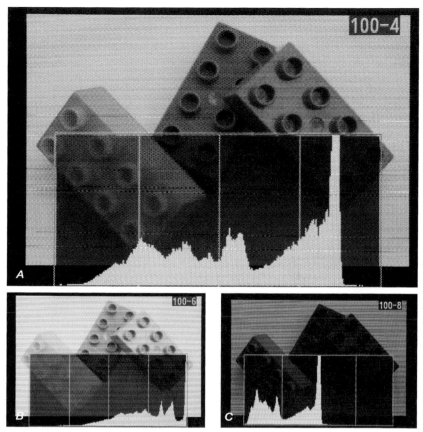

The three pictures shown here represent a range of exposures. Image A is properly exposed; the left and right-hand ends of the histogram curve stop on the bottom axis before reaching either side of the graph, indicating that all tones have been recorded. Image B is 2 stops overexposed; the curve is biased to the right side of the graph and it cuts off at a point high up along the right-hand vertical axis. In this case, highlight detail has been "blown-out" and not recorded. Image C is 2 stops underexposed; the curve is heavily biased toward the left side of the graph, with virtually no light tones recorded. In this case, digital noise is likely to be apparent.

dark areas. In these cases, the histogram curve will be biased to the right (light scenes) or the left (dark scenes), but provided the histogram curve stops on the bottom axis before it reaches either side of the graph, the image should still contain a full range of the available highlight or shadow tones in the subject or scene being photographed. Scenes that are low in contrast will have a curve that looks like a narrow spike and falls far short of either the left or right-hand sides of the graph. You have two choices as to how to deal with this situation; either use the *Tone Compensation* function within the *Optimize Image* Shooting menu option (see pages 130-131) to have the contrast control performed by the camera, or adjust the contrast level at a later stage using image-processing software.

Thumbnail Playback
If you wish to view multiple images at once on the LCD monitor, press the ⊙ button and rotate the main command dial; you can choose to view either four or nine images at one time. A yellow border surrounds the highlighted image. To scroll through the images use the Multi Selector. Once highlighted, you can press the center of the Multi Selector to show the image at full-frame, you protect an image by pressing the ⊙ button, and you can delete an image by pressing the ⊙ button. To scroll through the thumbnails a page at a time, press and hold the ⊙ button and rotate the sub-command dial. To return to full-frame image playback, hold the ⊙ button and rotate the main command dial until a single image fills the screen.

Playback Zoom
The image displayed on the monitor screen is usually too small to determine with any certainty whether or not it is sharp. The playback zoom feature allows you to enlarge the image by up to 25x (equivalent to a 400% view on a computer screen). To zoom into the image displayed on the monitor screen, press the ⊙ button. The image will appear slightly enlarged. To increase the degree of magnification, press and hold the ⊙ button and a red border with blue corner sections will appear superimposed over the displayed image. Continue to hold the ⊙ button down and rotate the main command dial to reduce the size of the red border and zero in on a section of the image. Release the ⊙

button to display the enlarged section. To select a different area of the image press the ● button again to show the red border and use the Multi Selector to move the border over the area of the image you wish to enlarge.

Rotating the main command dial will display, depending on the direction of rotation, either the next image or the preceding one stored on the memory card at the same degree of magnification. This is a useful feature if there are a number of similar images of the same subject and you want to check a specific detail such as a certain person's eyes in a group portrait. To exit the playback zoom feature, simply press the ● button again.

Protecting Images

To protect an image from inadvertent deletion, display the image on the LCD monitor in full-frame single image playback and press the ● button. A small key icon will appear in the upper left corner, superimposed over the image. To remove the protection, open the image and press ● again and check that the key icon is no longer displayed.

Note: Protected images are only protected from deletion, not from formatting. Be sure that you have transferred all the images on your memory card to a safe location (such as your computer) before formatting it.

Deleting Images

Images can be deleted using one of two routes. The quickest and easiest is to use press ● button when the image to be deleted is displayed on the monitor screen. The first press of the button opens a warning dialog box that asks for confirmation of the delete command. To complete the process, press the ● button again. To cancel the delete process, press the ● button to return to viewing the image. Images can also be deleted via the playback menu. There are two options: delete images individually, or delete all images stored on the memory card.

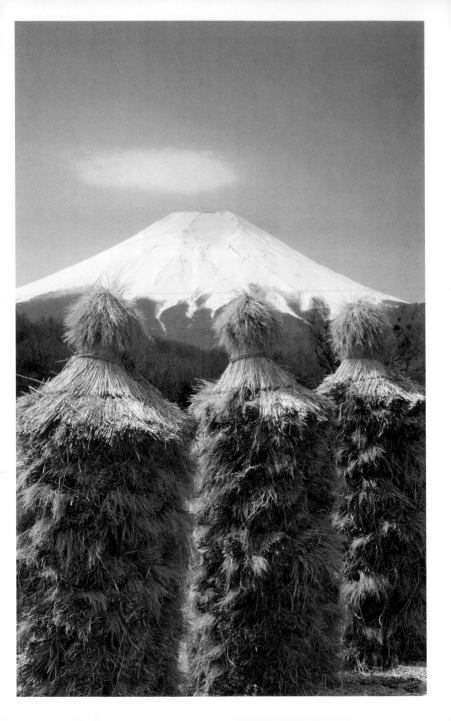

White Balance and Optimizing Images

We are all familiar with the way the color of sunlight changes during the course of a day from the orange/yellow colors immediately after sunrise, through the cooler look of light around midday, to the red/orange colors that appear as the sun sets. These changes are significant and our eyes can see them quite clearly. However, the color of light (not to be confused with the color of the objects from which it is reflected) changes in subtle ways at other times of the day and in different climatic conditions. Furthermore, different types of light sources, such a household bulb, or camera flashgun emit light of a different color. The color of light is referred to as its color temperature (see panel on page 112), and in many instances our eyes and brain are remarkably good at adapting to these changes in the color temperature of the light so that they are not apparent to us. Think about what you see when you stand outside a building in which the interior lamps are switched on in daylight – the light the lamps emit often appears very yellow, but if you look at the same building after dark the light from the lamps now appears to be white. This is an example of the adaptive process that our eyes and brain apply to light – one which cameras cannot perform!

Cameras have a fixed response to the color temperature of the light they record; film has a response limited to a specific color temperature (for daylight balanced film this is equivalent to direct sunlight at midday under a clear sky) but digital cameras such as the D200 are far more flexible, as they can process the picture data to equate to a variety of specific color temperatures, either automatically, or by selecting the color temperature manually. This function is known as the white balance control.

◁ *The D200 provides a sophisticated white balance capability, able to achieve an accurate color rendition in almost any lighting or photographic situation*

What Is Color Temperature?

The color of light is often referred to as its 'color temperature', which is expressed in units called degrees Kelvin (K). It sounds counter intuitive but warm light (red/orange tones) has a low temperature and cool light (blue tones) has a high temperature.

Why is this? Well, the color temperature of a light source equates to the color of something called a 'black body radiator'—a concept used by scientists that involves a theoretical object that can re-emit 100% of the energy it absorbs. As it is heated and becomes hotter, its color changes from black, to red, orange, yellow, and through to blue. The visual output of a light source is said to approximate to a 'black body' at the same temperature, thus at low color temperatures light contains a high proportion of red wavelengths, and at a high color temperature it comprises of blue wavelengths.

Direct sunlight under a clear sky at mid-day most commonly has a color temperature around 5500K, and the light emitted by a tungsten bulb, which has an orange hue, has a color temperature around 3000K.

Note: The color temperature of daylight will vary according to a number of factors, including time of day, time of year, latitude, altitude, and atmospheric and climatic conditions.

Digital cameras are very versatile and most allow you to set a specific color temperature, also referred to as the white balance. In addition, they often have automatic white balance capabilities, so when you view the image in the camera, or computer, the colors are matched to your chosen white balance value. Assuming this value corresponds to the color temperature of the prevailing light the scene will be rendered without any color casts. You can use the white balance feature creatively by setting an alternative value, which does not correspond to the prevailing light and create a deliberate color shift.

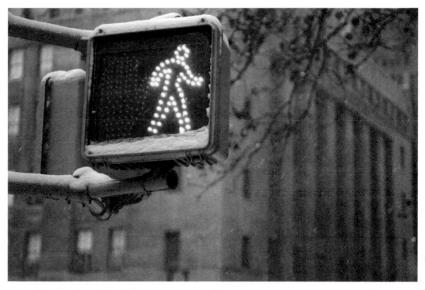

Predominently white scenes, such as snowscapes can sometimes fool the automatic white balance setting and read as gray. Use the Preset option PRE *for more control in setting your own white balance.*

White Balance Options

The D200 camera offers nine principal white balance options: *Automatic, Incandescent, Fluorescent, Direct Sunlight, Flash, Cloudy, Shade, Color Temperature, and Preset.*

A   *Automatic (3500 – 8000K)*

Nikon suggests that the D200 automatically measures light with a color temperature between 3500K and 8000K. In most instances the *Automatic*   **A**   option is very effective, but as with all automatic features on any camera you do need to think for yourself and step in to take control when appropriate. For example, if you shoot indoors under normal domestic type electric lighting, the color temperature is likely to be lower than 3500K. Alternatively, outdoors in bright overcast conditions the color temperature is likely to exceed 8000K!

☀ *Incandescent (3000K)*

Use this in place of the *Automatic* option, as its color temperature is closer to most tungsten-based interior lighting. You may find the result still looks too warm (red), so use the D200's white balance fine-tuning capability (see pages 117-118) to make further adjustments.

☼ *Fluorescent (4200K)*

Light emitted from fluorescent tubes is notorious for causing greenish color casts in pictures. This is due to the way these tubes work, and the variability in the color temperature of the light the produce. This option is accurate enough for any tubes that are described by their manufacturer as being "daylight" balanced.

☀ *Direct Sunlight (5200K)*

The *Direct Sunlight* ☀ option is intended for subjects or scenes photographed in direct sunlight during the middle part of the day (i.e. from around two hours after sunrise to two hours before sunset). At other times, when the sun is lower in the sky, the light tends to be "warmer", and shooting at those times with this white balance setting will produce pictures with a redder appearance.

Hint: White balance is very subjective, depending on the viewer, but to my eye Nikon's color temperature for the *Direct Sunlight* ☀ option is too low. When shooting in these conditions, I prefer to use either the *Flash* ⚡ , or *Cloudy* ☁ options.

⚡ *Flash (5400K)*

As its name implies, this option is intended whenever you use flash (Nikon refers to their own flash units as Speedlights) as the main light source.

Hint: In a similar way to the *Direct Sunlight* ☀ option I consider the color temperature of the Flash ⚡ option to be too low, since the color temperature of light emitted by Nikon Speedlights is generally in the range of 5500 – 6000K. Therefore I often select the *Cloudy* ☁ option when working with Nikon flash units as the main light source.

114

Cloudy (6000K)

The *Cloudy* option is for shooting under overcast skies, when daylight has a high color temperature. It ensures the camera renders colors properly without the typical 'cool' (blue) appearance, particularly in pale skin tones that can look "cold" in a photograph taken in these conditions.

Shade (8000K)

This option applies a greater degree of correction than the *Cloudy* option, and is intended for those situations when your subject or scene is in open shade beneath a clear, or nearly clear blue sky. Under these conditions, the lighting will be biased strongly towards blue due to the light reflected from the blue sky above.

Choose Color Temp. (2500 – 10,000K)

This option allows the user to select a range of specific color temperature values, expressed in degrees Kelvin (K). If you know the specific color temperature of the light source(s) illuminating the subject / scene the camera can be set to match it.

PRE *Preset*

Preset **PRE** allows the user to obtain a measurement of the color temperature of the light illuminating the subject or scene by making a test "exposure". You can also use an existing image stored on the memory card as a reference for the color temperature value.

Selecting a White Balance Option

The white balance options of the D200 camera can be selected in one of two ways:

Press the button on the rear of the camera and use the Multi Selector to open the Shooting menu . Navigate to the *White bal.* option and Multi Select right to open the options page. Scroll down the list to highlight your choice and Multi Select right again. If you select *Auto* or one

One way to set the white balance is to use the ● *button and navigate through the* ▣ *menu.*

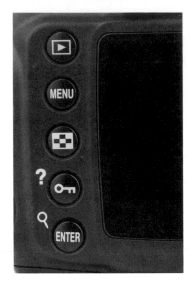

of the six pre-determined white balance values (Incandescent, Fluorescent, Direct Sunlight, Flash, Cloudy, or Shade), the next menu page shows the *Fine-tune* option (see below for details). Use the Multi Selector to set any fine-tune factor required (or leave it set to 0 if no adjustment is needed). Finally, Multi Select right to set the white balance (with or without a fine-tune factor applied).

Note: The fine-tune factor cannot be applied to the *Choose Color Temp.* and the *Preset* options.

Alternatively, and in my opinion the faster option, use the WB button on the top of the camera to select a white balance option. Press and hold this button, then rotate the main command dial to select a white balance option and the sub-command dial to set the fine-tuning factor (if required); as you do this the values are displayed in the control panel.

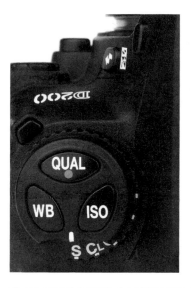

An alternate option for choosing a white balance setting is to press the WB button and scroll through the icons with the main command dial.

Note: If you select the *Choose Color Temp.* 🄺 option and hold down the WB button while rotating the sub-command dial, the color temperature value will change up and down the scale of available settings, depending on the direction the dial is rotated. The selected value is displayed in the control panel.

Fine-Tuning Your White Balance

In addition to the white balance options available on the D200 camera, regardless of whether the white balance is set automatically or manually, the camera allows you to fine-tune the color temperature value by increasing or decreasing it (excluding the *Choose Color Temp.* and *Preset* options). However, rather than express this fine-tuning factor in degrees Kelvin, Nikon use a system of whole numbers between −3 and +3. Negative numbers set a higher color temperature making pictures appear warmer (red cast), and positive numbers reduce the color temperature making pictures appear cooler (blue cast). If a fine-tuning factor other than +0 is selected and set, a pair of black arrows appear in the control panel beneath **WB** , as a reminder.

Hint: If you are unsure about which fine-tune factor to set, you can activate *WB Bracketing* via Custom Setting e5.

Hint: Nikon states that, excluding the *Fluorescent* white balance option, each +/- whole number increment is equivalent to a 10-MIRED (Micro Reciprocal Degree, a method of calculating color temperature) but they provide no information about what a MIRED value means in practical terms. If you assume a picture is recorded with a neutral white balance, at its 0 value, applying a -1 factor is like adding an 81-series (pale amber) filter. Thus -2 is equivalent to an 81A filter, -3 is equivalent to an 81B.

Creative White Balance

Do you want to get creative? It is easy with the white balance control. You do not have to set the white balance to match the color temperature of the prevailing light—try mismatching it! For example, rather than shoot a subject or scene lit by daylight using one of the daylight white balance values, set the white balance to *Incandescent* ☀ . Now your picture will have a strong blue color cast, as ever the great appeal of digital photography is the ability to experiment!

Remember, if the color temperature of the prevailing light is lower than the color temperature of the set white balance value, the subject or scene will be rendered with a warm (red/yellow) color cast. Conversely, if the color temperature of the prevailing light is higher than the color temperature of the set white balance value, the subject or scene will be rendered with a cool (blue) color cast.

K Choose Color Temp.

The *Choose Color Temp.* K sub-menu under the white balance option in the Shooting menu ⬛ allows the user to select one of 31 predetermined color temperature values ranging from 2500 to 10,000K, in increments of approximately 10 MIREDs.

	☀	▨	☀	⚡	☁	⌂⁄⁄.
+3	2,700 K	2,700 K	4,800 K	4,800 K	5,400 K	6,700 K
+2	2,800 K	3,000 K	4,900 K	5,000 K	5,600 K	7,100 K
+1	2,900 K	3,700 K	5,000 K	5,200 K	5,800 K	7,500 K
±0	3,000 K	4,200 K	5,200 K	5,400 K	6,000 K	8,000 K
−1	3,100 K	5,000 K	5,300 K	5,600 K	6,200 K	8,400 K
−2	3,200 K	6,500 K	5,400 K	5,800 K	6,400 K	8,800 K
−3	3,300 K	7,200 K	5,600 K	6,000 K	6,600 K	9,200 K

*The size of the increments for Fluorescent reflects the wide varia-
tions in color temperature among the many different types of fluorescent light sources, ranging from low temperature stadium lighting to
high temperature mercury vapor lamps.*

    As with other white balance options the *Choose Color
Temp.* **K** option can be selected via the **◘** menu, or
by pressing the WB button on top of the camera and rotating
the main command dial. If you use the **◘**   route, you can
select the specific color temperature value by scrolling
through the options then Multi Selecting right to select it. If
you use the WB button and command dial route, you can
select the value by pressing and holding the WB button
while rotating the sub-command dial. The color temperature
value is displayed in the control panel.

Using the Preset White Balance Feature

The *Preset* **PRE**   option allows you to manually set a white
balance value based on the light on the subject or scene
being photographed, and provides probably the most accurate way of setting a white balance value. The D200 offers
two methods of selecting a **PRE**   white balance value,
either by using the camera to measure light reflected from
a white or gray card test target, or by using the white balance value from a previous exposure as a reference.

119

Hint: In the instruction manual, Nikon suggests that you can use either a white or gray card as a reference target for the **PRE** white balance option. I strongly recommend that you use only a gray card, for two reasons—first, a white card often contains pigments used to whiten it, which can cause the camera to render colors inaccurately, and second, it is more difficult to expose correctly for a pure white subject and exposure errors can affect the white balance reading you obtain from the test target.

Hint: In place of a test target, such as a gray card, there are a number of products that can be attached directly to the lens and allow the camera to not only obtain a white balance measurement but also take an incident reading for the ambient light using its TTL metering system. Probably the best device I have used for this purpose is the ExpoDisc (www.expodisc.com).

Using The *Preset* Option: The **PRE** option involves a few more steps than the other white balance options. There are two methods available with the D200 for obtaining a value for a preset white balance. The first is direct measurement, and the second is copying the white balance from an existing picture or from Nikon Capture software (version 4.4 or later, including NX). The D200 can store up to five different values for a preset white balance. The white balance measured most recently will be stored as d-0. This can be copied to any one of the other four white balance files, d-1, d-2, d-3, and d-4. Likewise, a white balance copied from an existing image or created in Nikon Capture software can also be copied to the same white balance value files.

Direct Measurement: Select the **PRE** option, then place your test target (a gray card or other metering target) in the same light as the scene or subject to be photographed. Select manual focus and set the focus distance on the lens to the infinity point. The exposure mode you use is not critical but I recommend you use A (Aperture-Priority). Point the camera at your test target (make sure you do not cast a shadow over the test target card) and make sure that it fills the viewfinder frame (select manual focus and set the lens to infinity—there is no need to focus on the test target card). Then press the WB button on top of the camera and rotate the main command dial until *PrE* is displayed in the control panel. To use the new white balance value immediately, ensure that d-0 is selected for the white balance file by rotating the sub-command dial. Release the WB button briefly, and then press and hold it until *PrE* begins to flash in the viewfinder and control panel displays. Now press the shutter release. If the camera is able to obtain a measurement and set a white balance value *Gd* will appear in the viewfinder and *Good* will be displayed in the control panel; both icons will flash. The white balance is now set for the prevailing light falling on your subject or scene, and this value will be stored and retained, automatically, in d-0, replacing any previous value stored there, until you make another measurement. To retain the value at d-0, store it in one of the other four files (d-1 to d-4) before taking a new white balance measurement. If the camera is unable to set a white balance value, *no Gd* will flash in both the viewfinder and control panel. In this case repeat the process until a measurement is achieved.

Note: If no white balance value is measured for d-0, the color temperature will automatically be set to 5200K.

Preset White Balance Options
Open the *White balance* menu from the **◘** options, and select **PRE** . Multi Select to the right to open the white balance preset files d-0 to d-4. Multi Select up or down to highlight the required preset white balance value, which will be bound by a yellow frame. To view the options for the selected preset press the center of the Multi Selector; the following options are shown:

Option	Description
Set	Sets the white balance to the value of the selected preset and returns user to the shooting menu
Edit Comment	Rename the selected preset with a comment of up to 36 characters. The keyboard is displayed. Select characters as required and press ● to confirm comment.
Select Image **d-1 to d-4 only**	Image files stored on the memory card currently inserted in the camera are displayed as thumbnail images. Use the Multi Selector to select an image; press ● to view full image. Press the center of the Multi Selector to copy white balance value (and any recorded comment) of the selected image to the selected white balance preset. Only images recorded by the D200 can be used.
Copy d-0 **d-1 to d-4 only**	Copy the white balance (and any recorded comment) for the preset d-0 to the selected preset.

Hint: The ability of the D200 to store preset white balance values is very useful. If the camera is to be used at a variety of locations with different lighting conditions during the course of an event, a white balance value can be measured, stored, and named for each location in advance. The user then has to only recall the appropriate preset value for each location as the event progresses. Alternatively, if you frequent to a particular location, the white balance value for the lighting can be stored and recalled at will on each visit.

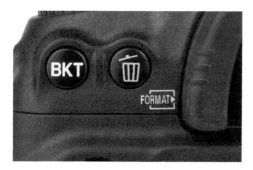

*To begin white bal-
ance bracketing,
select WB Bracketing
from Custom Setting
e5, then press the* ⊕
*button and rotate the
main command dial.*

White Balance Bracketing

The white-balance bracketing feature creates multiple copies
of a single image recorded by the camera, and each copy
has a different white balance value as determined by the settings the users selects.

Note: White-balance bracketing is not available with
Choose Color Temp. **K** or *Preset* **PRE** . The feature can-
not be used with the following image quality settings: NEF
(Raw), or NEF (Raw) + JPEG (Fine, Normal, Basic).

To select white-balance bracketing, choose *WB Bracketing*
from the options at Custom Setting e5 *(Auto BKT Set)*. Press the
⊕ button and rotate the main command dial to select the
number of shots in the bracketing sequence. However, if the
number of image files to be created exceeds the number of
remaining exposures on the memory card, *FULL* is displayed in
the control panel and *FuL* is shown in the viewfinder.

To select the adjustment to be applied rotate the sub-command dial. Each increment is a whole number (1, 2, or 3),
and represents a shift of approximately 10 MIREDs. After
making the single exposure the camera will process the data
to create the number of shots specified in the sequence by
the user; each file will have a different white balance value
according to the increment selected.

Control panel display	No. of shots	WB increment	Bracketing order
+ 3F I+·········ɪɪ̯̈·········−	3	+1	+1, 0, +2
+ 3F 2+·········ɪ̯ɪ̯̈·········−	3	+2	+2, 0, +4
+ 3F 3+·······ɪ··ɪ̯̈·········−	3	+3	3, 0, 6
-- 3F I+·········ɪ̯̈ɪɪ·········−	3	−1	−1, −2, 0
-- 3F 2+·········ɪ̯̈ɪ·ɪ·········−	3	−2	−2, −4, 0
-- 3F 3+·········ɪ̯̈··ɪ··ɪ·······−	3	−3	−3, −6, 0
+ 2F I+·········ɪ̯̈·········−	2	+1	0, +1
+ 2F 2+·········ɪ·ɪ̯̈·········−	2	+2	0, +2
+ 2F 3+·······ɪ··ɪ̯̈·········−	2	+3	0, +3
-- 2F I+·········ɪ̯̈ɪ·········−	2	−1	0, −1
-- 2F 2+·········ɪ̯̈ɪ·········−	2	−2	0, −2
-- 2F 3+·········ɪ̯̈··ɪ·······−	2	−3	0, −3
3F I+·········ɪ̯̈ɪɪ·········−	3	±1	0, −1, +1
3F 2+·········ɪ·ɪ̯̈ɪ·········−	3	±2	0, −2, +2
3F 3+·······ɪ··ɪ̯̈··ɪ·······−	3	±3	0, −3, +3
5F I+·········ɪɪ̯̈ɪɪ·········−	5	±1	0, −2, −1, +1, +2
5F 2+·········ɪ·ɪ̯̈ɪ·ɪ········−	5	±2	0, −4, −2, +2, +4
5F 3+·······ɪ·ɪ·ɪ̯̈·ɪ·ɪ·······−	5	±3	0, −6, −3, +3, +6
7F I+·······ɪɪɪɪ̯̈ɪɪɪ·······−	7	±1	0, −3, −2, −1, +1, +2, +3
7F 2+·····ɪ·ɪ·ɪ·ɪ̯̈·ɪ·ɪ·ɪ·····−	7	±2	0, −6, −4, −2, +2, +4, +6
7F 3+ɪ·ɪ·ɪ·ɪ̯̈·ɪ·ɪ·ɪ−	7	±3	0, −9, −6, −3, +3, +6, +9
9F I+·····ɪɪɪɪɪ̯̈ɪɪɪɪ·····−	9	±1	0, −4, −3, −2, −1, +1, +2, +3, +4
9F 2+·ɪ·ɪ·ɪ·ɪ·ɪ̯̈·ɪ·ɪ·ɪ·ɪ·−	9	±2	0, −8, −6, −4, −2, +2, +4, +6, +8
9F 3█·ɪ·ɪ·ɪ·ɪ̯̈·ɪ·ɪ·ɪ█	9	±3	0, −12, −9, −6, −3, +3, +6, +9, +12

To cancel the bracketing process, press the ⊛ button and rotate the main command dial until the number of shots in the bracketing sequence is zero and the white-balance bracketing indicator is no longer displayed in the control panel.

Optimizing Images

In addition to white balance, the D200 has several other controls that affect the appearance of your pictures. In an effort to make things easier for the user, Nikon has clustered these controls together in a series of pre-set options that can be applied to images captured in P, A, S, and M exposure modes.

Option	Description
Normal	The default setting tends to produce a slightly subdued looking image that benefits from slight enhancement of levels and contrast in post-processing. Useful if you intend to deal with images individually using a computer.
Softer	As the title suggests it produces images with slightly lower contrast and lower edge acuity. It is useful for portraits or pictures shot with flash as the main light source.
Vivid	Adds a little extra bite to images as color saturation and edge acuity is increased. Useful if you expect to print images direct from the camera without any post-processing.
More Vivid	An enhanced version of *Vivid*, this produces results akin to a high saturation color transparency film. Depending on how the images will be used, the level of sharpening applied in this option may be too high for many subjects.
Portrait	This option appears to produce results that are almost identical to the Normal option, particularly in terms of the contrast.
B&W	This option provides a "quick'n dirty" conversion that appears to just average out the red, green, and blue values to produce an image that looks as though a simple grayscale conversion has been applied to it. Far superior results can be achieved using a color image and converting it with image-processing software on the computer.
Custom	This is the only option that provides full control to the user for each attribute: sharpness, contrast, color mode, saturation, and hue.

It is vitally important to understand that the *Custom* option is the only one that allows you to set controls manually. If you select any of the other six options, the camera will assign controls automatically (see the table below). However, that is not the whole story! The D200 will seek to optimize each individual image according to the shooting conditions that prevail at the time of exposure. In other words, even if you shoot a series of pictures of a similar scene, the values assigned in the *Normal, Softer, Vivid, More Vivid, Portrait,* and *B&W* options may vary depending on the exposure and position of the subject within the frame area.

To ensure consistent results, use the *Custom* option but avoid selecting *Auto* for *Sharpening, Tone Compensation,* and *Saturation*, as you relinquish control of these attributes by doing so.

Optimize Image Options

Optimize	Color Mode	Tone	Hue	Saturation	Sharpen
Normal	*I*	*Auto*	*0*	*Auto*	*Auto*
Softer	*I*	*Less Contrast*	*0*	*Auto*	*Low*
Vivid	*III*	*Normal*	*0*	*Enhanced*	*Med. High*
More Vivid	*III*	*More Contrast*	*0*	*Enhanced*	*High*
Portrait	*I*	*Auto*	*0*	*Auto*	*Med. Low*
B&W	*I*	*Normal*	*0*	*Normal*	*Normal*

Hint: To maximize image quality, I strongly recommend using the *Custom* option.

Note: Unlike many previous Nikon cameras, in which the settings for *Color Space* and *Color Mode* were linked, these controls have been separated in the D200, offering more options for combinations of available settings.

Note: A color space describes the range (gamut) of colors that can be recorded by the camera. The color mode defines how accurate the rendition of the recorded colors will be.

Note: Color Mode II is only available when Adobe RGB—the color space that offers the widest range (gamut) of colors—is selected as the working color space. You will want to use Color Mode II to ensure the highest level of color accuracy, which is particularly useful if the images will be subject to extensive work in post-processing. If sRGB is selected as the color space when the color mode is set to Color Mode II, the mode will reset to either Color Mode I or III, depending on which one was selected most recently.

To select any of the *Optimize Image* controls open the Shooting ⬛ menu and navigate to the *Optimize Image* option. Multi Select right to open the next menu page, which lists the options available. Use the Multi Selector to scroll to the required option then Multi Select right to select it.

If you select *Custom* this action will open a sub-menu from which you can set each control option. Highlight the required option using the Multi Selector, then Multi Select right; scroll to the setting you want to change and select it by Multi Selecting right again. Finally, navigate to *Done* and Multi Select right to confirm and save the selected settings. If you do not select *Done*, the settings will not be saved.

Sharpen

Sharpening is a process applied to digital data that can increases the apparent sharpness (acuity) of a picture. It is not a method for rescuing an out-of-focus picture—remember once out-of-focus, always out-of-focus!

Sharpening is used to correct the side effects of converting light in to digital data, which often causes distinct edges between colors, tones, and objects in a digital picture to look ill defined (fuzzy). The D200 uses a technique that identifies an edge by analyzing the differences between neighboring pixel values. Then the process lightens the pixels immediately adjacent to the brighter side of the edge, and darkens the pixels adjacent to the dark side of the edge. This causes a local increase of contrast around the edge that makes it look sharper; the higher the level of sharpening applied, the greater the contrast at the edge.

The D200 offers seven levels of image sharpening:

BKT *Auto:* The camera processing applies a level of sharpening that varies according to how the camera analyzes the image data.

Note: Nikon gives no indication as to what the D200 does at this setting other than state that the level of sharpening can vary from image to image, even with subject / scenes of a similar type.

◇ 0 *Normal:* Apparently the camera applies a moderate amount of sharpening at a consistent level. I say "apparently," because again Nikon does not provide specific values for the level of sharpening the camera applies.

◇-2 *Low:* A lesser amount of sharpening is applied than Normal.

◇-1 *Medium Low:* The sharpening level is slightly higher than Low.

◇+1 *Medium High:* Sharpening is slightly higher than Normal.

◇+2 *High:* The D200 applies an aggressive level of sharpening, which may not be appropriate for some subject /scenes.

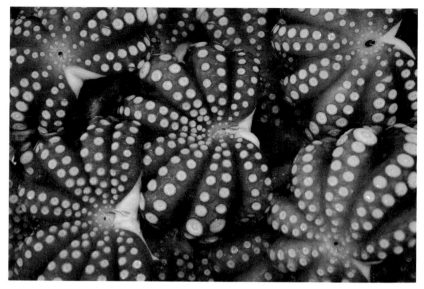

In-camera sharpening is useful for a touch of sharpness, but it will not sharpen an out-of-focus image!

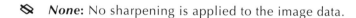 **None:** No sharpening is applied to the image data.

Hint: No single level of sharpening is suitable for all pictures taking situations. The level of sharpening should be based on your ultimate intentions for the image, (i.e. display on a web page, publication in a book or magazine, or producing a print for framing). Therefore, it is often preferable to apply sharpening in post-processing on a computer, particularly if you want to work on images for a range of different output purposes.

The following are my suggestions in regard to in-camera sharpening when shooting with the D200:

- For general photography using JPEG format files, set sharpening to *Low* or *Medium Low* if you intend to work on these images in post-processing.

- For general photography, using JPEG format files set sharpening to *Normal* if you intend to print pictures directly from the camera without any further post-processing.

- On those occasions when you need to expedite the output pictures for publishing on a web page, or in newsprint, use the JPEG format and set the sharpening level to *Normal* or *Medium High*. In this case, a slightly stronger degree of sharpening is more suitable, as images will be viewed on computer monitor screens or at low reproduction resolutions. Also, it saves valuable time in post-processing.

- If you shoot in the NEF file format, set sharpening to *None*.

Tone Compensation

Tone compensation allows you to adjust the contrast of an image. It works by applying a curve control similar to those used in post processing applications that alter the distribution of tones from the sensor data to fit the selected contrast range as defined by the contrast curve.

A **Auto:** The D200 uses its Matrix Metering system to assess the differences between the levels of brightness in the scene. If these are significant, the camera assumes the scene has high contrast and applies a compensation to lower it. Conversely, if a scene's contrast is low, the camera will increase image contrast.

◑0 **Normal:** The D200 applies a "standard" contrast curve that produces images with contrast somewhere between the extremes of Less contrast and More contrast.

◑− **Less Contrast:** This setting produces images with noticeably less overall contrast, which can be beneficial when shooting a subject or scene that contains light tones that are well illuminated. However, it can also affect the density of very dark tones resulting in a lack of depth.

Note: If you expect to perform post processing on your pictures you may wish to consider setting *Less Contrast*, as it is easier to increase contrast at this stage than reduce it.)

◐**+** *More Contrast:* Image contrast is boosted, which can be a benefit when shooting subjects or scenes that lack contrast. There is a risk that highlight detail will be "burnt out."

◐*◎* *Custom:* This option is only applicable if you have access to Nikon Capture 4.4 (or later, including Capture NX) software, because it allows you to write your own contrast curve and upload it to the camera. If no custom contrast curve is created and uploaded to the camera this option performs the same as Normal ◐**0** .

Color Mode

The D200 offers a choice of three color modes, which determine the accuracy of the colors recorded in an image. The color mode should be chosen based on the intended use for the image.

Mode I (sRGB): This is the default setting on the D200. Nikon recommends it for portrait pictures that will be used or printed without further modification, since the range of colors recorded by the camera is biased in favor of reproducing skin tones with a pleasant appearance (i.e. colors have an increase 'warmth').

Mode II (Adobe RGB): This color mode produces the most accurate rendition of colors recorded by the camera. Generally, it is the mode used by many photographers because it gives the widest range of options when it comes to the subsequent use of images.

Mode III (sRGB): This setting enhances the rendition of green and blue specifically, although yellow, orange, and red tend to look very strong as well. Nikon recommends that it should be used for "nature or landscape shots" that will be used or printed without further modification.

Unless you know your pictures will only ever be displayed on a computer monitor, or you will use a direct printing method with no intention of carrying out any post-processing on the computer, I would recommend using the Adobe RGB color space. It provides the widest range (gamut) of colors with a subtle rendition, and well-graduated tonal transitions, which increases the flexibility of an image that will be post-processed.

Hint: It is essential that your image manipulation application be set to the same Adobe RGB color space (i.e. you work with a color managed system), otherwise the application will likely assign its own default color space and you will lose control over the rendition of colors.

Saturation
Adjusting the saturation changes the overall vividness (chroma) of color without affecting the brightness (luminance) of an image.

A *Auto:* The D200 will adjust the level of saturation automatically according to the camera's assessment of the scene or subject.

&0 *Normal:* This is the default setting, and is probably the option to use for most situations, since the camera offers very limited control compared with a post-processing application.

&- *Moderate:* The vividness of colors is reduced but Nikon provides no information as to the level of adjustment that is applied.

&+ *Enhanced:* The vividness of colors is increased but Nikon provides no information as to the level of adjustment that is applied.

Hue
The RGB color model used by the D200 to produce images is based on combinations of red, green, and blue light. By

mixing two of these colors, a variety of different colors can be produced. If a third color is introduced, the hue of the final color is altered. For example, if the level of red and green data is increased relative to the blue data, the hue shifts (positive adjustment) to a warmer (red/yellow) rendition. If you apply a negative adjustment the hue shifts to a cooler (bluer) rendition, so for example red will shift toward purple. The control on the D200 allows you to set an adjustment of +/- 9° in increments of 3°.

Hint: Personally, I believe it is better to leave control of both color saturation and hue to the post-processing stage, as they can be controlled to a far greater degree using an image manipulation application on a computer. I would recommend that these controls be left set to *Normal* and 0° respectively.

Color Space

Color management is a huge topic, and a full discussion of it is totally beyond the scope of this book. Suffice to say that you should have a basic understanding of what a color space is, and thereby make an informed choice as to which of the two offered by the D200 you should use and why.

A color space (often referred to as a color gamut) defines the range of colors that can be reproduced by a device. This range will depend on a number of factors, but different devices will reproduce a different range of colors. A computer monitor, for example, will produce one range of colors, while a simple inkjet printer will reproduce another. Equally, the type of inks available for printing, or the type of phosphors applied to a monitor screen will determine the range of colors that can be reproduced.

The D200 allows the user to select either the sRGB or Adobe RGB color space. If you expect to shoot pictures that will be viewed exclusively on Web sites, or in some other electronic form, such as a computer monitor or television, the sRGB color space is probably the one to choose, as its narrower range of colors is more suited to these mediums. Equally, if you expect to print images directly from the camera / memory card using a DPOF or PictBridge compatible printing device, then one of the two sRGB color spaces available on the D200 is probably the best choice. However, the reduced range of colors in an sRGB space can limit flexibility when you want to make subtle adjustments to color in post processing.

The Adobe RGB color space offers a wider range of colors that can be used to reproduce a broader variety of subtle color adjustments. Colors recorded in this color space can frequently look less saturated when displayed on a computer monitor (particularly if the monitor has not been profiled to match the color space) or television screen, but the colors will be much closer to those of the original subject and consequently those you see when the image is reproduced in the form of a print. Therefore, if you intend to use pictures for printing on high-end inkjet or digital printers, or for high quality lithographic reproduction, the Adobe RGB color space is probably the best choice.

To select the color space, open the 📷 menu and highlight *Color Space*. Multi Select to the right then highlight the required option and Multi Select right again.

Image Storage

The D200 accepts two kinds of storage media: CompactFlash (Type I/II) and Microdrive. CompactFlash cards are memory cards, whereas Microdrives are actually just very tiny hard drives. The following sections will explain these two types of storage media in detail.

CompactFlash Cards
These solid-state memory cards are capable of retaining data even when they are not powered, and since they have no moving parts, they are reasonably robust. Obviously, you should treat any memory card with same care you would your camera equipment, but a minor knock or minor exposure to the

elements should not cause any problems. Total immersion in water, however, should be avoided! Typically, CompactFlash cards have a temperature operating range of -4F° to 167F°(-20°C to 75°C) and no altitude limit. Unlike film, they are not affected by ionising radiation from X-ray security equipment such as that used at airports, so you need not worry about passing your camera and memory cards through security checkpoints when travelling. You pictures will be unaffected.

Microdrives

As their name implies, Microdrives are miniature hard disk drives that have a platter that spins as an arm with a recording head that tracks across it to write the data to the disk. With all these moving parts, they are more susceptible to damage, particularly a shock as a result of an impact, and they are certainly far less resistant to the effects of moisture and temperature as compared to CompactFlash cards. They also have a considerably narrower temperature operating range of 41°F to 131°F (5°C to 55°C), and can become unreliable above an altitude of about 9,000 feet (3,000 m).

There are several other issues concerning Microdrives that you should be aware of:

- Due to all their moving parts, Microdrives consume far more power than CompactFlash cards do.

- Microdrives produce relatively high levels of heat during extended periods of use, which will inevitably increase the internal temperature of the camera. This may have undesirable consequences in terms of generating electronic noise.

- Like any mechanical device, Microdrives will eventually suffer the effects of wear and tear, and may subsequently fail.

Hint: When handling Microdrives, always hold them by the edges. Do not pinch them in the center of their two largest surfaces, as any force in this region that compresses the card casing can result in damage to the internal mechanism.

Formatting

The memory of a CompactFlash card or Microdrive has a similar structure to that of a hard disk drive with a file directory, file allocation table, folders, and individual files. As data is written to and erased from these storage media, small areas of their memory can become corrupted, causing files to become fragmented. By regularly formatting your storage media in-camera, the worst effects of fragmentation are generally cleaned up.

The process of formatting causes the existing file directory information to be overwritten so that it no longer points to the image data held on the card. This makes it extremely difficult to access any images that remain on the card after formatting, so you should always download all the files saved on your card before you format. If you should format a card inadvertently, however, it is often possible to recover the image files using software designed to recover data, provided no further data is written to the card. Since prevention is better than cure, always save you images to a computer or other storage device (and make a back up copy) before formatting a card.

Note: The D200 supports FAT32, which allows it to use memory cards with a capacity in excess of 2 GB. FAT16 is used when formatting any memory card already formatted in FAT16.

File Formats

The D200 saves images in two file formats: Joint Photographic Experts Group (JPEG) and Nikon's proprietary RAW file, the Nikon Electronic File (NEF). Using the JPEG format, the camera processes the sensor data to produce an image file while at the same time applying the current relevant camera settings. As part of this process, the 12-bit sensor data is reduce to 8-bits since JPEG is by nature a compression scheme. Current camera settings are then recorded into the relevant fields of the EXIF file that is appended to the image file data. The D200 does differ slightly from most other Nikon D-SLR cameras in so much as it modifies the image data at a 12-bit level before reducing it to 8-bits to comply with the requirements of the JPEG format. (This system was first seen in the D2X camera, and is also used by its successor the D2Xs.)

Using the NEF format, the camera deals with the sensor data in one of two ways, depending on whether you choose to save your NEF files in an uncompressed or compressed form. If the camera is set to record uncompressed NEF files, the original 12-bit data values from each pixel on the sensor are preserved. However, if the camera records compressed NEF files, some of the 12-bit data from the sensor is discarded in a process that Nikon describe as being "visually lossless" (see the section on pages 140-141 for an explanation of what actually occurs). Regardless of whether the camera saves uncompressed or compressed NEF files, the camera settings in use at the time the image was recorded are saved to the relevant fields in the EXIF file, and the camera also creates and stores a small "thumbnail" image, akin to a JPEG file, alongside the NEF file.

To summarize, the principal difference between the JPEG and NEF formats concerns how the camera deals with the data from the sensor that forms the image. Using the JPEG format, the camera produces an image based on the sensor data and the settings at the time of the exposure, selected either by you or the camera. JPEG files can still be worked on, if required, after they have been imported to a computer, though they arrive in an essentially "finished" state. Using the NEF format, on the other hand, requires the work involved in producing the finished image to be done by the photographer after the fact using NEF compatible software and a computer.

If you have the impression that in order to eek out every last ounce of quality the D200 has to offer you should shoot in the NEF format, you are not too far off the mark! However, while many photographers refer to the RAW/NEF format as being "better" than JPEG, I prefer to consider the issue in terms of the flexibility the two formats offer, and I recommend that you use the one that is best suited to your specific requirements. It is worth further examination of the attributes of each format so you can make an informed decision.

JPEG
The JPEG format has three attributes that can potentially influence image quality in an adverse manner:

- The in camera processing reduces the 12-bit color data from the sensor to 8-bit values when it creates a JPEG file. The D200 does, however, have the advantage of using the same processing regime as the pro-level D2Xs camera, so all in-camera adjustments to image attributes such as sharpening, contrast, and saturation, are made at a 12-bit level before the data is reduced to 8-bits. If you have no intention of carrying out any post processing work on your images, the reduction to 8-bits is of no real consequence. However, if you make significant changes to an image using software in post processing the 8-bit data of a JPEG file can impose limits on the degree of manipulation that can be applied.

- When the camera saves an image using the JPEG format it encodes most of the camera settings for attributes such as white balance, sharpening, contrast, saturation, and hue into the image data. If you make an error and inadvertently select the wrong setting, you will need to try and undo your mistake in post processing. Inevitably this is time consuming and there is no guarantee it will be successful.

- The technology of digital imaging is fast paced, and the electronics used in any particular camera are only as good as the day the manufacturer decided on their specification and finalized the design of the camera. Granted, most modern cameras can have their firmware (installed software) upgraded by the user and, to some extent, this helps off set obsolescence, but it is only effective for so long. By processing images using computer software you can often take advantage of the very latest advances in image processing, which are unavailable in-camera.

NEF—Nikon's Proprietary RAW File

Using NEF has only one real disadvantage to my mind that of the extra time you will need to invest in post processing each image to produce a finished picture. The larger file size of the NEF format can be an issue in terms of the amount of available storage both as far as memory card capacity, and external storage for archiving your pictures. Equally, there can be limitations with some third party software when it comes to its ability to read and interpret Nikon NEF files. The benefits of NEF include:

• More consistent and smoother tonal graduations

• Color that is more subtle and accurate to the original subject or scene

• A slight increase in the level of detail that is resolved

• The ability (within fairly limited parameters) to adjust exposure in post processing to correct for slight exposure errors

• The ability, in post processing, to correct and/or change image color by resetting attributes such as the white balance value, contrast, saturation, and hue

Note: Most modern software is capable of reading NEF (RAW) files generated by the D200. There are a wide variety of third party RAW file converters that enable NEF (RAW) files to be opened in most popular digital imaging software. For compatibility between NEF (RAW) files from the D200 and Nikon software you will require: PictureProject 1.6.1, Nikon View 6.2.7, or Nikon Capture 4.4.0. The latest iterations of Nikon View and Capture, View Pro and Capture NX also provide compatibility.

Compressed NEF (RAW)

If the camera is set to record uncompressed NEF (RAW) files the original 12-bit data values from each photosite (pixel) on the sensor is preserved (hence the name of the format – RAW). However, if the camera records compressed NEF (RAW) files some of the 12-bit data from the sensor is discarded.

Nikon describes the compression applied to NEF (RAW) files as being "visually lossless," by which they mean it is impossible to differentiate the compressed files from the original data. The "compression" process used by Nikon is selective; it only works on certain image data while leaving other data unaffected. Nikon's use of the word "compression" in this context is rather misleading, as the process involves two distinct phases. The first phase sees certain tonal values grouped and then rounded, and the second phase is the point at which a conventional lossless compression is applied. During the first phase of the compression process, the values that represent the very dark tones are separated from the rest of the data. Then, data with values that represent the remaining tones is divided into groups, but this process is not linear. As the tones become lighter, the size of the group increases, so the group with the lightest tones is larger than a group containing mid-tone values. A lossless compression is then applied to each individual dark tone value and a rounded value is applied to each group in the mid and light tones.

When an application such as Nikon View or Nikon Capture opens a NEF (RAW) file it reverses the lossless compression process. The individual dark tone values are unaffected (remember the compression is lossless) but, and here is the twist, each of the grouped values for the mid and light tones must be expanded to its appropriate range on 12-bit scale. Since the rounding error in each group becomes progressively larger as the tonal values it represents become lighter and lighter, the "gaps" in the data caused by the rounding process also become progressively larger at lighter tonal values.

It is important to put these data "gaps" into perspective. A single compression/decompression cycle performed on a NEF (RAW) file produces an image that is indistinguishable from one produced from an uncompressed NEF (RAW) file. Because the human eye does not respond in a linear way to increased levels of brightness, it is incapable of resolving the very minor changes that take place even in the lightest tones where the rounding error is greatest and therefore the data "gap" is largest (remember Nikon's phrase – "visually lossless").

Furthermore, our eyes are generally only capable of detecting tonal variations equivalent to those produced by 8-bit data, and since even a compressed NEF (RAW) file has the equivalent to more than 8-bit data, the data "gaps" caused by Nikon's "compression" process are of no consequence.

Similarly, many photographers will ultimately reduce their 12-bit NEF (RAW) files to 8-bit RGB-TIFF or JPEG files prior to printing, which masks any loss of tonal graduation caused by compressing NEF (RAW) files.

It is worth mentioning that, in spite of what I have just described above, there is a small latent risk that the data loss caused by compression of NEF (RAW) files might manifest in the highlight areas of an image that is subjected to a significant level of alteration during post-processing (e.g. considerable color shift, or excessive sharpening).

Which Format?
In considering the attributes of JPEG and NEF (RAW) many photographers make an analogy with film photography. They consider the NEF (RAW) file as though they have the original film negative to work from, and the JPEG file as being akin to a machine-processed print. I do not disagree, but this is where my point about flexibility of the two formats comes back to be relevant. Not every photographer has the desire, ability, or time to spend post-processing NEF (RAW) files. The good news is that we have a choice, so consider the points made in this section and make your decision about which format to use based on the format that is most suited

to your purposes. If you have sufficient storage capacity you could select one of the NEF (RAW) + JPEG combinations from the *Image Quality* options, as the D200 can save a copy of a single image in both formats.

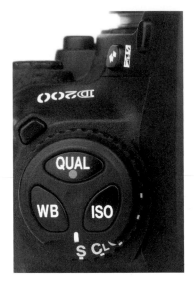

Use the QUAL button to quickly navigate through your quakity options and choose the best quality for your intended use.

Image Quality and Size

The D200 allows you to save JPEG files at three different levels of quality:

- **FINE** – uses a low compression of approximately 1:4
- **NORMAL** – uses a moderate compression ratio of approximately 1:8
- **BASIC** – uses a high compression ratio of approximately 1:16

Each JPEG file can also be saved by the D200 at one of three different sizes:

- **L** – Large (3872 x 2592 pixels)
- **M** – Medium (2896 x 1944 pixels)
- **S** – Small (1936 x 1296 pixels)

Note: As the processing involved in the creation of a JPEG files uses compression that discards data, you should select the lowest level of compression to maintain the highest image quality. A file saved at the FINE setting will be visually superior to a file saved at the BASIC setting.

Note: JPEG compression can generate visual "artifacts"; the higher the compression ratio, the more apparent these become. If you are shooting for web publication this is unlikely to be an issue but if you intend to make prints from your JPEG file pictures you will probably want to use the Large FINE settings.

NEF (RAW) files can be saved in either an uncompressed or compressed form. A compressed NEF (RAW) file is approximately 40 - 50% smaller than the uncompressed NEF (RAW) file. There is no size option with NEF (RAW) files since the D200 always uses the full 3872 x 2592 resolution of the sensor.

Note: NEF (RAW) files taken with the D200 using the B&W option in the Optimize Image menu are only slightly smaller than color files, because the NEF (RAW) retains all the original RAW data including the color information. Consequently, a black-and-white NEF (RAW) file can be converted to produce a color image by selecting a color mode option in the Advanced Raw tool palette of Nikon Capture 4 (requires 4.4.0, or later, and includes Capture NX)

Note: Compressed black-and-white NEF (RAW) files are slightly smaller than color NEF (RAW) files due to thumbnail image embedded in the NEF (RAW) file being a smaller grayscale file, with no color information.

Setting Image Quality and Size
To set image quality (format) on the D200, open the shooting menu ◘ and Multi Select up or down to highlight the *Image Quality* option; Multi Select right to open the list of quality options and highlight the required setting. Alternatively, and in my opinion by far the more convenient

way to select image quality is to use the button and dial method. Press and hold the **QUAL** button then rotate the main command dial; the selected value is displayed in the control panel. There are seven options available: NEF (RAW), JPEG Fine, JPEG Normal, JPEG, Basic, NEF (RAW) + JPEG Fine, NEF (RAW) + JPEG Normal, and NEF (RAW) + JPEG Basic.

To set image size for JPEG format files on the D200, open the ![camera icon] menu and use Multi Select up or down to highlight the *Image Size* option; press Multi Select right to open the list of options then highlight the required setting. Alternatively, and in my opinion by far the more convenient way to select image quality is to use the button and dial method. Press and hold the **QUAL** button then rotate the sub command dial; the selected value is displayed in the control panel, as L (large), M (medium), or S (small).

File Compression

In addition to the image quality settings that apply a varying degree of compression to the image data when saving JPEG format files the D200 has two further options in respect of JPEG compression. Open the ![camera icon] menu and Multi Select up or down to highlight the *JPEG Compression* item. Multi Select right to open the next menu page and Multi Select up or down to select one of the two options:

Size Priority – Image files are compressed to a near uniform size, which results in a variation of quality dependent on the level of fine detail in the subject or scene. The more detail the subject or scene contains, the more likely the image quality will be reduced. This is the default setting.

Optimal Quality – Image files are compressed to a varying size to allow for different levels of detail in the subject or scenes being photographed. Unless you really need files of a consistent size, or image storage capacity is an issue, I recommend you use this option in preference to *Size Priority*.

144

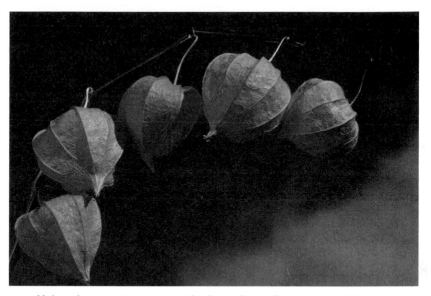

Unless image storage capacity is an issue, I recommend that you always use the highest quality and lowest compression settings for your images.

To choose compression for NEF (RAW) files, open the ⬛ menu and Multi Select up or down to highlight the *RAW Compression* item. Multi Select right to open the next menu page and Multi Select up or down to select the *Comp. NEF (RAW)* option.

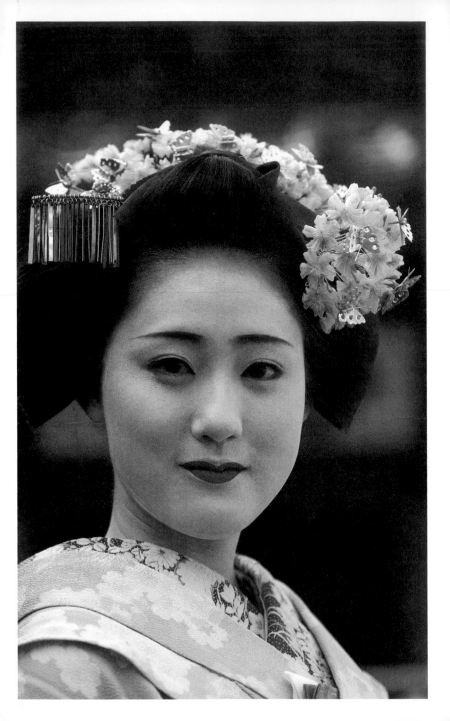

The Autofocus System

The autofocus system of the D200 has a number of aspects that make it quite different from any of the focusing systems used in any previous Nikon digital SLR cameras. While there are some similarities with the focusing system used in the D2-series cameras, the overall coverage of the autofocus sensing areas and the ability of the user to combine the function of some of these AF areas sets the D200 apart.

The D200's AF Sensor Module

The D200 has an entirely new autofocus (AF) module: the Multi-Cam 1000. As its name implies, the sensor has a total of 1000 photosites to analyze contrast in the subject or scene it is pointed at. When the contrast level is determined to be at a maximum, focus is attained. The 1000 photosites on the sensor module are divided in to eleven defined sensing areas. Each one of the eleven sensing areas is aligned, approximately, to the eleven small squares marked on the focusing screen and arranged in an elongated diamond pattern orientated to the center of the viewfinder frame.

Only the central sensing area is a cross-type; this area is sensitive to detail in both a horizontal and vertical orientation, therefore, it is the most reliable. The remaining ten sensing areas are line-types; these are only sensitive to detail in a direction that is perpendicular to the orientation of the sensing area. The sensing areas above and below the central focusing point are arranged horizontally, so they detect

The D200 features an innovative, new Multi-Cam 1000 focusing system. For pictures like this, set the focus mode selector to "S" for single servo AF. This choice activates focus-priority and the camera will not fire until focus is confirmed.

detail aligned with the short vertical edge of the viewfinder frame. The other eight sensing areas area aligned vertically, so they detect detail aligned with the long horizontal edge of the viewfinder frame.

Hint: Sometimes when using one of the line-type sensing areas the AF system will "hunt" (i.e. the camera will drive the focus of the lens back and forth but it is unable to attain focus). This is indicative of the detail in the subject being aligned in the same orientation as the focus sensing area. If this occurs try tilting the camera slightly (10 – 15°); this is often sufficient to allow the camera to acquire focus. Once focus is confirmed, lock it (see page 160) and recompose the picture before releasing the shutter.

The three sensing areas that form a column on either side of the central focusing point can be set to perform as a single focus sensing area depending on the option selected via Custom Setting a3 (*Focus Area Frame*). This means that the D200 can perform autofocus with either the original 11 sensing areas or 7 sensing areas. To achieve this, the camera employs a system of electronic masking to define the active portion of each sensing area. To support the functionality of the autofocus system, the display on the focusing screen is dynamic; when Custom Setting a3 is set to *Normal Frame*, the selected AF point is surrounded by a pair of bold brackets. If you switch to *Wide Frame*, the area defined by these brackets is increased to correspond to the greater coverage of the focus sensing areas. The user's choice of a specific sensing area and sensor area coverage has a profound effect on the abilities of the camera to perform autofocus (see page 163 at the end of this chapter).

Focus Modes

The D200 offers three principal methods of focusing known as focus modes: S (single-servo) autofocus, C (continuous-servo) autofocus, and M manual focus. To select a focus mode, rotate the focus mode selector (located on the camera front to the left of the lens mount and below the lens release

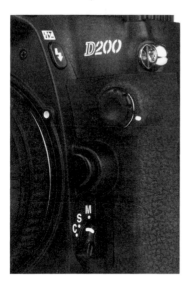

Use the focus mode selector to choose single-servo autofocus, continuous-servo autofocus, or manual focus.

button) until the white index mark is aligned with appropriate letter for the mode you wish to use.

S - Single-Servo Autofocus: As soon as the shutter release button is pressed, the D200 begins focusing the lens. The shutter can only be released once focus has been attained and the focus indicator ● is displayed in the viewfinder. The camera will only initiate predictive focus tracking in this autofocus mode if it detects that the subject was moving when focus was first attained (see pages 152-153 for more about predictive focus tracking).

C - Continuous-Servo Autofocus: When the shutter release button is pressed halfway, the D200 focuses the lens, continuously shifting focus to follow the subject if the camera-to-subject distance changes, regardless of whether the subject moves constantly or stops and starts periodically, until either the shutter is released or you remove your finger from the shutter release button. If the shutter release is pressed all the way down, the shutter will operate whether the camera has attained focus or not. Predictive focus tracking is active at all times in this autofocus mode.

M - Manual Focus: The user must rotate the focusing ring of the lens to achieve focus. There is no restriction on when the shutter can be operated, but the focus confirmation signal
● still functions, which is particularly useful for low light or low contrast scenes.

Note: To use manual focus, the focus mode selector must be set to M with most AF-Nikkor lenses. However, if the lens you are using has a switch that allows you to select an M/A (manual/autofocus) mode you need only touch the focusing ring and the lens can be focused manually. As soon as you release the focusing ring, the camera will resume autofocus operation. If the lens attached to the camera has an M/A mode option, the focus mode selector lever on the D200 does not need to be set to M in order to use manual focus.

Note: The focus mode selector represents, for me at least, one of the few weak points of the D200 design. I consider the profile of the lever to be too high; on a number of occasions while handling my D200, I have inadvertently moved it from the S position (single-servo mode) to the C position (continuous-servo mode). Since each of these two focusing modes cause fundamental differences in the way the camera focuses, the consequences of this flaw are potentially serious. I know that many other photographers have experienced the same issue. Furthermore, from the number of D200 bodies that I have tested I have determined that the resistance of this lever varies tremendously from body to body. You may be lucky and have a camera with a lever that is held in place firmly once set, but otherwise you'll need to check the position of the lever with due diligence!

Single-Servo vs. Continuous-Servo

It is important that you appreciate the fundamental difference between the S (single-servo) and C (continuous-servo) autofocus modes. In S focus mode, the shutter cannot be released until focus has been acquired; Nikon refers to this mode as having "focus priority." Even if the shutter release is pressed all the way down, operation of the shutter is disabled until the camera has attained focus. In most shooting conditions, par-

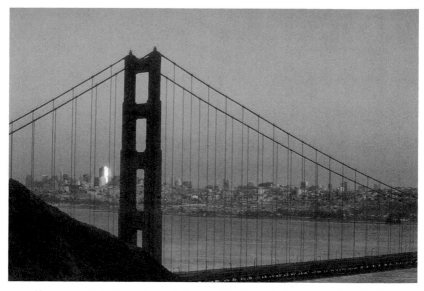

If you wish to use manual focus, the D200's focus mode selector should be set to M. However, if the lens in use has an M/A switch, you can simply turn the lens' focusing ring to focus manually manual. When you remove your hand from the focusing ring, the lens will resume autofocus.

ticularly in good light, this delay is so brief that it is not perceptible and it is has no practical consequence. However, under certain conditions, such as in low-light or when photographing subjects with low contrast, there is often a discernable lag between pressing the shutter release button and the shutter opening, because, generally, it takes the camera longer to establish focus in these circumstances. Conversely, in C focus mode, the shutter will operate immediately when you press the shutter release button all the way down, regardless of whether focus has been achieved; Nikon refers to this mode as having "release priority."

Some photographers assume, mistakenly, that if the shutter is released before the camera has attained focus, the picture will always be out-of-focus. To the contrary, in C focus mode, the combination of constant focus monitoring and predictive focus tracking is normally successful in causing the focus point to be shifted within the split second delay between the reflex mirror lifting and the shutter opening to obtain a sharp picture. Even if the camera's calculations are slightly off, minor focusing errors are often masked by the depth-of-field. However, when using C focus mode to photograph a subject that is moving (or likely to move), it is imperative that the camera is given sufficient time to assimilate focusing data to perform the focusing action; either press and hold the shutter release button halfway down or press and hold the AF-ON button in advance of releasing the shutter (see pages 201-202 for details on Custom Setting a6 and its options when using the AF-ON button).

Note: The focus priority and release priority assigned to S focus mode and C focus mode, respectively, can be reversed using Custom Settings a2 and a1. I recommend that changes from the default settings should only be made once you understand how the focusing system works, and then only if the specific shooting situation requires the priorities be reversed.

Predictive Focus Tracking

Whenever the shutter release is pressed all the way down to activate the shutter mechanism, there is a short delay between the reflex mirror lifting out of the light path to the camera's sensor and the shutter actually opening. If a subject is moving toward or away from the camera, the camera-to-subject distance will change during this delay. In these circumstances, the D200 uses its predictive tracking system to shift the point of focus on the lens to allow for the change in camera-to-subject distance, regardless of whether the subject is moving at a constant speed, is accelerating, or decelerating. Predictive focus tracking is always initiated when the camera detects the camera-to-subject distance changing (i.e., the subject is moving toward or way from the camera). The camera achieves this by comparing multiple samples of contrast levels as it monitors subject movement; based on this data, the camera shifts the focus point accordingly.

It is important to understand the distinction between how predictive focus tracking (which operates whenever the D200 performs autofocus) works in single-servo mode versus the way it functions in continuous-servo mode. In single-servo, predictive focus tracking is only initiated if the camera detects the subject to be moving toward or away from the camera at the time focus is attained. If the subject is stationary when focus is attained, the focus distance on the lens is locked at that specific camera-to-subject distance. If the subject then moves before the shutter is released, the lens is not re-focused. In continuous-servo mode, predictive focus tracking is initiated as soon as the camera detects subject movement, regardless of whether this occurs while the camera is establishing focus or after focus is attained; in this focus mode, the camera monitors focus constantly before the shutter is released.

Note: Using AF-S type lenses (which have an internal focusing motor that provides faster focusing) increases the chance of attaining sharp focus with a moving subject.

Note: The D200 instruction manual implies that predictive focus tracking only operates in C (continuous-servo) mode; in fact, the camera always uses predictive focus tracking when it detects a moving subject in both S and C autofocus modes.

Autofocus Lock-On

In an effort to prevent the camera from re-focusing on an object that appears briefly between the intended subject and the camera, once the camera has established focus on the subject, the D200 will deliberately delay shifting focus. Nikon refers to this feature as autofocus Lock-On; the length of the delay before the camera shifts focus can be controlled using Custom Setting a5 (*Lock-On*). However, if you want to photograph a subject where the camera-to-subject distance is changing abruptly during a series of shots, the *Lock-On* feature can prevent the camera from following focus on the subject. In this case, I recommend selecting either *Short* (to reduce the delay to its minimum), or *Off* (the camera will refocus immediately) from the options in Custom Setting a5.

Note: Nikon has not published the specific duration of the various delay periods that can be selected using Custom Setting a5.

The Trap Focus Technique

It is possible to use the functionality of the focus system in the D200 to perform the trap focus technique. Trap focus allows the camera to be pre-focused at a specific point and have the shutter released automatically as soon as a subject passes through it. Provided you can predict the path of the subject, this technique can be very effective. Trap focus with the D200 can be set as follows. Set Custom Setting a6 (*AF Activation*) to AF-ON Only (focusing is only performed when the ⬤ button is pressed, and not when the shutter release button is pressed). Choose S focus mode, single autofocus area mode (refer to the following section), and if the lens has a focus mode switch on it set it to A or M/A. Pre-focus the lens on the point through which the subject will pass by aligning the selected autofocus sensing area with it and push the ⬤ button. Keep the camera active by maintaining full pressure on the shutter release button. When the subject covers the selected autofocus sensing area, the camera will detect focus and the shutter will be released.

Autofocus Area Modes

The D200 has four autofocus area modes (not to be confused with the three focusing modes described earlier in this chapter) that determine how the eleven autofocus sensing areas are used: single area AF, dynamic area AF, group dynamic AF (with or without closest subject priority), and dynamic area AF with closest subject priority. The autofocus area mode is selected using the AF-area mode selector on

154

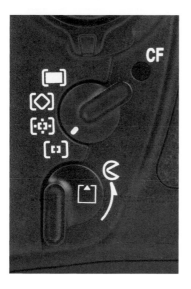

Use the AF-area mode selector to choose single area AF [ɪ] *dynamic area AF* [·:·] *group dynamic AF* [◇] *or dynamic area AF with closest subject priority* [■] *.*

the camera back just below the Multi Selector. The four options available operate as follows:

[ɪ] **Single area AF:** The D200 uses only the single autofocus sensing area currently selected for focusing; the camera takes no part in choosing which sensor to use. The selected area is highlighted in the viewfinder.

[·:·] **Dynamic Area AF:** Initially, the D200 uses the autofocus sensing area currently selected for focusing. Then, if the camera detects that the subject is moving, it evaluates information from the other autofocus sensing areas and will shift focusing to another sensor area if necessary. The selected area is highlighted in the viewfinder and remains highlighted even if the subject leaves it.

[◇] **Group Dynamic AF:** A group of AF sensing areas (either four arranged in a diamond or triangle pattern or three arranged in a line) can be chosen to control focus depending on what you select via Custom Setting a5 (*Pattern Selection in Group Dynamic AF*). You select the pattern of focus sensing areas to be used by the camera, as well as whether the cam-

155

era will place priority on the central focus sensing area in the selected group (*Center Priority*) or automatically select the focus sensing area that covers the object deemed to be closest to the camera (*Closest Subject Priority*).

[■] **Dynamic Area AF with Closest Subject Priority:** The camera evaluates information from all eleven of its autofocus sensing areas and always selects and uses the sensor area that detects the object that is closest to the camera. I say "object" rather than "subject" because the camera may not focus on the intended subject! You have no control over which sensor area is used for focusing when in this mode.

Selecting an Autofocus Area
To select the autofocus area or group of areas that the D200 will initially use to attain focus:

- Rotate the focus selector lock (which surrounds the Multi Selector on the camera back) counterclockwise so the two white dots are aligned.
- If the camera is not already active, press the shutter release button halfway and release it.
- Then Multi Select up, down, left, or right to change the selected autofocus area or group of areas.

Note: Selection of the autofocus area can be set so that it wraps around from one side of the viewfinder screen to the other as you scroll by selecting Wrap from Custom Setting a8 (*Focus Area*). If you press and hold the Multi Selector in a particular direction, the autofocus area selection will scroll continuously in that direction. This enables the selected autofocus area to be shifted from one side of the frame area to the other rapidly.

Overview

If you are new to Nikon's AF system, it will probably take a while to get used to the functionality of the various focus modes and focus area modes. Therefore, you may wish to re-read the sections above and refer to the following table that summarizes the D200's autofocus operations.

AF Mode	AF Area Mode	Selection of Focus Area
Single-servo	Single	You
Single-servo	Dynamic	You
Single-servo	Group dynamic	You [1, 2]
Single-servo	Dynamic-area with closest subject priority	Camera
Continuous-servo	Single	You
Continuous-servo	Dynamic	You
Continuous-servo	Group dynamic	You [1, 2]
Continuous-servo	Dynamic-area with closest subject priority	Camera

1. In group dynamic AF area mode, you select the group of focus sensing areas (the central area is used initially).

2. If group dynamic with closest subject priority is chosen, the camera selects the focus sensing area from the selected group that covers an object deemed to be closest to the camera.

Hint: I recommend avoiding the use of group dynamic with closest subject priority or dynamic-area with closest subject priority AF area modes since you have no control over which autofocus sensing area is being used by the camera.

Hint: When using group dynamic AF area mode, Custom Setting a4 (*Pattern Selection in Group Dynamic AF*) allows the user to select the pattern of autofocus sensing areas as well as which sensor within the pattern will be used initially. In my opinion, the pattern with three autofocus sensing areas combined with central sensor selection (*Center Priority*) offers the greatest level of user control.

Focus Zone Selection

Focus screen display with 11-area Normal Frame selected.

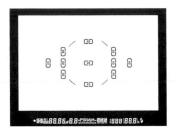

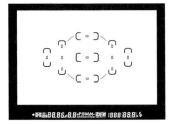

Focus screen display with 7-area Wide Frame selected.

As if the options available for focus mode and focus area mode were not enough, the D200 adds a further twist to its autofocus system by offering two further options to control the coverage of autofocus areas in   (single-area AF) and (dynamic-area AF) modes. In these two AF area modes, it is possible to select either normal or wide zone coverage for the autofocus areas via Custom Setting a3 (*Focus Area Frame*); the available options are shown in the following table.

Option	Description
Normal Frame	All eleven autofocus sensing areas are available
Wide Frame	Number of autofocus sensing areas is reduced to seven but each has a wider zone of coverage

The options are displayed in the control panel and viewfinder as follows:

Option	Control Panel	
	Single-area AF	**Dynamic-area AF**
Normal Frame		
Wide Frame		

To select the zone of coverage for the autofocus sensing areas, go to Custom Setting a3 (*Focus Area Frame*) and highlight the required option before Multi Selecting right to confirm the selection.

Hint: Use the *Normal Frame (11 areas)* option when photographing a static or slow moving subject, as this allows precise placement of the point of focus on the subject. If the subject is moving, particularly if the movement is somewhat erratic, or the nature of the shooting situation provides little time to frame the shot, I recommend selecting the *Wide Frame* option. However, it is worth remembering that if the focus area in the *Wide Frame* option is placed over a subject or part of a subject in which there are numerous potential points of focus, focus precision may be unpredictable. In this situation, use the *Normal Frame* option.

Note: It is also possible to select the zone of coverage for the autofocus areas by using the FUNC. button and the sub-command dial. Open Custom Setting f4 and use the *Focus Area Frame* option. To set the focus area frame, press the FUNC button and rotate the sub-command dial; *Wide Frame* is selected when WIDE is displayed in the control panel.

Focus Lock

Once the D200 has attained focus, it is possible to lock the autofocus system so the shot can be recomposed and focus retained even if the subject is no longer covered by an auto-focus sensing area.

S – (single-servo) autofocus: Pressing the shutter release button halfway will activate autofocus; as soon as focus is attained, the focus indicator ● is displayed in the viewfinder and focus is locked; it will remain locked while the shutter release button is depressed halfway. Alternatively, press and hold the AE-L/AF-L button to lock focus; once focus is locked using the AE-L/AF-L button, it is not necessary to keep the shutter release button depressed.

C – (continuous-servo) autofocus: The autofocus system remains active, constantly adjusting the focus point, while the shutter release button is held halfway down. To lock focus in this focus mode, press and hold the AE-L/AF-L button.

Hint: Use Custom Setting c2 to assign the function of the AE-L/AF-L button; it can be used to lock exposure and focus, exposure only, or focus only.

Hint: Once focus has been locked in either S or C focus mode, ensure the camera-to-subject distance does not alter. If it does, reactivate autofocus and refocus the lens at the new distance before using the autofocus lock option.

Buildings with repetitive squares or rectangles are often difficult ⇨ *subjects for any AF system. However, you may be able to acquire focus along an edge with a lot of contrast (such as where a building meets the sky). In this case, depress the shutter release partway to lock focus and then recompose the picture, as desired.*

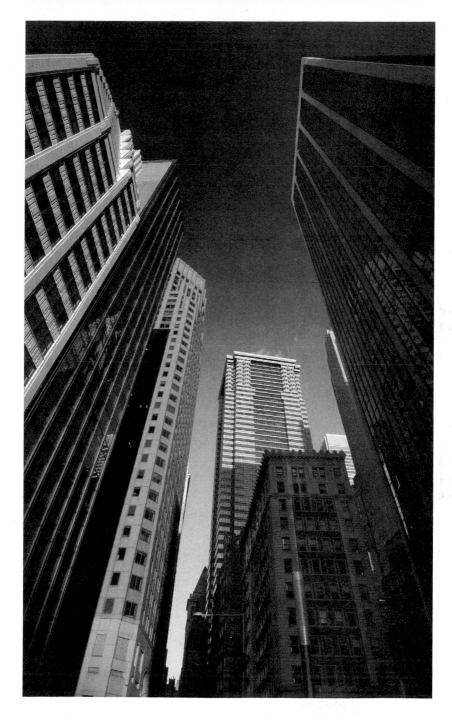

AF Assist Illuminator

The D200 has a small built-in white light known as the AF assist illuminator that is designed to facilitate autofocus in low light conditions. It is located on the front of the camera between the finger grip and the viewfinder head. Whatever the intentions of the camera's design team were, it is my opinion that this feature is largely superfluous! Here are a few reasons why I suggest using Custom Setting a9 (*AF Assist*) to cancel the lamp's operation:

- The lamp only works if you have an autofocus lens attached to the camera and the focus mode is set to S (single-servo) with either the center focus area or center focus area group selected, or the closest subject priority feature active.

- It is only usable with focal lengths from 24 – 200mm.

- The operating range is restricted to between 1 foot 8 inches – 9 feet 10 inches (0.5 – 3.0 m).

- Due to its location, many lenses obstruct its output, particularly if they have a lens hood attached.

- The lamp overheats quickly (six to eight exposures in rapid succession is usually sufficient) and will automatically shut down to allow it to cool. Plus, at this level of use, it also drains battery power faster.

Hint: Provided the conditions described above are met it is possible to use the built-in AF assist illuminator lamp of either the SB-600 or SB-800 Speedlight, or the SU-800 Speedlight commander unit (operation of the camera's lamp is disabled in these circumstances). If you want to use either the SB-600 or SB-800 off-camera, the SC-29 TTL flash head has a built-in AF-assist lamp that attaches to the camera's accessory shoe.

Limitations of AF System

Although the autofocus system of the D200 is very effective, there are some circumstances or conditions that limit its performance:

- Low light

- Low contrast

- Highly reflective surfaces

- The subject is too small within the autofocus sensing area

- The subject has very fine detail

- The autofocus sensing area covers a regular geometric pattern

- The autofocus sensing area covers a region of high contrast

- The autofocus sensing area covers objects at different distances from the camera

If any of these conditions prevent the camera from attaining focus, either switch to manual focus mode or focus on another object that is the same distance from the camera as your subject and use the focus lock feature to lock focus before recomposing the shot.

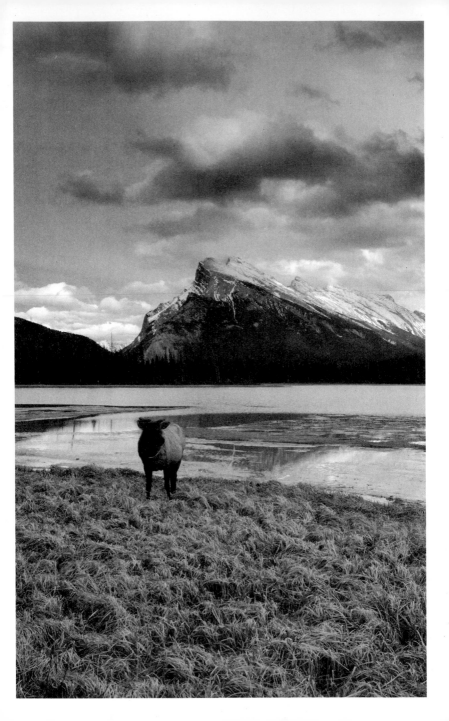

Playback, Shooting, and Setup Menus

The D200 makes extensive use of a sophisticated and comprehensive menu system that is displayed on the LCD monitor. It is divided into five main sections:

▶ **Playback Menu** – This menu is used for reviewing, editing, and managing the pictures stored on the memory card.

🖿 **Shooting Menu** – This menu is used to select more sophisticated camera controls that have a direct influence on the quality and appearance of the pictures recorded by the camera. The 🖿 menu also contains several special features such as the image overlay tool, configuring multiple exposures, and using time-lapse photography.

✐ **Custom Settings Menu** – As the title of this menu suggests, the options available here allow you to select and set a wide range of controls to fine tune camera operation to meet your own specific requirements. The ✐ menu will be covered in detail in the next chapter.

Ⓨ **Setup Menu** – This menu is used to establish the basic configuration of the camera; once the settings for the items in the Ⓨ menu are made, they do not need to be changed very often.

◁ *Use the D200's menu system to optimize the camera for your style of shooting.*

▤   **Recent Settings** – While not an independent menu itself, this useful feature lists the fourteen most recently used options from the Shooting and Custom Settings menus; it can also be used to create a customized menu from these two menus that saves you having to scroll through all the options of both so that frequently used options can be accessed more efficiently.

Accessing the Menus

To access any menu, push the ⊙ button and Multi Select left to highlight one of the five tabs used to identify each menu. From top to bottom, they are ▶ Playback menu, ◻ Shooting menu, ⌀ Custom Settings menu, ⋔ Setup menu, and ▤ Recent Settings menu. You navigate to the specific menu item you require by using the Multi Selector. To display the options available for each menu item, Multi Select right on the desired item.

Note: The menus have multiple pages, so keep scrolling up or down to access options not shown on the first page of the menu.

Note: If a menu item or menu item sub-option is displayed in gray, it is not currently available.

   To exit the menu system, press the shutter release button halfway or press the ⊙ button twice. Many of the options within the menu system can be set using buttons and dials located on the camera body; where such an alternative route is available I recommend using it, as this will improve the efficiency of camera handling and reduce battery power consumption by avoiding use of the monitor screen. In the following sections, I will deal with the features and functions controlled by the Playback, Shooting, Setup, and Recent Settings menus. In cases where certain features are discussed in detail elsewhere in the book, I have given the relevant page reference. (The Custom Settings menu and its many features and functions are detailed in the next chapter.)

▶ Playback Menu

The Playback menu will only be displayed if a memory card is currently installed in the camera.

Delete

Using the *Delete* option in the Playback menu allows you to erase individual images, a group of images, or all of the images on the card.

Hint: To deleting images one by one, it is quicker and easier to use the ⊖ button on the rear of the camera. However, to erase a group of images the *Delete* option will probably save a lot of time.

To delete a group of images:
* Select *Delete* from the Playback menu.
* Choose *Selected* from the options list.
* Thumbnails of all of the images stored on the card will be displayed on the LCD monitor, regardless of whether they are stored in different folders. Scroll through the images using the Multi Selector; a yellow frame will form a boundary around the selected image. To see an enlarged view of the image, press and hold the ⊕ button.
* To select the highlighted image for deletion, press the center of the Multi Selector. A small icon of a trashcan will appear in the upper right corner of the thumbnail image.
* Once all the files to be deleted have been selected, press the ⊛ button.
* The total number of images to be deleted will be displayed, along with two options: *No* or *Yes*. Select the required option and press the ⊛ button to complete the process.

Note: Images that have been hidden will not be displayed, and therefore cannot be selected for deletion.

To delete all images:
- Select *Delete* from the Playback menu.
- Select *All* from the options list.
- Highlight *Yes* or *No*.
- Press the ⓔⓝⓣⓔⓡ button to complete the process.

Note: This process cannot delete pictures that have been protected.

Hint: If you want to delete a high volume of pictures, you may want to hook the camera up to the EH-6 AC adapter or load your memory card into a card reader to erase the images using your computer. Erasing a lot of images using the camera can take some time and use up a lot of battery power.

Playback Folder

The *Playback Folder* option allows you to determine which images on the installed memory card will be displayed during playback. There are three options available:

- *ND200* – Displays all the images recorded by the D200 from all folders.

- *All* - All of the images stored on the card displayed, regardless of which camera was used to record them, provided they conforms to the Design Rule for Camera File System (DCF). All Nikon digital cameras and most other current digital cameras are DCF compatible.

- *Current* - Only the images in the folder currently set for image storage (via the Folders option in the Shooting menu) are displayed.

To make your selection:
- Select *Playback Folder*.
- Highlight the required option and Multi Select right to confirm your choice.

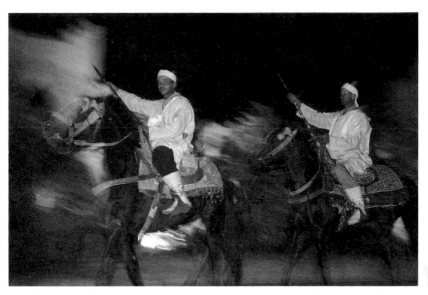

The Slide Show feature is a great way to share your favorite photos with family and friends.

Slide Show

The *Slide Show* option allows you to view all of the images stored on the current memory card in sequential order. This can be a useful and enjoyable feature, especially if the camera is connected to a television for viewing.

To use *Slide Show*:
• Select *Slide Show* from the Playback menu.
• Start will be highlighted; to commence the slide show immediately, Multi Select right.
• To select the duration of display for each image, highlight *Frame Interval* and Multi Select right to display the four options: 2, 3, 5, or 10 seconds. Highlight the desired elction and Multi Select right to confirm and return to the main Slide Show page.
• Repeat the second step to commence the slide show.

There are a variety of control options when the *Slide Show* function is active:

- To return to the previous image, Multi Select left.
- To skip to the next image, Multi Select right.
- To display image information, Multi Select up or down until the required page is displayed.
- To pause the slide show, press the ⊛ button. A sub-menu with three options will be displayed: *Restart*, *Frame Interval*, or *Exit*. Highlight the desired option and Multi Select right.
- To stop the slide show, press the ⊛ button, the shutter release button, or ⊡ button.

At the end of the slide show, the same menu displayed when the slide show is paused will be shown: *Restart*, *Frame Interval*, or *Exit*. Highlight the desired option and Multi Select right.

Note: Images that have been hidden do not appear during the slide show. (Refer to the following section for instructions on how to hide an image.)

Hint: The *Slide Show* function consumes a lot of power, especially if a large number of images are stored on the memory card. Ensure that your battery is fully charged or use the EH-6 AC adapter.

Hide Image

The *Hide Image* option enables the user to hide or reveal selected images. Images that are hidden cannot be viewed during normal image playback; these hidden images can only be seen in the *Hide Image* menu, and they are also protected against deletion. They can only be deleted from the memory card if it is formatted.

Note: Remember, formatting does not actually delete the image file data; it merely overwrites the file directory on the memory card so that the camera can no longer navigate to the image files stored on it. It is sometimes possible to recover files from a card that has been formatted, but the chances of success diminish as more new data is saved on the card after the formatting process. In any case, you should not depend on being able to access images on the memory card after you have formatted it, even though it is possible.

To use *Hide Image*:
• Select *Hide Image* from the Playback menu.
• The next page shows *Select/Set* and *Deselect All?*.
• To select images to hide, choose *Select/Set*. Thumbnails of all the images stored on the card will be displayed on the monitor screen, regardless of whether they are stored in different folders. Scroll through the images using the Multi Selector; a yellow frame will form a boundary around the selected image. To see an enlarged view of the image, press and hold the ⊕ button.
• To select the highlighted image to be hidden, press the center of the Multi Selector. A small icon of a frame with a diagonal line through it will appear in the upper right corner of the thumbnail image.
• Once you have selected all the images you wish to be hidden, press the ⊕ button to hide all selected images.

To reveal only selected images:
• Select *Hide Image* from the Playback menu then highlight Select/Set and Multi Select right.
• Thumbnails of all of the images stored on the card will be displayed on the monitor screen, irrespective of whether they are hidden or not and regardless of whether they are stored in different folders.
• To select a highlighted hidden image to be revealed, press the center of the Multi Selector when the hidden image is highlighted. The small icon of a frame with a diagonal line through it that denotes a hidden image will disappear.
• Once you are finished selecting those hidden images that are to be revealed, press the ⊕ button.

To reveal all images:
• Select *Hide Image* from the Playback menu then highlight *Deselect All?* And Multi Select right.

- A message is displayed in the monitor screen: *No images will be hidden*. OK? Highlight *Yes* or *No* accordingly and Multi Select right to confirm your choice.

Print Set

The *Print Set* option enables you to create and save a set of images to be printed automatically by a compatible printing device. This feature will communicate which images should be printed, how many prints of each image, and the information that is to be included on each print. This information is saved on the installed memory card in the Digital Print Order Format (DPOF) to be read subsequently by a DPOF compatible printing device. (See pages 290-291 for more information on DPOF.)

Display Mode

The *Display Mode* option determines which pages of image information are displayed during single-image playback, in addition to the Basic Information and File Information pages. There are five options: *Data (two-pages)*, *Histogram*, *Highlights*, *RGB Histogram*, and *Focus Area*.

To use *Display Mode*:
- Select *Display Mode* from the Playback menu.
- Highlight each option you wish to have access to during single-image playback one by one and Multi Select right to select them. A checkmark will appear in the box to the right of each option that has been selected.
- When you have selected all the information pages you wish to appear, highlight *Done* and Multi Select right.

Refer to pages 102-106 for details on the various information pages.

Image Review

The *Image Review* option determines whether or not an image will be displayed on the LCD monitor immediately after it is recorded.

Hint: There are situations when reviewing every image recorded by the camera is either impractical or unnecessary. Since the LCD monitor consumes a relatively large amount of power, it is often prudent to switch the Image Review function to Off in order to conserve the camera's battery power.

To use *Image Review*:
- Select *Image Review* from the Playback menu.
- Highlight *On* or *Off* and Multi Select right to confirm your choice.

After Delete

The *After Delete* option enables you to select whether the next or previous image (based on the order in which they were recorded) is displayed after an image has been deleted.

To set *After Delete*:
- Select *After Delete* from the Playback menu.
- Highlight either *Show Next* (the default), *Show Previous*, or *Continue as Before* and Multi Select right to confirm your selection.

Hint: Sometimes I wonder if features such as the *After Delete* option are included just for the sake of doing so! It adds what I consider to be unnecessary complexity to a camera that is already loaded with options, features, and functions. Personally, I leave this option at its default setting and forget it is there.

Rotate Tall

The *Rotate Tall* option allows pictures taken in the vertical (portrait) format to be displayed on the LCD monitor in the orientation in which they were shot. However, viewing images this way will decrease the overall size of the image to about 2/3 the size of an image viewed using the full viewing area of the screen.

Note: The *Auto Image Rotation* option in the Setup menu must be turned on for the *Rotate Tall* function to operate (see page 189).

To activate *Rotate Tall*:
- Select *Rotate Tall* from the Playback menu.
- Highlight *Yes* or *No* and Multi Select right to confirm the choice.

📷 Shooting Menu

Shooting Menu Bank

The D200 can store all the Shooting menu options in one of four separate banks, allowing the user to store four different configurations of camera settings for quick and easy access. Changes made in one bank do not affect the settings in the other three. This feature can be particularly useful if you shoot various types of subjects that require different shooting setups (i.e., you can set one bank up for portrait photography and another for sports). So, rather than having to change a group of settings each time you photograph a certain type of subject, you simply switch to the relevant bank of settings. Likewise, if the camera is used by a variety of different photographers, each one can store their own group of settings in a specific bank. The default bank is A.

To access the *Shooting Menu Bank* feature:
- Select *Shooting Menu Bank* from the Shooting menu.
- Highlight the name of the bank you wish to select, then Multi Select right to open that particular bank.

   The default names for the banks are A, B, C, and D but these can be changed for easy reference. For example, you may wish to name them for a particular type of photography (i.e., portrait, landscape, etc.), or alternatively, you could identify a particular bank by using the name of the photographer whose settings are saved there. The name of the bank is limited to 20 characters.

To rename a shooting bank:
- Select *Shooting Menu Bank* from the Shooting menu.
- Select *Rename* and Multi Select right.
- Highlight the bank you wish to rename, then Multi Select right to open the keypad of characters.

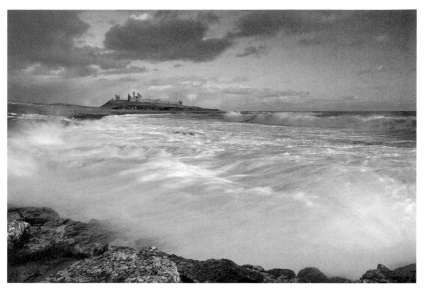

Shooting menu banks are useful for grouping settings used for particular types of photography, such as landscapes or portraits.

- To enter a new shooting bank name, highlight the character you wish to input and press the center of the Multi Selector to select it. If you enter the wrong character inadvertently, use the 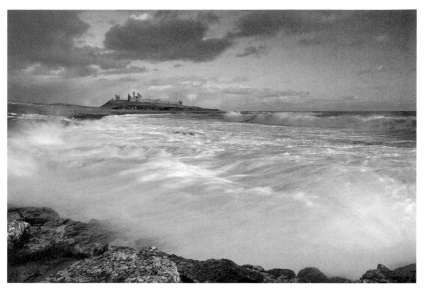 button in combination with the Multi Selector to move the cursor over the unwanted character, then press the button to erase it.
- Press the button to save the name and return to the Shooting Menu Bank options list.

Menu Reset

The *Menu Reset* option allows you to restore all settings in the current shooting bank back to their default values. This will not affect most of the Custom Settings. A list of the affected settings and their defaults can be found below.

To use *Menu Reset*:
- Select *Menu Reset* from the Shooting menu.
- Highlight *Yes* or *No* and Multi Select right to confirm.

Option	Default	Option	Default
File naming	*DSC*	**Multiple Exposure**[2]	
Optimize Image	*Normal*	*Number of Shots*	*2*
Color Space	*sRGB*	*Auto Gain*	*On*
Image Quality	*JPEG Normal*	**Interval Timer Shooting**[3]	
Image Size	*Large*	*Start Time*	*Now*
JPEG Compression	*Size Priority*	*Interval*	*00:01:00*
NEF Raw Compression	*NEF Raw*	*No of intervals*	*1*
White Balance	*Auto*[1]	*No of shots*	*1*
Long Exp. Noise reduction	*Off*	*Start*	*Off*
High ISO noise reduction	*ON (Normal)*	**Non-CPU lens data**	
ISO sensitivity	*100*	*Focal length*	*N/A*
		Maximum Aperture	*N/A*

[1] Fine tuning reset to 0.
[2] Applies to all banks.
[3] Applies to all banks.

Note: The default settings for *Image Quality*, *Image Size*, *White Balance*, and *ISO Sensitivity* can also be reset using the two button reset option described on pages 100-101.

Folders

The D200 uses a folder system to organize images stored on the memory card installed in the camera. The Folders option allows you to select which folder the images you are currently recording will be saved in, as well as enabling you to create new folders. If you do not use any of the Folders options, the camera creates a folder named 100ND200, automatically, in which the first 999 pictures recorded by the camera will be stored on the memory card. If you were to exceed 999 pictures, the camera creates a new folder named 101ND200, and so on for each set of 999 pictures.

You can also create your own folder(s). The folder title is always prefixed by a three digital number between 100 and 999, assigned by you; the suffix "ND200" remains the same. If you use multiple folders, you must select one as the active folder to which all images will be stored until an alternative folder is chosen or the maximum capacity of 999 pictures in the active folder is exceeded, in which case the D200 will create a new folder and assign a three-digit prefix with an incremental increase of one (i.e., if folder 100ND200 became full, the D200 would create folder 101ND200 and any new pictures would be stored in this new folder).

Note: If the folder that has reached full capacity is folder number 999ND200, the camera will disable the shutter release button, preventing you from making an exposure. You will have to create a new folder with a lower number, or choose another folder on the card that still has space to hold new images.

To create a new folder:
• Select *Folders* from the Shooting menu.
• Highlight *New* and Multi Select right.
• Designate the number of the new folder by Multi Selecting up or down until the desired number is displayed.
• Multi Select right to confirm the new folder title.

To select an existing folder:
• Select *Folders* from the Shooting menu.
• Highlight *Select Folder* and Multi Select right.
• Highlight the folder you wish to use, then Multi Select right to confirm your selection and return to the Shooting menu.

Note: When the camera is first turned on, you can create a new folder by pressing the ⊙ button. The new folder will have a prefix number one higher than the current folder number. However, if the current folder is empty, no new folder can be created.

Hint: Folders may be useful if you expect to take pictures of a variety of subjects (e.g. you go away on a touring vacation and want to file your images on the memory card(s) location-by-location. You can create a folder for each location and select this as the active folder accordingly).

Hint: Personally, using multiple folders is time consuming, potentially confusing, and fraught with danger! If you have more than one Nikon digital camera and move cards between them the individual cameras will not be able to handle images in folders created by another camera. If the second camera then creates a new folder it will have a higher prefix number than the folder created by the first camera. Even multiple folders created by the D200 can present problems, as images will be saved to the currently selected folder with the highest prefix number. I would rather use a browser application such as PictureProject or Nikon View Pro to transfer and organize my images.

File Naming

The file names of all images you take with the D200 contain three letters, a four-digit number, and the three-letter file extension (.JPG or .NEF). The default for the three letters in the name is DSC, and depending on the selected color mode, they will have an underscore mark either as a prefix to denote Adobe RGB or as a suffix to denote sRGB (i.e., _DSC0001.JPG denotes a JPEG file, number 0001, saved in the Adobe RGB color space). The File Naming option allows you to select three letters of your choice (this section of the file name must contain three letters, no more or less).

To use *File Naming*:
• Select *File Naming* from the Shooting menu by highlighting it and Multi Selecting right.

178

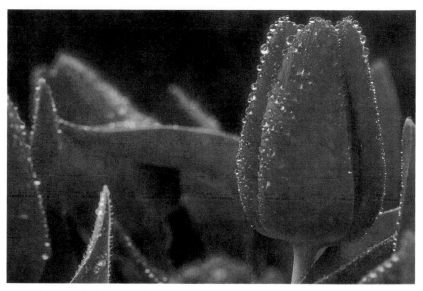

The D200's Optimize Image feature allows you change aspects such as sharpening and contrast in-camera.

- *File Naming* is highlighted on the next screen; Multi Select right to open the keyboard.
- To enter the new name, highlight the character you wish to input and press the center of the Multi Selector to choose it. If you enter the wrong character inadvertently, use the ⊗ button in combination with the Multi Selector to move the cursor over the unwanted character, then press the 🗑 button to erase it.
- Press the ⊛ button to save the name and return to the Shooting menu. All subsequent images recorded by the camera will contain the three new letters within their file name.

Optimize Image

The *Optimize Image* option allows you to make changes to sharpening, contrast, color mode, saturation and hue based on the current shooting situation and/or your preferences. This function was covered in detail on pages 124-133.

Color Space

The range of colors present in an image recorded by the D200 is determined by the *Color Space* setting. The D200 provides two options for color space: Adobe RGB and sRGB. The color space determines the range (gamut) of colors that will be available in an image file for color reproduction, and should be chosen according to how the image will be processed after it has been exported from the camera. Refer to pages 133-134 for full details.

Image Quality

The *Image Quality* option allows you to select the file format for images recorded by the camera. You can also select whether or not compression is applied to NEF files and the degree of compression applied to JPEG files. Refer to pages 142-144 for full details.

Image Size

The *Image Size* feature determines the file size or resolution of an image and is expressed as a numbers of pixels. See pages 142-144 for full details.

Note: Adjustments made to the *Image Size* menu option will only apply to images saved using the JPEG format. NEF files are always saved at the camera's highest resolution.

JPEG Compression

The complexity of the scene being recorded will affect the size of an image file captured using the JPEG format. Usually, a more intricate scene will require more information to be recorded, which increases the file size. However, the *JPEG Compression* option enables you to determine whether the camera places a priority on recording JPEG files at a fixed size or varies the file size to optimize image quality. See pages 138-139 and 144 for more about JPEG compression.

NEF/RAW Compression

The D200 provides the option of saving NEF files in either an uncompressed or compressed form. Compressed NEF files are approximately 40 – 50% smaller than uncompressed files, which increases the number of pictures that can be stored in any given storage capacity. Nikon states that NEF/RAW compression is "visually" lossless. For more information, refer to pages 140-141 and 145.

White Balance

The *White Balance* option allows you to select the color temperature to which the images you are shooting will be balanced. The various *White Balance* options are covered in detail on pages 113-115.

Long Exp. NR

Images taken at shutter speeds of 8 seconds or longer will often exhibit a higher level of electronic noise. Noise is the result of amplification processes that are applied to the data captured by the sensor. It manifests as irregularly placed bright, colored pixels that disrupt the appearance of an image, particularly in areas of even tonality. Long exposure noise reduction, abbreviated to *Long Exp. NR* in the Shooting menu, will help reduce the appearance of noise when using long exposure times.

To set *Long Exp. NR*:
• Select *Long Exp. NR* from the Shooting menu.
• Highlight *On* or *Off* and Multi Select right to confirm your choice.

If *On* is selected, the processing time for each recorded image will increase by 50 – 100%. While the image data is being processed, **Job** **nr** will appear in place of the shutter speed and aperture value displays in the control panel. No other pictures can be taken while **Job** **nr** is displayed.

The process used by the D200 to perform long exposure noise reduction involves the camera making a second exposure known as a "dark frame" exposure, during which the shutter remains closed but the camera maps the sensor and records the values of each pixel. Sometimes a pixel can retain a value that is erroneous; this often occurs if the sensor gets hot due to protracted use, as would occur during a long exposure or due to a high ambient atmospheric temperature. After mapping the sensor for "hot" (overly bright) pixels, the camera subtracts the "dark frame" pixel values from the pixel values of the main exposure in an effort to reduce the effect of noise in the final image.

Hint: Nikon states that the long exposure noise reduction feature of the D200, when switched on, will operate whenever the shutter speed exceeds 8 seconds. Personally, I have found that the in-camera signal processing of the D200 is so effective that using this feature is not really necessary until a shutter speed of 30 seconds or longer is used.

High ISO NR
At high ISO values, the presence of electronic noise in an image increases due to the greater degree of signal amplification that takes place during in-camera processing (it is analogous to the more visible grain structure of higher ISO film). The high ISO noise reduction feature, abbreviated to *High ISO NR* in the Shooting menu, helps to reduce the amount of noise in images taken at ISO settings above 400. For more information about ISO sensitivity ratings and the D200, refer to pages 79-82.

ISO Sensitivity
The *ISO Sensitivity* setting allows you to change the D200's relative sensitivity to light. ISO sensitivity is the digital equivalent to film speed. It emulates the sensitivity to light of film bearing the same ISO number. The higher the ISO number, the more sensitive a film is to light. In the D200 the ISO sensitivity is a measure of the degree of amplification applied to the signal from the sensor, since the sensitivity of the sensor is fixed at its base level, which is equivalent, approximately, to ISO100. Refer to pages 79-82 for more details on ISO sensitivity and the D200.

Image Overlay
Image Overlay is one of two methods available on the D200 that enable the user to combine multiple images. In the case of this feature, it is limited to using a pair of NEF files and

182

combining them to form a single, new image (the original image files are not affected by this process). The images do not have to be taken in consecutive order but must have been recorded by a D200 and be stored on the same memory card. Refer to pages 75-76 for details about this feature.

Multiple Exposure

The other method of combining images using the D200 is through the *Multiple Exposure* feature. This enables you to combine multiple exposures (up to a maximum of 10) into a single image. However, the images must be shot in consecutive order, and they are not saved as individual files once they are combined into a single image. For more information, see pages 76-77.

Interval Timer Shooting

The *Interval Timer Shooting* feature of the D200 enables the user to set the camera to take a set number of pictures of the same scene over a period of time at a predetermined interval, a technique often called time-lapse photography. It has applications for both scientific and artistic purposes. This feature is covered in detail on pages 77-79.

Non-CPU Lens Data

The D200 can be used with non-CPU type lenses. By registering details of the lens (focal length and maximum aperture) in the *Non-CPU Lens Data* feature, the functionality of many of the options and settings available with CPU-type lenses are also available with non-CPU type lenses. This enables the use of color matrix metering, the display of aperture value, control of flash output for balanced fill-flash, and inclusion of information about the lens in the shooting data stored by the camera with each image file. See pages 267-270 for more about using non-CPU type lenses with the D200.

⚐ Setup Menu

The ⚐ menu is used to establish the basic configuration of the camera; once the settings for the items in this menu are made, they are not often changed.

Format

A new memory card should always be formatted when it is first placed into the D200. It is also good practice to format your memory card whenever you insert it into the camera. This is particularly important if you use your memory cards with multiple camera bodies.

To format a memory card:
• Select *Format* from the Setup menu.
• Select *Yes* or *No*.
• Press the ⬤ button to confirm your selection.

To help prevent accidental deletion of image files, *No* is highlighted by default when you enter the *Format* sub-menu. If you select Yes, the camera will display the following message on the monitor screen: WARNING ALL IMAGES WILL BE DELETED. During the formatting process, FORMATTING will be displayed on the LCD monitor.

Note: Make certain that the power to the camera is not interrupted during formatting. A loss of power could damage the card, so ensure the battery is fully charged or use the optional EH-6 AC adapter.

Note: The D200 supports FAT32, which allows it to use a memory cards with a capacity in excess of 2GB. FAT16 is used when formatting any memory card already formatted in FAT16.

Note: The formatting process does not actually delete the image files, it only overwrites the file directory on the memory card so that it is no longer possible to access the image files stored on it. If you should format a card inadvertently, it may be possible to recover lost image files using software designed for this purpose provided no new data has been written to the card.

Note: The most convenient way to format a card is to use the two-button method; press and hold the ⊕ and ⬛ buttons until F o r appears blinking in the control panel screen. Then press ⊕ and ⬛ buttons again until F o r appears continuously.

LCD Brightness

The brightness of the LCD monitor on the back of the camera is set to a default value. However, this can be adjusted to help improve the visibility of any displayed image or page of information. This feature can be particularly helpful when trying to review images in bright outdoor light.

To adjust *LCD Brightness*:
• Select the *LCD Brightness* option from the Setup menu.
• Adjust the brightness value up or down using the Multi Selector.
• Select OK to set the brightness value you have chosen.

Note: A negative adjustment will darken the screen while a positive adjustment will brighten it. The screen displays a grayscale to help you judge the brightness effect on the full tonal range present in your images.

Note: You should only review images on the LCD monitor to check the composition of the picture and use the histogram displays to make a broad assessment of overall exposure accuracy. Due to the limitations of the LCD monitor, it is pointless to try to judge color fidelity or any nuances of tonal graduation.

Mirror Lock-Up

This feature is for cleaning or inspecting the low pass filter; it should not be confused with the mirror lock-up shooting mode (see pages 39-40). It is essential that the power supply to the camera is not interrupted in any way when the *Mirror Lock-up* function is active, particularly if you have any cleaning utensils in the camera at the time, as the reflex mirror will drop to its normal position with potentially dire consequences. Make sure the camera battery is fully charged, or preferably, use the optional EH-6 AC adapter.

Note: This option will not function if the battery charge indicator displayed in the control panel shows a level of ⬚⬚⬚ or less.

To use *Mirror Lock-Up*:
- Select *Mirror Lock-Up* from the Shooting menu.
- Highlight *Start* and Multi Select right. (A message with instructions on how to proceed will be displayed on the monitor screen and a series of dashes will appear in the control panel.)
- Press the shutter release button fully so the mirror will lift and the shutter opens. Proceed with any necessary inspection or cleaning.
- To return the reflex mirror to its normal position, be sure that any and all tools or instruments are out of the way of the reflex mirror, then turn the power switch to the OFF position.

Note: Exceptional care should be taken whenever the *Mirror Lock-Up* function is in use, as the low pass filter is exposed. There is an increased risk that unwanted material like dust or moisture might enter the camera, so always keep the camera facing down. In this situation, gravity is your best friend!

Video Mode

Video Mode allows you to tell the D200 what type of signal is being used by any video equipment (such as a DVD player or a television) you wish to connect your camera to for image review or playback. This should be set before connecting your camera to the device with the supplied A/V cord.

To set *Video Mode*:
• Select *Video Mode* from the Setup menu.
• Use the Multi Selector to choose either *NTSC* or *PAL*, then Multi Select right to confirm your selection.

World Time

World Time enables you to set and change the date and time recorded by the camera's internal clock, as well as decide how it will be displayed. Once you have selected *World Time* from the Setup menu, four options are displayed: *Time Zone, Date, Date Format,* and *Daylight Savings Time.* Each one requires the user to input information.

To set *Time Zone*:
• Select *Time Zone* from the *World Time* options list.
• Scroll right or left through the world map until the relevant time zone is highlighted, then press the ⊙ button to select it.

To set *Date*:
• Select *Date* from the *World Time* options list.
• Scroll up or down to set each portion of the date and time settings.
• Press the ⊙ button to confirm.

To set *Date Format*:
• Select *Date Format* from the *World Time* options list.
• Select the desired configuration for the date display, then Multi Select right to confirm your selection.

To set *Daylight Savings Time*:
• Select *Daylight Savings Time* from the *World Time* options list.
• Select *ON* or *OFF* depending on the time of year or the location in which the camera is to be used.
• Select *OK* to confirm the selection.

Language

The *Language* option on the D200 allows you to select one of 13 languages for the camera to use when displaying menus and messages.

To set *Language*:
• Select *Language* from the Setup menu.
• Highlight the desired language from the list displayed and Multi Select right to confirm your selection.

Image Comment

The *Image Comment* feature allows you to attach a short note to an image file. Comments can be up to 36 characters long and may contain letters and/or numbers. Since the process requires each character to be input individually, this is not a feature you will use for every picture. However, as a way of assigning a general comment such as the name of a location or event, or to identify your pictures with a note as to their authorship or copyright, this feature is very useful.

To use *Image Comment*:
• Select *Image Comment* from the Setup menu.
• Highlight *Input Comment* and Multi Select right.
• To enter your comment, highlight the character you wish to input and press the center of the Multi Selector to choose it. If you accidentally enter the wrong character, use the 🔍 button in combination with the Multi Selector to move the cursor over the unwanted character, then press the 🗑 button to erase it.
• Press the 🔘 button to save the comment and return to the *Image Comment* sub-menu.
• To actually attach the comment to your photographs, scroll down to the *Attach Comment* option and select Set. A small check mark will appear in the box to the left of the option.
• Finally, once you have completed this process, highlight *Done* and Multi Select right to confirm.

Note: If you wish to exit this process at any time without attaching the comment, prior to selecting *Attach Comment*, simply press the ⬤ button.

When the check mark is present beside the *Attach Comment* option, the saved comment will be attached to all subsequent images shot on the camera. To prevent the comment from being attached to an image, simply return to the *Image Comment* submenu and uncheck the *Attach Comment* box. The comment will remain stored in the camera's memory and can be attached to future images by rechecking the *Attach Comment* box.

The first twelve characters of the comment will be displayed on the fourth information page during image playback. The full comment can be viewed when using the supplied Picture Project software or other Nikon software, such as Nikon Capture 4 (version 4.4 or later), Nikon Capture NX, Nikon View (version 6.2.7), or Nikon View Pro.

Auto Image Rotation

The D200 automatically recognizes the orientation the camera is in as it records an image (i.e., horizontal, vertical, rotated 90° clockwise, rotated 90° counterclockwise). At its default setting, the camera stores this information so the image can be automatically rotated during image playback or when viewing images on the computer with compatible software. If you do not want the camera to record the shooting orientation, the *Auto Image Rotation* feature can be set to *Off*.

Note: The *Rotate Tall* option must be turned on via the Playback menu for the image to be viewed in the orientation in which it was originally taken (see pages 173-174).

Recent Settings

This great feature of the D200 can be accessed from the main menu list and shows the last fourteen items you have used from the Custom Settings and Shooting menus and how they are currently set. The Recent Settings 🗐 menu acts as a short cut to accessing these items rather than you having to navigate through the other two menus should you wish to change any of them again. Simply press the 🔘 button and select 🗐 , use the Multi Selector to highlight the required menu item, then Multi Select right to open it and display its options.

The *Recent Settings* option listed in the Setup menu enables you to make choices regarding the configuration of this feature. There are two options: *Lock Menu* and *Delete Recent Settings*. *Lock Menu* allows you to lock the current set of options listed in the Recent Settings menu so thate items cannot be removed from or added to the list. *Delete Recent Settings* erases the current list of items, even if they have been locked, making it possible to display new selections.

Note: The *Lock Menu* option can be useful if you expect to be photographing subjects or scenes under similar conditions for a protracted period and will only want access to a specific range of items from the Custom Setting and Shooting menus.

USB

This menu item allows you to select the correct USB interface option for your particular computer's operating system. This enables the transfer of images from the camera using Nikon software, or controlling the camera using Nikon Capture 4 (version 4.4, or later), or Nikon Camera Control Pro software. Use the table below to select the appropriate USB option for your operating system.

Note: The selection for the USB option should be made before connecting your camera to your computer using the supplied USB cable.

To select *USB*:
• Select *USB* from the Setup menu.
• Highlight *Mass Storage* or *PTP* (Picture Transfer Protocol), then Multi Select right to confirm your selection.

Operating system	Supplied software	Nikon Capture 4 Camera Control
Windows XP Home Edition Windows XP Professional	Choose **PTP** or **Mass Storage**	
Mac OS X		
Windows 2000 Professional Windows Millennium Edition (Me) Windows 98 Second Edition (SE)	Choose **Mass Storage**	Choose **PTP**
Mac OS 9	Not supported	

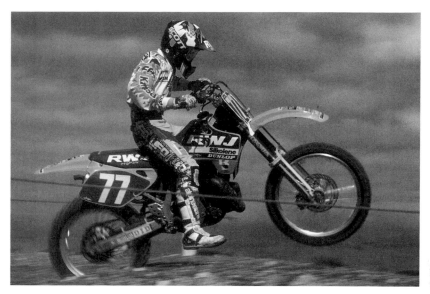

Use the Dust Off Ref Photo feature to reduce the appearance of shadows in your image caused by dust particles on the low pass filter.

Dust Off Ref Photo

The *Dust Off Ref Photo* option on the D200 is specifically designed for use with the Image Dust Off function in Nikon Capture 4 (version 4.4 or later). The image file created by this function creates a mask that is overlaid electronically onto an NEF file to enable the software to reduce or remove the effects of shadows that are cast by dust particles on the surface of the low pass filter.

Note: This function can only be used with NEF files. It is not available for JPEG files.

Note: To obtain a reference image for the *Dust Off Ref Photo* function, you must use a CPU-type lens, and Nikon recommends use of a lens with a focal length of 50mm or more.

To use *Dust Off Ref Photo*:

- Select *Dust Off Ref **Photo*** from the Setup menu.
- Multi Select right on *Start* to begin the process. A message instructing you to take a picture of a bright, featureless white object 10 cm (about 4 inches) from the lens will be displayed in the monitor screen.
- Point your camera at a white featureless subject at the requested distance from the lens, press the shutter release button halfway, and focus will be set to infinity. Alternatively, you can select manual focus and set the lens to infinity yourself.
- Depress the shutter release button the rest of the way to record the image.

Note: If the lighting conditions for your subject are too bright or too dark, the camera will display the error message INAPPROPRIATE EXPOSURE CONDITIONS on the LCD monitor. In these conditions, it is not possible to complete the process; you will need to increase or decrease the level of illumination of the test target accordingly.

Once you have recorded the reference photo, it can be displayed in the camera. It appears as a grid pattern and data is shown within the image area. These files cannot be viewed using a computer.

Note: You can identify the *Dust Off Ref* Photo file by its file extension, which is .NDF.

This is Dust Off Ref Photo file as seen on the LCD monitor.

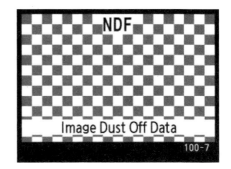

Battery Info

The EN-EL3e rechargeable battery has an electronic chip in its circuitry that allows the D200 to report detailed information regarding the status of the battery. To access this information, select *Battery Info* from the Setup menu and three parameters concerning the battery will be displayed on the monitor screen (see the table below).

Parameter	Description
Bat. Meter	Current level of battery charge expressed as a percentage.
Pic. Meter	Number of times the shutter has been released with the current battery since it was last charged. This number will include shutter release actions when no picture is recorded (e.g. to record a *Dust Off Ref Photo* frame, or measure color temperature for a preset white balance value).
Charg. Life	Displays the condition of the battery as one of five levels (0 – 4); level 0 indicates the battery is new, and level 4 indicates the battery has reached the end of its charging life and should be replaced.

Note: If the MB-D200 battery pack is fitted to the D200 and has two EN-EL3e batteries inserted, the *Battery Info* display will show information for each battery separately; it is listed as *L Slot* for the battery in the left hand chamber and *R Slot* for the battery in the right hand chamber. If AA sized batteries are inserted in the MS-D200 battery holder, no information about the batteries is available.

Firmware Version

When *Firmware Version* is selected from the Setup menu, the current version of the firmware installed on the camera is displayed on the monitor screen.

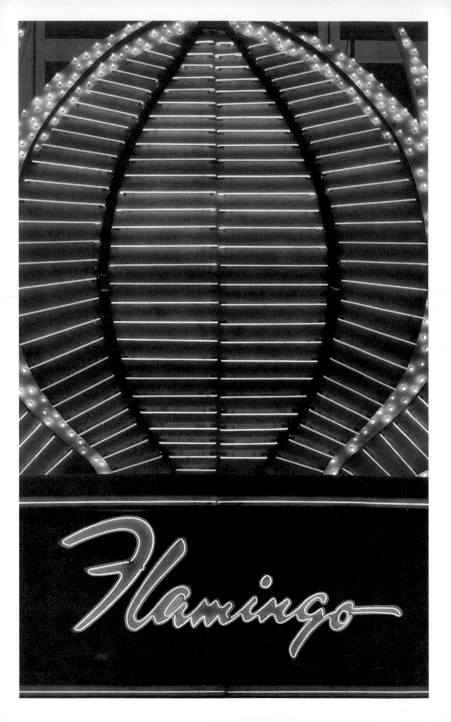

Custom Settings Menu

The Custom Settings menu ✐ allows the user to fine tune the performance of the D200 to satisfy their particular requirements and adapt the camera to meet the demands of specific shooting situations. It is comprised of a comprehensive set of no less than 45 items, each with a range of options that cover virtually every aspect of camera operation. The items are grouped logically by the nature of their function, as set out in the table below:

Group		Custom Settings
a	*Autofocus*	a1 – a10
b	*Metering/Exposure*	b1 – b7
c	*Timers/AE&AF Lock*	c1 – c5
d	*Shooting/Display*	d1 – d8
e	*Bracketing/Flash*	e1 – e8
f	*Controls*	f1 – f7

Selecting Custom Setting Options

As with the other camera menus, you will use the Multi Selector to navigate through the Custom Setting menu. To access this menu, simply press the ● button, highlight ✐ , then Multi Select right to display the list of six Custom Setting groups, plus the *C: Bank Select* and *R: Menu Reset* options. Highlight the required group and Multi Select right to display a full list of the items in that group. To access and/or activate any of these internal menu items, simply highlight your choice and Multi Select right.

◁ *Use the D200's Custom Settings menu to customize many of the camera's buttons, dials, and functions and optimize ease-of-use for your style of photography.*

C: Bank Select

The D200 can store a full range of custom settings in one of four different banks. Alterations made to custom settings in one bank have no affect on the settings in the other three banks. To select a particular bank, highlight *C: Bank Select* and Multi Select right. A list of four banks (identified as A, B, C, and D) is displayed. Each bank of settings can be renamed using the *Rename* option in the Shooting menu, and each bank can be configured with a different combination of custom settings to allow the user to switch swiftly between one range of settings to another. If the selected bank has been modified from its default settings, CUSTOM is displayed in the control panel and an asterisk is shown beside each altered item in all the different groups of items.

R: Menu Reset

To reset a particular custom bank to the default settings, use the *R: Menu Reset* option. Select the custom setting bank to be reset, highlight *R: Menu Reset*, then Multi Select right. Highlight Yes and Multi Select right to confirm. The default custom settings are set out in the table below:

	Custom Setting	Default
a1	All Mode Priority	FPS rate
a2	All Mode Priority	Focus
a3	Focus Area Frame	Normal Frame (11 Areas)
a4	Group DynamicAF	Pattern 1/Center Area
a5	Lock On	Normal
a6	AF Activation	Shutter/AF ON
a7	AF Area Illumination	Auto
a8	Focus Area	No Wrap
a9	AF Assist	On
a10	AF ON for MB D200	AF ON+Fecas Area
b1	ISO Auto	Off
b2	ISO Step Value	1/3 Step
b3	EVStep	1/3 Step

	Custom Setting	Default
b4	ExpComp/Finelune	1/3 Step
b5	Exposure comp.	Off
b6	Center Weighted	ø 8mm
b7	Fine Tune Exposure	0*
c1	AE Lock	AE L/AF L Button
c2	AE L/AF L	AE/AF Luck
c3	Auto Meter Off	6s
c4	Self Timer	10s
c5	Monitor Off	20s
d1	Beep	High
d2	Grid Display	Off
d3	Viewfinder Warning	On
d4	Shooting Speed	3 fps
d5	Exp. Delay Mode	Off
d6	File No. Sequence	Off
d7	Illumination	Off
d8	MB D200 Batteries	LR6)AA size Alkaline)
e1	Flash Sync Speed	1/250s
e2	Flash Shutter Speed	1/60s
e3	Built in Flash	TTL
e4	Modeling Flash	On
e5	Auto BKT Set	AE & Flash
e6	Manual Mode Bkting	Flash/Speed
e7	Auto BKTOrder	MTR>Under>Over
e8	Auto BKT Selection	Manual Value Select
f1	**Center Button**	
	Shouting mode	CenterAF Area
	Playback Mode	Thumbnail Os/Off
f2	Multi Selector	Do Nothing
f3	Photo Info/Playback	Info AV/PB 40,
f4	FUNC. Button	FV Lock
f5	**Command Dials**	
	Rotate Direction	Normal
	Change Main/Sob	Off
	Aperture Selling	Sub command Dial
	Menus and Playback	Off
f6	Buttons and Dials	Default
f7	NoMemory Card?	Disable Shutter

a Autofocus

a1: AF-C Mode Priority Selection

This setting controls whether an exposure is made whenever the shutter release is pressed (release priority) or only when focus has been attained (focus priority) in continuous-servo autofocus mode. Here are this setting's options:

- **FPS Rate** – Exposure can be made whenever the shutter release is pressed. This is the default setting.

- **FPS Rate + AF** – An exposure can be made whenever the shutter release is pressed. However, in continuous shooting mode, the effective frame rate is reduced to help improve the accuracy of focus in low light or low contrast conditions.

- **Focus** – The shutter can only be released once focus has been attained, although focus does not lock in continuous-servo autofocus mode.

Hint: I recommend leaving this item set to the default option, at least until you are familiar with the focusing system of the D200.

a2: AF-S Mode Priority Selection

This setting controls whether an exposure can be made only when focus has been attained (focus priority) or whenever the shutter release is pressed (release priority) in single-servo autofocus mode. Regardless of the selected option, focus is always locked when the focus indicator ● is displayed in the viewfinder. Here are this setting's options:

- **Focus** – An exposure can be made only when focus has been attained and the focus indicator ● is displayed in the viewfinder. This is the default selection.

- **Release** – An exposure can be made whenever the shutter release is pressed.

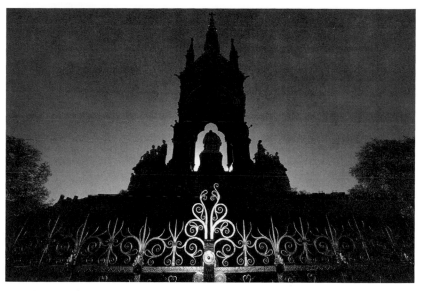

The AF-C Mode Priority Selection feature allows you to customize the D200 to make an exposure only when focus has been attained or whenever the shutter release button is pressed.

Hint: As with the previous setting, I recommend leaving this item set to the default option, at least until you are familiar with the focusing system of the D200.

a3: Focus Area Frame Selection

The D200 can be configured to use either eleven or seven autofocus sensing areas when either ⟦ ⟧ single servo AF or ⟦ ⟧ dynamic area AF is selected for the autofocus area mode. Here are this setting's options:

- *Normal Frame (11 Areas)* – The camera uses all eleven of its autofocus sensing areas. This is the default setting.

- *Wide Frame (7 Areas)* – The camera uses seven autofocus sensing areas.

Hint: The default setting of Normal Frame (11 Areas) is useful for focusing on a specific part of a subject or scene, particularly when you have time to compose the picture with precision. The Wide Frame (7 Areas) option is useful for shooting situations when the subject is moving, or when maintaining a precise composition is difficult.

a4: Pattern Selection in Group Dynamic AF

This item determines the grouping of autofocus sensing areas in group dynamic AF. It also controls whether the camera gives priority to the subject in the center focus area of the selected group. Here are this setting's options:

- *Pattern 1/Center Area* – Focus sensing areas are grouped in pattern 1 (see the following table) and the camera focuses using the center focus area of the selected group. If the subject moves out of this area, the camera will focus using information from the other focus sensing areas in the group. This is the default setting.

- *Pattern 1/Closest Subject* – Focus sensing areas are grouped in pattern 1 (see the following table) and the camera selects the focus area in the selected group that reports focus on the closest object to the camera. If the subject moves out of this area, the camera will focus using information from the other focus sensing areas in the group.

- *Pattern 2/Center Area* – This option is like *Pattern 1/ Center Area* except that the focus areas are grouped in pattern 2 (see the following table).

- *Pattern 2/Closest Subject* – This option is like *Pattern 1/ Closest Subject* except that focus areas are grouped in pattern 2 (see the following table).

Hint: I recommend you avoid any option that uses closest subject priority, as you have less control over focusing when compared with the center-priority options.

	Pattern 1	**Pattern 2**
Center Area		
Closest Subject		

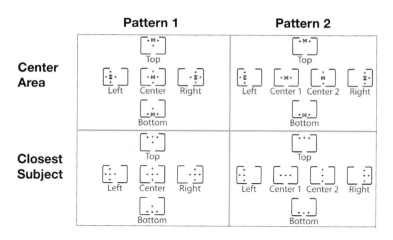

a5: Focus Tracking with Lock-On

This item determines how the autofocus system adjusts to abrupt changes in the camera-to-subject distance. This setting's options are *Long*, *Normal* (the default), *Short*, and *Off*. For each of the length options, the D200 delays adjusting the focus point when the camera-to-subject distance changes suddenly. The purpose is to prevent the camera refocusing inadvertently when an object passes briefly between the camera and the subject. Nikon does not provide any information on the duration of the three delay options, so you may want to do some experimenting to see which of them works best for you. Selecting the *Off* option means that the camera readjusts focus right away when the camera-to-subject distance changes suddenly.

Hint: To ensure that the D200 can perform follow-focus efficiently and effectively, uninhibited by any user selected delay, I recommend setting the *Off* option for this item.

a6: AF Activation

This item determines whether both the shutter release button and the AF-ON button can be used to activate autofocus or whether autofocus is only activated when the AF-ON button is pressed. This setting's options are:

- **Shutter/AF-ON** – Autofocus is activated with either the shutter release button or the AF-ON button. This is the default setting.

- **AF-ON Only** – Autofocus is only activated by pressing the AF-ON button.

a7: AF Area Illumination

To facilitate the identification of the active autofocus sensing area, particularly in low light situations, this option allows you elect for the active autofocus sensing area to be highlighted in red. Here are your options:

- **Auto** – The selected autofocus sensing area is highlighted in red if required, depending on the level of ambient illumination. This is the default setting.

- **Off** – The selected autofocus sensing area is not highlighted.

- **On** – The selected autofocus sensing area is always highlighted in red, regardless of the level of ambient illumination.

Hint: The default option of *Auto* is probably the best for most shooting situations. However, you may wish to consider setting the *Off* option for this item if you expect to shoot rapid sequences of frames, as displaying the active focus area does introduce a very slight delay in shutter operation.

a8: Focus Area Selection

This item controls how the selection of an autofocus sensing area is performed. Here are this setting's options:

- **No Wrap** – Pressing the Multi Selector to the right, for example, has no effect if the right-hand autofocus sensing area is already selected.

- **Wrap** – This allows the selection of autofocus sensing areas to "wrap around" from top to bottom, bottom to top, left to right, and right to left of the frame area.

Hint: I recommend setting the *Wrap* option for this item, as it helps to speed up selection of the focus sensing area.

a9: Built-in AF Assist Illuminator

The D200 has a built-in lamp that activates to assist autofocus operation in low light shooting situations. This Custom Settings menu item determines whether the lamp operates or not. Here are your options:

*   *On* – The built-in lamp that activates to assist autofocus operation in low light shooting situations. This is the default setting.

*   *Off* – The lamp does not light up, regardless of the level of ambient illumination.

Hint: The AF assist lamp is of little practical value, so I recommend you set the *Off* option for this item.

a10: AF-ON Button for MB-D200 Battery Pack

This item determines the function assigned to the AF-ON button on the MB-D200 battery pack when it is fitted to the D200. The options are:

*   *AF-ON + Focus Area* – The AF-ON button on the MB-D200 performs the same function as the AF-ON button on the camera; focus area can be selected by pressing the AF-ON button on the MB-D200 and rotating the sub-command dial. This is the default setting.

*   *AF-ON* – The AF-ON button on the MB-D200 performs the same function as the AF-ON button on the camera.

*   *AE-L/AF-L + Focus Area* – The AF-ON button on the MB-D200 performs the same function as the AE-L/AF-L button on the camera; focus area can be selected by pressing the AF-ON button on MB-D200 and rotating the sub-command dial.

*   *AE-L/AF-L* – The AF-ON button on the MB-D200 performs the same function as the AE-L/AF-L button on the camera.

- **Focus Area** – The focus area can be selected by pressing the AF-ON button on MB-D200 and rotating the sub-command dial.

- **Same as FUNC. button** – The AF-ON button on the MB-D200 performs the same function as the FUNC. button on the camera using Custom Setting f4 (see pages 220-221).

Hint: The choice you make here will be determined by the shooting situation; for general photography, the default setting is probably the most useful since you can select the autofocus sensing area without having to take your eye from the viewfinder.

b Metering/Exposure

b1: ISO Sensitivity Auto Control

The D200 can be set to adjust the ISO sensitivity level to maintain what Nikon refers to as "optimal exposure." The adjustment can be applied to any ISO sensitivity level up to ISO 1600. Here are this setting's options:

- **Off** – ISO sensitivity remains fixed at the level you select.

- **On** – The camera adjusts the ISO sensitivity level. The minimum value set is approximately equivalent to ISO 200; the maximum level is selected via the *Max. Sensitivity* option. In P and A exposure modes, ISO sensitivity is adjusted to prevent overexposure at a shutter speed of 1/8000 or to prevent underexposure at the shutter speed value selected from the *Min. Shutter Speed* option. In S exposure mode, the camera adjusts the ISO sensitivity if the limit of the exposure metering system is exceeded and under- or overexposure would result. In M exposure mode, the camera adjusts the ISO sensitivity if exposure cannot be achieved at the selected shutter speed and aperture values. Regardless of the exposure mode being used, the ISO sensitivity cannot be raised above ISO 1600 by this option.

- **Max. Sensitivity** – Use this sub-menu to select the maximum ISO sensitivity level that can be set by the camera.

- **Min. Shutter Speed** – Use this sub-menu to select the minimum (longest) shutter speed at which the camera will initiate adjustment of the ISO sensitivity value.

Hint: My advice is to avoid this Custom Settings menu option. You never know what ISO level the camera has set despite ISO-AUTO being displayed in the viewfinder and the control panel to indicate that the function is active. Since noise increases as the ISO sensitivity is raised, I prefer to retain total control of the ISO value to minimize noise levels.

b2: ISO Sensitivity Step Value
Use this item to select the increment when adjusting ISO sensitivity. Your options are *1/3 Step* (default), *1/2 Step*, and *1 Step*.

Hint: This item can be useful in situations when you want to use the lowest ISO sensitivity level to maintain image quality but still be able to adjust exposure while continuing to use your selected shutter speed and lens aperture. To provide the finest degree of control, stick with the default *1/3 Step* option.

b3: EV Steps for Exposure Control
Use this item to set the increment when adjusting shutter speed, lens aperture, and exposure bracketing. Your options are *1/3 Step* (default), *1/2 Step*, and *1 Step*.

Hint: I recommend sticking with the default 1/3 Step option to provide the finest degree of exposure control.

b4: Steps for Exposure Comp and Fine Tuning
Use this item to select the size of the increment when setting your exposure compensation level and exposure fine-tuning level. Your options are *1/3 Step* (default), *1/2 Step*, and *1 Step*.

Hint: As with the last two settings, I recommend sticking with the *1/3 Step* default option to provide the finest degree of exposure control.

b5: Easy Exposure Compensation

This item controls whether the ⊟ button is required to set an exposure compensation value. Here are your options:

- *Off* – Set exposure compensation by pressing the ⊟ button and rotating the main command dial. This is the default.

- *On* – Set exposure compensation by rotating one of the command dials; there is no need to press the ⊟ button. This option is not available with manual exposure mode. Which command dial sets the exposure compensation will depend on which exposure mode you are in and which option you selected via Custom Setting f5 (see page 222).

- *On (Auto Reset)* – This option works just like On except that exposure compensation set using a command dial is cancelled when the camera is turned off or the exposure meter turns off.

Hint: This item introduces additional complexity to the D200, especially if you have other Nikon cameras (film or digital) that do not offer this level of control. Most modern Nikon cameras use a combination of pressing a button and turning a command dial to set exposure compensation, so I suggest that if you have other cameras this item should be set to the default option of *Off*.

b6: Center-Weighted Area

In center-weighted exposure metering, the D200 assigns approximately 75% of the metering influence to a circular area in the center of the frame. This Custom Settings menu option allows you to select the diameter of the circular metering area or have the camera average the exposure reading across the entire frame area. Your options are *6mm, 8mm (default), 10mm, 13mm,* and *Average*.

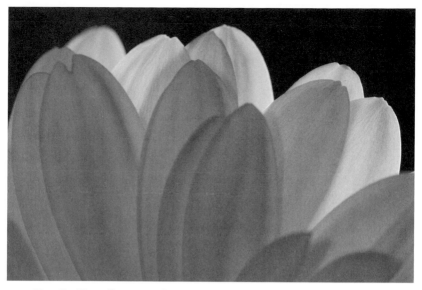

Use the Easy Exposure Compensation feature if you wish to access exposure compensation at the touch of a button, without turning the main command dial.

Hint: This is very much a personal preference item; I do not use center-weighted metering, so I leave it set to the default *8mm* circle. The smaller the circle you use, the more precise metering you can perform on a specific area of the frame.

b7: Fine Tune Optimal Exposure

This option enables you to fine-tune exposure measurement; it can be set independently for each metering method over a range of +/- 1 EV. Highlighting *No* will exit the item without adjusting exposure. Highlighting *Yes* and Multi Selecting right will open a sub-menu that displays the three metering methods. Highlight the desired metering method and Multi Select right to open another sub-menu that displays the exposure adjustment value.

Hint: I recommend you avoid this item if you use Matrix metering, as it will adjust exposure by unknown amounts based on each and every subject or scene that it meters from. However, if you use the spot metering function to take a meter reading from a known test target, this item is useful to ensure the meter reading suggested by the camera matches the reflectivity of the test target. For example, if you use an 18% gray card as a test target, you will probably want to set a fine tune value of +1/3 to +1/2 EV due to the way the camera meter is calibrated.

c Timers/AE&AF Lock

c1: AE Lock Buttons

This option determines how the exposure value can be locked. Here are this setting's options:

- **AE-L/AF-L Button** – Exposure can only be locked by pressing the AE-L/AF-L button. This is the default option.

- **+Release Button** – Exposure can be locked by pressing the AE-L/AF-L button or by pressing the shutter release button halfway.

Hint: This is a matter of personal preference, but it can be convenient to have exposure locked by just pressing the shutter release button if you wish to recompose the picture after taking a meter reading from the subject.

c2: Assignment of AE-L/AF-L Button

The AE-L/AF-L button can be allocated a variety of functions:

- **AE/AF Lock** – Both exposure and focus are locked when the ● button is pressed and held down. This is the default setting.

- **AE Lock Only** – Exposure is locked but focus continues to operate when the ● button is pressed and held down.

208

- *AE Lock Hold/Reset* – Exposure is locked when the ● button is pressed and remains locked until it is pressed again, the shutter is released, or the exposure meter turns off.

- *AE Lock Hold* – Exposure is locked when the ● button is pressed and remains locked until it is pressed again or the exposure meter turns off.

- *AF Lock* – Focus is locked when the ● button is pressed and held down but exposure values can be altered.

c3: Auto Meter-Off Delay
This item determines how long the camera exposure meter remains active when no other camera operation is performed. Your options are *4s, 6s* (default), *8s, 16s,* or *No Limit.*

Hint: To prevent undue drain on the battery, I recommend using either the default setting of *6s* or the *8s* option, as these provide a good compromise between having sufficient time to read and assess the meter reading and conserving battery power.

c4: Self-Timer Delay
The duration of the shutter release delay in self-timer mode is controlled by this item. Your options are *2s, 5s, 10s* (default), or *20s.*

Hint: Set the duration of the delay to match the shooting situation; using a duration that is unnecessarily long will just increase drain on the battery power.

c5: Monitor-Off Delay
This option determines how long the LCD monitor remains on if no other camera operation is performed. Your options are *10s, 20s, 1min., 5min.,* or *10min.*

Hint: Use the shortest duration to prevent undue drain on the battery power.

Note: If the EH-6 AC adapter is used, the exposure meter will not turn off and the monitor will only switch off after ten minutes, regardless of the options selected via Custom Setting c3 and c5.

d Shooting/Display

d1: Beep
Controls the volume of the audible warning that sounds when the self-timer function is counting down or when the camera attains focus in single-servo AF mode with focus priority, selected via Custom Setting a2. Your options are High (default), *Low*, or *Off*.

Hint: The audible warning can be a distraction in many shooting situations, so I recommend selecting *Off* for this setting.

d2: Viewfinder Grid Display
When this option is set to *On*, a pattern of grid lines is displayed in the viewfinder. *Off* is the default.

Hint: This is very useful feature for any photography that requires precise alignment of elements in the picture, such as a horizon or the surface of water. I like to keep this option in the Recent Settings menu so that it is accessible at short notice (see pages 189-190 for more about the Recent Settings menu).

d3: Viewfinder Warning Display
At the default setting of *On*, the camera will display a warning in the viewfinder to indicate low battery, no memory card inserted, or that the *B&W* option is selected in the *Optimize Image* feature in the Shooting menu.

Hint: I recommend leaving this setting at its default option of *On*.

d4: CL-Mode Shooting Speed

This item determines the frame rate of the camera when the shooting mode is set to CL (continuous low-speed). It also determines the frame rate for single-frame and mirror-up modes when using the interval timer feature. This setting's options are frame rates of *4 fps, 3 fps* (default)*, 2 fps,* and *1 fps*.

Hint: I never use the CL shooting mode, as I prefer to have the camera shoot at its fastest rate, taking individual frames in rapid succession in CH (continuous high-speed) shooting mode. Your own specific shooting requirements will determine the choice you make for this item.

Note: The effective frame rate can be influenced by the shutter speed and the capacity of the buffer memory.

d5: Exposure Delay Mode

This item enables the camera to delay the release of the shutter by approximately 0.4s after the shutter release button is pressed. Its purpose is to help reduce the risk of camera vibration, which might affect the sharpness of a picture. You can select either *On* or *Off*.

Hint: Since the camera has a proper mirror lock-up mode that can be used in conjunction with a remote shutter release to prevent camera shake, I see little worth in using this item. For that reason I recommend leaving set to its default option of *Off*.

d6: File Number Sequence

This setting controls whether file numbering continues in a consecutive sequence from the last number used when a memory card is formatted, a new folder is created, or a new memory card is inserted in the camera. Here are this setting's options:

*   *Off* – File numbering is reset to 0001 whenever a memory card is formatted, a new folder is created, or a new memory card is inserted in the camera.

- **On** – File numbering continues consecutively from the last number used or from the largest number in the current folder (whichever is higher) when a memory card is formatted, a new folder is created, or a new memory card is inserted in the camera. If the current folder contains a photograph numbered 9999, a new folder will be created automatically and numbering is reset to 0001.

- **Reset** – This selection is just like *On* except that the file number for the next exposure is assigned by adding one to the largest file number in the current folder.

Hint: If you expect to shoot pictures using more then one memory card, I strongly suggest that you use set this feature to *On*. Otherwise, you will end up with duplicate file names, which could become very confusing once images are saved to your computer.

d7: LCD Illumination
This setting controls operation the illumination of the control panel's LCD screen. *Off* is the default; the panel only illuminates when the power switch it rotated past the ON position and released. If you select the *On* option, the backlight remains on while the exposure meter is active.

Hint: Since the use of the backlight will increase drain on the battery power, I recommend leaving this item set to its default option of *Off*.

d8: MB-D200 Battery Type
To ensure efficient and proper operation of the MB-D200 battery pack when fitted with AA size batteries, use this Custom Settings menu item to input the type of battery that is inserted in the MS-D200 battery holder. Yor options are *LR6(AA-size Alkaline)*, *HR6(AA-size NiMH)*, *FR6(AA-size Lithium)*, and *ZR6(AA-size Ni-Mn)*.

Hint: Although I would suggest that use of AA batteries in the MB-D200 battery pack should only be considered as an emergency measure, if you have to resort to using such batteries, ensure the correct type is selected for this item.

e Bracketing/Flash

e1: Flash Sync Speed Setting

Use this item to select the flash synchronization speed. Your options are shutter speeds between 1/250 and 1/60, plus 1/250s (Auto FP).

Hint: If you use the SB-800, SB-600, or SB-R200 Nikon Speedlights I recommend using the *1/250s (Auto FP)* setting if you expect to be shooting with fill-flash outdoors on a bright day. Otherwise, leave this item set to the *1/250s* default option to ensure the maximum flash shooting range. (In FP high-speed auto flash, the Speedlight emits a series of rapid pulses of light rather than a single flash and, as a consequence, flash shooting distances are reduced as the shutter speed is raised above 1/250).

Note: The *1/250s (Auto FP)* option is only supported when using a Speedlight compatible with the Nikon Creative Lighting System; this includes the SB-800, SB-600, and SB-R200 Speedlights.

e2: Slowest Speed When Using Flash

Use this item to select the slowest flash synchronization speed in A and P exposure modes when using front-curtain sync, with or without red-eye reduction. You can select from shutter speeds between 1/60 and 30 seconds.

Hint: I recommend using a shutter speed at which you are confident you can hold the camera steady, otherwise there is a risk that any part of the picture illuminated by ambient light will not be sharp due to the effects of camera shake. For most practical flash photography purposes, this will be around 1/30 to 1/15. At longer shutter speeds, use a tripod or some other form of camera support.

e3: Built-in Flash Mode

Use this item to select the flash mode for the built-in Speed-light of the D200. Here are this setting's options:

- **TTL** – The camera uses its 1,005-pixel RGB sensor (the same sensor used for Matrix metering) to control flash output automatically; it performs multi sensor balanced fill-flash (monitor pre-flashes are used), and distance information is included with a D- or G-type lens. Standard TTL flash is used if the camera is set to spot metering.

- **Manual** – The flash can be set to deliver a specific amount of light between its maximum output and 1/128 of its maximum output. The guide number (in manual flash mode only) is 42 feet (13 m) at ISO 100.

- **Repeating Flash** – The flash can be set to emit a sequence of outputs during a single exposure to produce a strobe-light effect. This item has three internal options: *Output* (similar to manual flash where the output of the flash is set to a specific level between 1/4 and 1/128), *Times* (choose the number of times the flash fires, dependent on the shutter speed used and frequency for flash outputs), and *Interval* (used to set the frequency of flash outputs).

- **Commander Mode** – This item is for using the built-in Speedlight as a master flash to control one or more remote Speedlights in up to two separate groups. All Speedlights must be compatible with the Advanced Wireless Lighting system; these include the SB-800, SB-600, and SB-R200 Speedlights.

Hint: The options available within Custom Setting e3 provide a variety of ways for using the built-in Speedlight. Refer to pages 224-259 for more information about using flash with the D200.

Option	Description
Built-in	Choose flash mode for built in flash (commander flash).
TTL	i-TTL mode. Menu of flash compensation values will be displayed; choose value between +3.0 and 3.0EV in steps of 1/3EV. At settings other than ±0, 🔲 will be displayed in control panel and viewfinder.
M	Choose flash output level for built in flash from values between Full Power and 1/128 Power (1/128 Of full power). 🔲 flashes in control panel and viewfinder.
—	Built-in flash does not fire, but AF-assist illuminator lights. Built-in flash must be raised to allow monitor preflashes to fire. Icon is not displayed in control panel flash-sync mode display.
Group A	Choose flash mode for all flashes in group A.
TTL	i-TTL mode. Menu of flash compensation values will be displayed; choose value between +3.0 and 3.0EV in steps of 1/3 EV.
AA	Auto aperture (not available with SB-600 and SB-R200 Speedlights). Menu of flash compensation values will be displayed; choose value between +3.0 and -3.0EV in steps of 1/3EV.
M	Choose flash output level for flashes in Group A from values between Full Power and 1/128 Power (1/128 of full power).
—	Flashes in Group A do not fire.
Group B	Choose flash mode for all flashes in group B.
TTL	i-TTL mode. Menu of flash compensation values will be displayed; choose value between +3.0 and 3.0EV in steps of1/3 EV.
AA	Auto aperture (not available with optional SB-600 and SB-R200 Speedlights). Menu of flash compensation values will be displayed; choose value between +3.0 and 3.0EV in steps of 1/3EV.
M	Choose flash output level for flashes in Group B from values between Full Power and 1/128 Power (1/128 of full power).
—	Flashes in Group B do not fire.
Channel	Choose from channels 1-4. All Speedlights in both groups must be set to same channel.

e4: Preview Button Activates Modeling Flash

Pressing the Depth-of-Field Preview button will cause either the built-in flash or an external flash unit (including the SB-800, SB-600, and SB-R200 Speedlights) to emit a very rapid series of low intensity light pulses that act as a modeling light so you can assess the effect of the flash illumination. You can turn this feature *On* (default) or *Off*.

Hint: Due to low intensity and brevity of the light pulses emitted by this feature, it is only useful at short shooting distances. However, if you take an external Speedlight off-camera using a dedicated TTL flash cord such as the SC-28, it can be helpful in assessing the position and nature of shadows cast by the flash.

e5: Auto Bracketing Set

This item allows you to decide which settings are affected when the automatic bracketing feature is used. Here are your options:

- *AE & Flash* – The camera brackets the exposure for both ambient light and flash output. This is the default setting.

- *AE Only* – The camera only brackets the ambient light exposure.

- *Flash Only* – The camera only brackets the flash output level.

- *WB Bracketing* – The camera brackets the white balance value when recording pictures in the JPEG format.

Note: The *WB Bracketing* option is not available for NEF or NEF+JPEG files.

Hint: Choice of the options available within this item will be a matter of personal preference based on the prevailing shooting conditions.

e6: Auto Bracketing in M Exposure Mode

This setting adds refinement to the *AE&Flash* and *AE Only* options of Custom Setting e5 when using Manual exposure mode. Here are this setting's options:

- **Flash/Speed** – The camera will bracket shutter speed and flash output level if *AE&Flash* is selected at Custom Setting e5, or just the shutter speed if *AE Only* is selected at e5. This is the default setting.

- **Flash/Speed/Aperture** – The camera will bracket shutter speed, aperture, and flash output level if *AE&Flash* is selected at e5, or just the shutter speed if *AE Only* is selected at e5.

- **Flash/Aperture** – The camera will bracket aperture and flash output level if *AE&Flash* is selected at e5, or just the aperture if *AE Only* is selected at e5.

- **Flash Only** – The camera will bracket just the flash output level if *AE&Flash* is selected at e5.

Hint: The choice you make within this item will be a matter of personal preference based on the prevailing shooting conditions.

e7: Auto Bracketing Order

This option allows you to select the order in which the camera makes exposures in a bracketing sequence. Your options are:

- **MTR>Under>Over** – "Correct" exposure is followed by an underexposed, then an overexposed frame. This is the default setting.

- **Under>MTR>Over** – An underexposed frame is taken first, followed by the "correct" exposure, then an overexposed frame.

Hint: This is a matter of personal preference, but whichever you choose, I recommend you use one option consistently so when you assess exposure you always know which frame is which in the sequence.

e8: Auto Bracketing Selection Method
This item allows you to decide how selection of a bracketing sequence is performed. Your options are:

- **Manual** – Press the 🔘 button and rotate the main command dial to select the number of shots in the sequence; rotate the sub-command dial to select the increment in the sequence. This is the default setting.

- **Preset** – Press the 🔘 button and rotate the main command dial to turn bracketing on or off; press the 🔘 button and rotate the sub-command dial to select the number of exposures and the increment in the bracketing sequence.

Hint: The Manual option requires the number of exposures to be set to 0 to switch the bracketing feature off, which can trip some users up. To ensure that bracketing is cancelled, you may prefer to select the Preset option

f Controls

f1: Multi Selector Center Button
The center of the Multi Selector can be used to select a variety of camera operations in both the shooting mode and playback mode. If you select *Shooting Mode* from this setting, your options are:

- **Center AF Area** – Pressing the center of the Multi Selector chooses the center autofocus sensing area or center autofocus area group. If *Pattern 2* is selected from Custom Setting a3, the center of the Multi Selector can be used to switch between the two center focus groups. This is the default setting.

- **Illuminate AF Area** – Pressing the center of the Multi Selector illuminates the active autofocus sensing area or focus area group in the viewfinder.

- **Not Used** – Pressing the center of the Multi Selector has no effect when the camera is in shooting mode.

If you select *Playback Mode* from this setting, your options are:

- **Thumbnail On/Off** – Pressing the center of the Multi Selector will cause the display to switch between single image and multiple image playback. This is the default setting.

- **Histogram On/Off** – Press the center of the Multi Selector to turn the histogram display on or off.

- **Zoom On/Off** – Press the center of the Multi Selector to enlarge the image displayed on the monitor screen, and press it again to return to either single image or multiple image display. This option has a sub-menu that allows you to choose the degree of magnification.

Hint: Personally, I do not find the *Shooting Mode* options all that helpful, so I leave it set to *Not Used* to avoid any confusion when handling the camera. However, the ability to display the histogram quickly is very useful, so I do recommend selecting *Histogram On/Off* from the *Playback Mode* options.

f2: When Multi-Selector Is Pressed
The Multi Selector switch can be used to activate the exposure metering system or the autofocus system using the following options:

- **Do Nothing** – Pressing the Multi Selector has no affect on the exposure metering or autofocus systems. This is the default setting.

- **Reset Mtr-Off Delay** – Pressing the Multi Selector activates the exposure metering system.

- **Initiate Autofocus** – Pressing the Multi Selector activates the exposure metering system and focuses the lens when the camera is set to S (single-servo) or C (continuous-servo) autofocus modes.

Hint: Choice of the options available within this item will be a matter of personal preference based on the prevailing shooting conditions. I recommend the *Initiate Autofocus* option if you are shooting fast-paced action such as sports as it can speed up camera handling.

f3: Role of Multi-Selector in full-frame Playback

This item determines the way in which using the Multi Selector will display both images for playback and the image information pages. Here are your options:

- **Info▲▼/PB◀▶** – Press the Multi Selector up or down to change image information pages and left or right to scroll through stored images. This is the default setting.

- **Info ◀▶/PB▲▼** – Press the Multi Selector left or right to change image information pages and up or down to scroll through stored images.

Hint: This is a matter of personal preference, but I recommend you select one and use it consistently to avoid confusion when reviewing images.

f4: Assign FUNC. Button

The FUNC. button (located on the camera front below the Depth-of-Field Preview button) can be assigned to perform a variety of functions. Here are this setting's options:

Hint: When using flash, the *FV Lock* option is useful, and when shooting in ambient light, I find the ability to select spot metering at the touch of a button very useful, as I stay in Matrix metering for most other circumstances.

Option	Description
FV Lock (default)	If built in flash or optional CLS compatible Speedlight is used, flash value locks when FUNC. button is pressed. Press again to cancel FV lock.
FV Lock/Lens Data	As above, except that if built in flash is lowered or optional CLS compatible Speedlight is not attached, FUNC. button and command dials can be used to specify focal length and aperture of non CPU lenses.
1 Step Spd/Aperture	If FUNC. button is pressed when rotating command dials, changes to shutter speed (exposure modes S and M) and aperture (expo-sure modes A and M) are made in increments of 1 FV.
Same as AE L/AF L	FUNC. button performs same functions as AE-L/AF-L button.
Flash Off	Flash will not fire in photos taken while FUNC. button is pressed.
Bracketing Burst	While FUNC. button is pressed, all shots in exposure or flash bracketing program will be taken each time shutter release button is pressed. In continuous high speed and continuous low speed modes, camera will repeat bracketing burst while shutter release button is held down. If white balance bracketing is selected, camera will take photos at up to 5fps (single or contin-uous high speed mode) or 1 4fps (continuous low speed mode) and perform white balance bracketing on each frame.
Matrix Metering	Matrix metering activated while FUNC. button is pressed.
Center weighted	Center weighted metering activated while FUNC. button is pressed.
Spot metering	Spot metering activated while FUNC. button is pressed.
Focus Area Frame	Press FUNC. button and rotate command dials to cycle between normal and wide focus areas.

f5: Customize Command Dials

This item provides additional functionality to the main and sub-command dials. Here are your options:

- **Rotate Direction** – Select *Normal* (the default) to have the command dials operate normally, as described in this book. Select *Reverse* if you wish to reverse the rotation of the command dials.

- **Change Main/Sub** – Select *Off* (the default) to have the main command dial control the shutter speed and the sub-command dial controls the aperture. Select *On* to reverse there roles.

- **Aperture Setting** – Selecting *Sub-command Dial* (the default) means the aperture can only be adjusted using the sub-command dial (or the main command dial if *On* is selected from *Change Main/Sub*). Selecting *Aperture Ring* means that the aperture can only be adjusted using the lens aperture ring; this option is selected automatically when a non-CPU lens is used.

- **Menus and Playback** – Select *Off* (the default) to use the Multi Selector to choose images for display, highlight thumbnails, and navigate through menus. Select *On* to have the main command dial perform the same function as pressing the Multi Selector to the left or right and have the sub-command dial perform the same function as pressing the Multi Selector up or down. (This option has no effect on the function of the command dials during playback zoom.

Hint: Personally, I leave each option set to its default to avoid confusion when I use other Nikon camera models that do not offer the alternatives that can be set here. If you use other Nikon camera models, I recommend you do the same.

f6: Setting Method for Buttons and Dials

Normally to make a range of adjustments to the D200 requires a button to be pressed and held down while rotating a command dial. This item allows you to make the same adjustment by pressing and releasing the appropriate button and then rotating the appropriate command dial. Your options are as follows:

- **Default** – An adjustment is made by pressing and holding the appropriate button while rotating the appropriate command dial.

- **Hold** – An adjustment is made by pressing and releasing the appropriate button while rotating the appropriate command dial; to exit this feature press the button again, press the shutter release, or wait 20 seconds (unless *No Limit* is selected at Custom Setting c3).

Hint: What was the Nikon design team thinking of? I recommend you avoid this item and leave it set to *Default*. The title of the Hold option is totally misleading since you do not hold the button down, and it is highly likely that you will forget to exit the feature and then wonder why the camera cannot be operated after you have made an adjustment.

f7: Disable Shutter If No Memory Card

This item allows the shutter to operate without a memory card being installed in the camera. Here are your options:

- **Release Locked** – The shutter release is disabled if no memory card is installed in the camera. This is the default setting.

- **Enable Release** – The shutter release will operate even if no memory card is installed in the camera.

Hint: Disaster looms, potentially, with this item unless it is set to the default *Release Locked*. You do not want the camera to operate as though it is recording pictures when in fact there is no memory card installed!

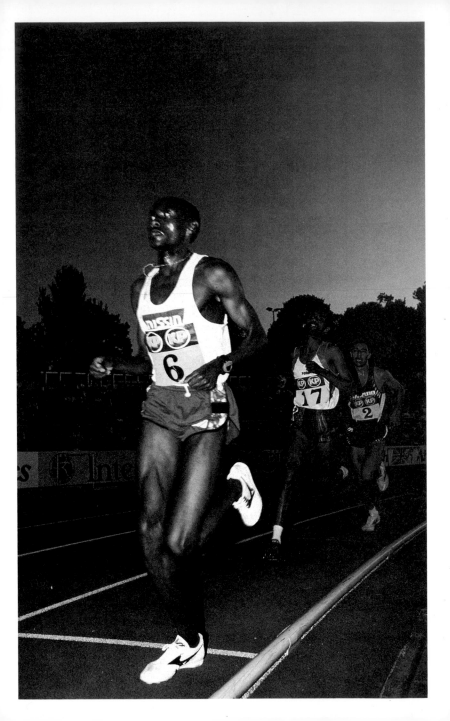

Nikon Flash Photography

Before we take a look at the flash capabilities for the D200, it is essential to understand the basic principles of flash photography.

The Inverse Square Law

This important principle states that when you double your distance from a light source, the intensity drops by a factor of four. This occurs because, as it travels away from its source, light spreads out and covers an area that is four times larger. Since a flash unit emits a precise level of light, it will only light the subject correctly at a specific distance, depending on the intensity of the light. Also, if the flash correctly exposes the subject, anything closer to the flash will be overexposed and anything further away will be underexposed.

Flash Synchronization Speed

The duration of the pulse of light from a Speedlight is extremely brief. Due to the design of the focal plane shutters used in Nikon cameras, each model has a specific shutter speed above which it is not possible to synchronize the flash. This is known as the maximum flash synchronization speed.

◁ *Nikon manufactures some of the world's most sophisticated flash equipment. This action shot was created with the D200 and external SB-800 Speedlight flash.*

If a Speedlight is fired at a shutter speed that is faster than the maximum flash sync speed, the shutter blades will obscure part of the film or digital sensor, preventing the flash's output from reaching this area. The D200, however, will automatically default to the maximum flash sync speed if a higher shutter speed is set inadvertently.

Note: In Auto FP High-Speed sync mode it is possible to use shutter speeds that exceed the normal maximum flash sync speed (see pages 250-251.)

Guide Numbers

The Guide Number (GN) is a useful and important specification to know about your Speedlight(s). It is the way the output of the flash is quantified and it tells us whether a specific flash can generate enough light for a proper exposure.

The higher the GN, the more light the flash produces. But you need to check closely how the GN is expressed, since the information will vary considerably depending on these factors: the sensitivity (ISO rating), the units of distance (feet or meters), the angle of coverage of the flash tube (usually given as an equivalent to a lens focal length), and use of attachments that modify the path of light from the flash tube.

Direct Flash

Direct flash represents the most straightforward and unsophisticated way of lighting a subject. It offers the maximum efficiency because the light travels the shortest possible route, is not diffused, and it maintains a constant color temperature (assuming you do not filter the flash head). However, the quality of the light is harsh, uncompromising, and flat, particularly if the Speedlight is mounted on the camera directly above the lens axis. Shadows cast by direct flash are deep and distinct with hard edges. That is not to say that direct flash does not have its uses—that is the delight of having control over your light source—you can use it as you see fit!

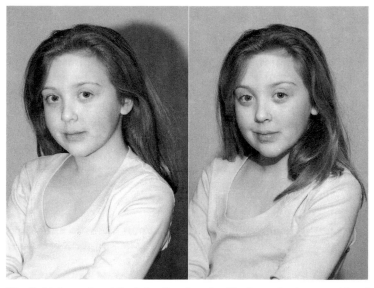

The light from direct flash is often harsh with deep shadows and hard edges. By bouncing the flash from an off-camera position, the light is softened and shadows drop down behing the subject where they are less noticeable.

Bounce Flash

This involves lighting the subject indirectly by "bouncing" the light from the flash off a nearby surface, such as a wall or ceiling. The SB-600 and SB-800 feature a flash head that can be tilted and/or swung to angle the direction of the light output. This affects both the quality and quantity of light that illuminates the scene. One of the most important decisions you will make when using bounce flash is the choice and location of the bounce surface. When choosing a bounce surface you should ensure that it is not colored. This is because the reflected light will include the surface color, causing a noticeable and generally unwanted color cast throughout picture.

To strike a balance between the proximity of the bounce surface and the amount of diffusion that you want it to create, generally, it is better to keep the bounce surface close to the flash to minimize the distance the light has to travel and thus maximize the amount of light available to illuminate the scene. It is often better to use a portable bounce surface with known reflective qualities. The SB-800 features a small "bounce card" that extends from the top of the flash head) for this purpose. It will reflect a small amount of subtle fill-light directly at the subject.

Balanced Fill-Flash

Usually, to produce a complementary exposure between a subject and its surroundings, you will want to balance the light from the flash with the ambient light. When the D200 is used with a D or G-type Nikkor lens and its built-in Speedlight, or an external SB-600 or SB-800 Speedlight, and is set to Matrix metering, it will use 3D Multi-sensor Balanced Fill-flash. In this mode, the camera attempts to balance the ambient light with the flash output. The system used in the D200 is Nikon's third generation of through-the-lens (TTL) flash exposure control. This is known as i-TTL (intelligent TTL), and it represents Nikon's most sophisticated flash exposure control system to date; it is part of a wider set of flash features and functions that Nikon calls the Creative Lighting System (CLS).

Note: Currently the internal Speedlights of the D70-series and D200, and the SB-800, SB-600, and SB-R200 external Speedlights are the only Nikon flash units that support CLS. If any other Nikon Speedlight is attached to the D200, TTL flash exposure control is not available.

The Creative Lighting System

During 2003 Nikon raised the bar a considerable distance for photography with portable, camera mounted, flash units by introducing the SB-800 Speedlight and D2H digital SLR camera—the first two components of the Creative Lighting System (CLS). The CLS encompasses a range of features and functions that are as much a part of the cameras that support it as the Speedlight units themselves. These features include: i-TTL, Advanced Wireless Lighting (wireless I-TTL control of multiple Speedlights), Flash Value (FV) Lock, Flash Color Information Communication, Auto FP High-Speed Sync, and Wide-Area AF-Assist Illuminator. The CLS has expanded to include the D2-series, D200, D80, D70-series, D50, and F6 cameras, with the SB-800, SB-600, SB-R200 Speedlights, and SU-800 Wireless Speedlight Commander (although the D70-series and D50 camera models do not support all the features of the CLS).

i-TTL (Intelligent TTL) Flash Exposure Control

Nikon's latest TTL flash exposure control technology, i-TTL, offers an enhanced and refined method of controlling flash exposure, using one or two pre-flash pulses. These have a shorter duration and higher intensity than those used for the TTL and D-TTL methods of previous Nikon cameras and Speedlights. Currently, the D200 supports i-TTL with compatible Speedlights (its built-in Speedlight, SB-800, SB-600, and SB-R200).

Note: Due to its design, the SB-R200 cannot be mounted on the accessory shoe of a camera; it can only be used as a remote flash wirelessly controlled by either the SU-800 Commander unit, an SB-800 Speedlight, or the built-in Speedlight of the D70-series and D200 cameras.

There are several key differences between the i-TTL system used with the D200 and the earlier TTL and D-TTL systems. These include:

- i-TTL uses fewer monitor pre-flashes, but they have a higher intensity. The greater intensity of the pre-flash pulses improves the efficiency of obtaining a measurement from the TTL flash sensor and by using fewer pulses, the amount of time taken to perform the assessment is reduced.

- The D200 uses its 1005-pixel RGB sensor, located in the viewfinder head, to assess the pre-flash output. Therefore, monitor pre-flashes are always emitted before the reflex mirror is raised, regardless of whether the camera is used with a single CLS compatible Speedlight or multiple CLS compatible Speedlights in the Advanced Wireless Lighting system.

The following is a summary of the sequence of events used to calculate flash exposure in the D200, when used with a single or multiple compatible Speedlights and a D or G-type Nikkor lens:

1. When the shutter release is pressed, the camera reads the focus distance from the D or G-type lens.

2. The camera sends a signal to the Speedlight to initiate the pre-flash system, which then emits one or two pulses of light.

3. The light from these pre flashes is bounced back from the scene, through the lens, where the camera's reflex mirror directs it to the i-TTL flash sensor in the camera's viewfinder head.

4. The i-TTL flash sensor information is then analyzed with information from the camera's TTL ambient exposure sensor and the focus information. The camera's microprocessors determine the amount of light required from the Speedlight(s). The duration of the flash discharge is set accordingly.

5. The reflex mirror lifts up out of the light path to the shutter and the shutter opens.

6. The camera sends a signal to the Speedlight(s) to initiate the main flash discharge, which is quenched the instant the amount of light pre-determined in Step 4 has been emitted.

7. The shutter closes at the end of the predetermined shutter speed duration and the reflex mirror is lowered to its normal position.

Note: The emission of the monitor pre-flashes occurs before the reflex mirror is raised. This can be a problem, if the pre-flashes cause the subject to blink just as the shutter opens.

Flash Output Assessment

The crucial phase in the sequence described above is step 4, when the required output from the flash is calculated. Nikon technicians and engineers claim that, in addition to the amount of light detected by the TTL flash sensor, three distinct elements are considered during this process when the camera is set to Matrix metering 〔•〕 :

• **Brightness**—The camera assesses the overall level of brightness using its 1005-pixel RGB sensor, located in the viewfinder head. This occurs regardless of whether the camera is used with single or multiple Speedlights.

• **Contrast**—The relative brightness of each metering segment in its Matrix metering system is compared by the camera, which is pre-programmed to recognize specific patterns of light and dark across the metering segment array. (For example, outer segments that record a high level of brightness and a central segment that detects a lower level of brightness would indicate a strongly backlit subject at the center of the frame.) The camera compares the detected pattern with patterns pre-stored in its database of example exposures. If the first comparison generates conflicting assessments, the segment pattern maybe re-configured and further analysis is performed. Finally, if any segment reports an abnormally high level of brightness in comparison to the others (e.g. a highly reflective surface in part of the scene causes a specular reflection, such as glass or a mirror), the camera will usually ignore this information in its flash exposure calculations.

- **Focus Information**—This is provided in two forms; camera-to-subject distance, and the level of focus (or defocus) at each focus sensor. Compatible cameras use both forms in tandem, not only to assess how far away the subject is likely to be but also its approximate location within the frame area.

Usually the focus distance information influences which segment(s) of the Matrix metering sensor and TTL flash sensor affect overall exposure calculations. For example, assuming the subject is positioned in the center of the frame and the lens is focused at a short range, the camera will place more emphasis on the outer metering segments and less on the central ones. An exception to this occurs if the camera detects a very high level of contrast between the central and outer sensors; it may—and often does—reverse the emphasis and weights the exposure according to the information received from central sensors. Conversely, if the subject is positioned in the center of the frame and the lens is focused at a mid to long range, the camera will place more emphasis on the central metering segments and less on the outer ones. Essentially what the camera is trying to do in both cases is prevent overexposure of the subject, which, it assumes is in the center or the frame.

Note: The focus distance information requires a D or G-type lens to be mounted on the camera.

Individual focus sensor information is integrated with focus distance information, as each AF sensor is checked for its degree of focus. This provides the camera with information about the probable location of the subject within the frame area. Using the examples given in the previous paragraph, the camera notes that the central AF sensor has acquired focus, although the outer AF sensors each report defocus. Therefore exposure is calculated on the assumption that the subject is in the center of the frame and the camera biases its computations according to the focus distance information it receives from the lens, as described.

However it is important to understand that other twists occur in this interaction between exposure calculation and focus information. For example, if you acquire and lock focus on a subject using the center AF sensor and then recompose the shot, so that the subject is located elsewhere in the frame, and the central AF sensor no longer detects focus, the camera will, generally, use the exposure value it calculated when it first acquired focus. However, if it detects that the level of brightness detected by the central metering segment has now changed significantly from the point when focus was acquired with the subject in the center of the frame the camera can—and often does—adjust its exposure calculations but not necessarily for the better!

Note: To help improve flash exposure accuracy in situations when the photographer wishes to recompose the picture, after acquiring focus, Nikon introduced the Flash Value (FV) lock feature on CLS compatible cameras (see below for a full description).

The Built-in Speedlight

The D200 has a built-in Speedlight (Nikon's proprietary name for a flash unit) that has a Guide Number of 42 (ft) 13 (m) at ISO 200. It can synchronize with the shutter at speeds up to 1/250 second. It has a minimum range of 2 ft (.6 m) below which the camera will not necessarily calculate a correct flash exposure. Operation of the built-in Speedlight must be activated manually by pressing the   button, which cause the flash head to lift.

The built-in Speedlight draws its power from the camera's main battery; so extended use of the flash will have a direct effect of battery life. As soon as the flash unit pops up, it begins to charge. The flash ready symbol appears in the

While the D200's built-in Speed-light has limited power, it comes in handy in low light situations with close subjects or for use as fill flash in harsh outdoor light.

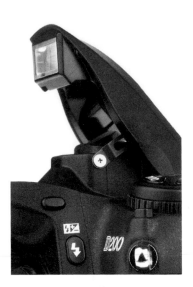

viewfinder to indicate charging is complete and the flash is ready to fire. If the flash fires at its maximum output, the flash ready symbol will flash for approximately three seconds after the exposure has been made, as a warning of potential underexposure.

Note: The flash ready symbol operates in the same way when an external Speedlight is attached and switched on.

Using the D200 with External Speedlights

In addition to the built-in Speedlight the D200 offers full i-TTL flash exposure control with two external Speedlights that are compatible with the CLS: the SB-600 with a GN of 98 (ft) 30 (m) at ISO100 and the flash head at 35mm, and the SB-800 GN 125 (ft) 38 (m) at ISO100 and the flash head at 35mm. Both models can be attached to the camera directly or with a dedicated TTL remote flash cord.

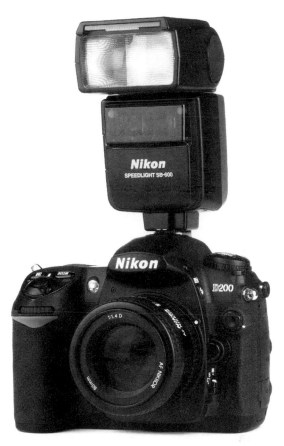

The D200 is fully compatible with CLS external flash units, such as this Speedlight SB-600.

Note: The D200 does not support TTL flash exposure control with any other Nikon Speedlight that is designed to be attached to a camera's accessory shoe (hot-shoe).

Note: The SB-R200 can only be controlled as part of a wireless flash system.

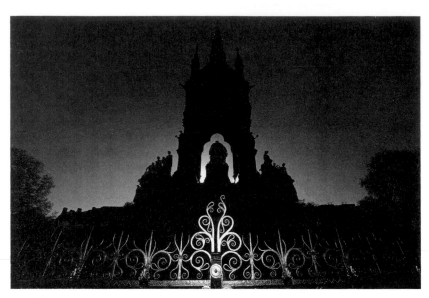

The flash unit's zoom head can also be used as a creative tool. Here it was set manually to the 105mm position and the flash was used as a spotlight to highlight the lower center of the photo.

Aside from being more powerful, the SB-600 and SB-800 Speedlights are considerably more versatile than the camera's built-in unit. Their flash heads can be tilted and swiveled for bounce flash. They also have an adjustable auto zoom-head, which controls the angle-of-coverage of the flash beam. The SB-800 adjusts to match focal lengths of 24-105mm and the SB-600's adjusts for focal lengths of 24-85mm. Both also feature a wide-angle diffuser for a focal length of 14mm.

Hint: Unlike earlier Nikon Speedlights, which cancelled monitor pre-flashes if the flash head was tilted or swiveled for bounce flash photography, the SB-800 and SB-600 emit pre-flashes regardless of the flash head orientation.

Focal Lengths and Zoom Heads

When the SB-800 and SB-600 adjust their zoom heads to match the lens focal lengths in use, it is assumed that the flash is being used with a film camera and not a digital SLR. The D200's DX-format sensor is smaller than the 35mm film frame and thus, has a reduced angle-of-view due to this smaller sensor size (for more information see pages 261-263). Therefore, at a given focal length setting, the flash will be illuminating a greater area than is necessary with the D200. This means you will be restricting your shooting range and squandering flash power. Use the following table to maximize the performance of an external Speedlight by manually adjusting the zoom head as indicated:

Focal length of lens (mm)	Zoom head position (mm)
14	20
18	24
20	28
24	35
28	50
35	50
50	70
70	85
85	105 [1]

[1] - *Available on SB-800 only.*

SB-800 Manual Zoom Head Adjustment
On the SB-800, to adjust the zoom head position manually, press either the ▦ , or ▦ button; a small M will appear above ZOOM in the Speedlight's LCD panel.

To cancel the manual zoom head feature press either the ▦ or ▦ button, until the focal length displayed matches the focal length set on the lens.

SB-600 Manual Zoom Head Adjustment

By pressing the zoom button, the zoom head position can be adjusted manually. To indicate that you are using the manual zoom feature, a small M appears above ZOOM in the LCD panel zo^MoM .

To cancel the manual zoom head feature, press the zoom button until the focal length that is displayed matches the focal length set on the lens.

Note: For more information, refer to the Speedlight instruction book or my book, Magic Lantern Guides: Nikon AF Speedlight Flash System, also published by Lark Books.

TTL Flash Modes

The D200 supports the following methods for TTL control flash exposure with either its built-in Speedlight or a compatible external Speedlight.

3D Multi-Sensor Balanced Fill-Flash

This is the most sophisticated version of Nikon's TTL flash exposure control system, but it is only available when a D or G-type lens is attached to the D200 camera body. The camera takes the following factors in to consideration when calculating the required flash output: focus distance information from the lens (hence the "3D" designation), information from the camera's TTL light metering system, and information based on the assessment of the monitor pre-flashes emitted immediately prior to the exposure. This system is particularly effective at detecting instances where the background is abnormally light (e.g. sky) or dark (e.g. dimly lit interior), or there are highly reflective surfaces in the scene (e.g. glass or a mirror), and generally does not consider them in flash exposure computations, as normally such factors would have an adverse affect on exposure accuracy.

Multi-Sensor Balanced Fill-Flash

This is essentially the same as 3D multi-sensor balanced fill-flash, except focus distance information is not taken into consideration during flash exposure calculations. The icons displayed on Nikon Speedlights to indicate you are in either 3D Multi-sensor Balanced Fill-flash or Multi-sensor Balanced Fill-Flash are identical! The only way to determine which mode the camera/flash is using to calculate flash exposure is to be aware of which mode is supported by the camera and with which lenses. For example, if you attach a non-D or non-G type autofocus lens to the D200, flash exposure control will default to Multi-sensor Balanced Fill-flash. The D200 can perform Multi-sensor Balanced Fill-flash with a non-CPU lens mounted on the camera, provided the relevant lens data is input via the Non-CPU Lens Data option in the shooting menu.

Standard i-TTL Flash

This differs from the automatic balanced flash control methods described above because the TTL flash sensor determines the output of the flash, exclusively. Any measurement of the ambient light performed by the camera's TTL metering system remains wholly independent; it is not integrated in any way with the flash exposure calculations.

Note: Standard i-TTL flash has very important implications when mixing ambient light with light from a Speedlight for the fill-flash technique, as any compensation factor selected for either the ambient exposure, the flash exposure, or both will be applied at the level pre-determined by the photographer.

Note: Selecting spot metering on the D200 will cause the flash exposure control to default to standard i-TTL Flash

Understanding Nikon's Terminology

Many photographers fail to understand how their choice of exposure mode can affect the appearance of a photograph made with a mix of ambient light and flash. All too often they assume that, since the camera is performing Automatic Balanced Fill-flash (3D Multi-sensor or multi-sensor), both the subject and background will be rendered properly. Their frustration deepens when they realize that any exposure compensation factor that they apply on the camera, Speedlight, or both, is often either overridden or ignored completely!

So what is going on? The first clue to this conundrum is quite obvious: read the title again—Automatic Balanced Fill-flash.

The photographer is not the one in control here: it is the camera that is responsible for all exposure decisions in the balanced fill-flash options, when the camera is set to any of the automatic exposure modes (P, A, and S), and all flash exposure decisions in the balanced fill-flash options when the camera is set to manual exposure mode.

Furthermore, if you select either Aperture-Priority (A), or Program (P) exposure modes, the available shutter speed range is restricted to between 1/250 and 1/60 second. If the level of ambient light requires a shutter speed outside of this range, as is usually the case when shooting in low-light conditions, like a dimly lit interior, the areas of the scene lit predominantly by ambient light will be underexposed.

Hint: If you habitually use Aperture-Priority (A) exposure mode with flash, consider setting Slow-sync flash mode (do not confuse this with Rear-sync mode), as it overrides this restriction on shutter speed range, and allows the full range of speeds available on the camera, between the maximum flash sync speed and the slowest shutter speed to be used; so areas lit by ambient light appear more balanced with those lit by flash.

Note: Alternatively, on the D200 it is possible to select the slowest shutter speed to be used with flash when the camera is set to either Aperture-Priority (A) or Programmed-automatic (P) exposure modes; this option is found in the custom settings menu e2 (Flash Shutter Speed).

The second clue is the word Balanced, which means that the camera uses both its TTL metering system to measure ambient light and its TTL flash sensor to measure flash output and combine these to create an approximately equal exposure from both light sources. For example, a background lit by ambient light and a subject in the foreground lit by the flash is each exposed at a similar level. The camera achieves this more often than not by compensating the exposure for either the ambient light, the flash, or both. As mentioned above, any exposure compensation factor applied by the photographer is frequently overridden, or even ignored, because with all the Automatic Balanced Fill-flash options, the camera and flash operate automatically; this makes consistent repeatable results difficult to accomplish.

The third part of this generic term Automatic Balanced Fill-flash just serves to confuse users even further! Fill-flash is a recognized lighting technique, where the flash is used to provide a supplementary light to the main ambient light source and, as such, its output is always set at a level below that of the ambient light. Generally, the purpose of this fill light from the flash is to provide additional illumination in the shadows and other less well-lit areas of a scene to help reduce the overall contrast range; many photographers also use the technique to put a small catch light in their subject's eyes.

Nikon's use of the term fill-flash is misleading on two counts in the context of the title Automatic Balanced Fill-flash: first, depending on the prevailing light conditions, generally when the level of ambient light is very low, using one of the Automatic Balanced Fill-flash options will often cause the Speedlight to become the principal light source for illuminating the scene and second, as discussed above, balanced implies that the exposure for the ambient light and flash comprise equal proportions.

Note: Whenever you see the term Automatic Balanced Fill-flash, remember that existing ambient light and flash will be mixed to produce the final exposure; how the two light sources are mixed and in what proportion will depend on the combination of camera, lens, exposure mode, and selected flash exposure control option. In my opinion a more accurate term for this system would be Automatic Balanced Flash.

Non-TTL Flash Modes (SB-800 Speedlight)

When using the SB-800 external Speedlight with the D200 there are two additional non-TTL flash modes available.

(AA) Auto Aperture

In this mode the SB-800 reads the sensitivity (ISO) setting and lens aperture from the D200 automatically, and receives the "fire flash" signal from the camera as well. It can be used in A and M exposure modes. Thereafter the system uses a sensor on the front panel of the Speedlight to monitor the flash exposure and as soon as this sensor detects that the flash output has been sufficient, the flash pulse is quenched. If, between exposures, you decide to alter the focal length or change the lens aperture the Speedlight will adjust its output accordingly to maintain a correct flash exposure. The problem with this option is that the sensor does not necessarily "see" the same scene as the lens, which can lead to an inaccurate flash exposure.

(A) Automatic (non-TTL)

This is the only automatic (non-TTL) flash mode available with other DX-type Speedlights, or with the SB-800. It can be used in A and M exposure modes. Similar to the AA mode, a sensor on the front of the SB-800 monitors flash levels and shuts off the flash when the Speedlight calculates that sufficient light has been emitted. However, the lens aperture and sensitivity (ISO) values must be set manually on the Speedlight to ensure the subject is within the flash shooting range. As with the AA mode, the sensor does not necessarily "see" the same scene as the lens, which can lead to an inaccurate flash exposure.

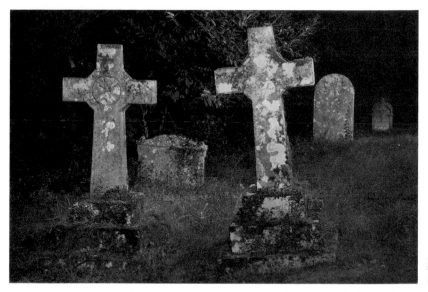

Here, non-TTL automatic A mode was used for the technique of "painting" with light from the flash.

Manual Flash Mode (Built-in Speedlight)

In Manual flash mode the user sets the output of the Speedlight (built-in or external) to a fixed level. It is necessary to calculate the correct lens aperture as determined by the flash to subject distance and the Guide Number (GN), of the Speedlight.

At its base sensitivity in Manual operation, of ISO 100 (equivalent) the built-in Speedlight of the D200 has a Guide Number (GN) of 42/13 (ft/m). The output level of the built-in Speedlight is determined by custom setting e3, where a value between 1/1 and 1/128 can be selected.

Since there is only one specific exposure value for any given level of sensitivity at a particular flash-to-subject distance, it is necessary to calculate the lens aperture required to record a proper exposure. Use the following equation:

Aperture = GN / Distance

So, for example, using the built-in Speedlight of the D200 set to its full output (1/1) and a shooting distance of exactly 7.5 ft (2.286 m), the lens aperture for a correct exposure of the subject will be f/5.6. (5.6 = 42/7.5 or 5.6 = 13/2.286).

Note: Similar calculations will have to be performed when using an external Speedlight in Manual flash mode. Check the Guide Number for the Speedlight model and ensure that you conduct the calculations using the same unit of distance throughout.

Repeating Flash (Built-In Speedlight)

This mode is accessed via custom setting e3 (Built-in Flash Mode). The flash will fire repeatedly, while the shutter is open to produce a strobe-lighting effect.

Press ☉ left or right to select one of the three values that must be set and use ☉ to select its value. Press ⬤ to return to the custom setting menu once all the required settings have been made.

Option	Description
Output	Select the required flash output (it is expressed as a fraction of the maximum output)
Times	Select the number of times the flash will fire at the selected output level. Depending on the shutter speed used, and the frequency selected at the Interval option, the number of frames may be less than selected.
Interval	Select the frequency at which the flash fires (per second – Hz)

Output	Times (Number of times the flash will fire)
1/4	2
1/8	2-5
1/16	2-10
1/32	2-10, 15
1/64	2-10, 15, 20, 25
1/128	2-10. 15. 20. 25, 30, 35

Flash Sync Modes

Not to be confused with Flash Modes available with the D200, as described above, the Flash Sync (synchronization) modes determine when the flash is fired and how it combines with the shutter speed. These apply to the built-in Speedlight, and the external SB-800 and SB-600 Speedlights.

To set a flash sync mode on the D200, press and hold the ⚡ button and rotate the main command dial to scroll through the various options, until the icon for the required mode appears in the control panel.

⌐⁵ Front-Curtain Sync
In this mode, the flash fires as soon as the shutter has fully opened. In P and A exposure modes, this will be combined with a shutter speed between 1/60th and 1/250th second, unless a lower speed has been selected via custom setting e2 (Slowest Speed When Using Flash). In S and M exposure modes the Speedlight synchronizes at shutter speed between 30 seconds and 1/250 second.

⊛⁵ Red-eye Reduction
In this mode, the D200 activates the AF-assist lamp on the front right side of the camera body to light for approximately

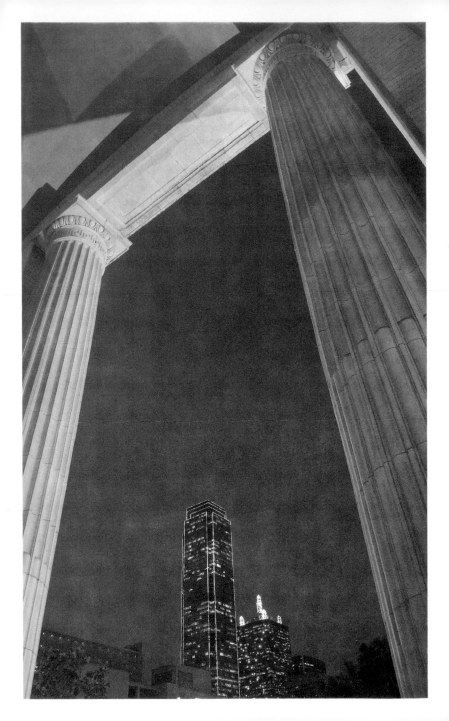

one second, before the main exposure, in an effort to reduce the size of a subject's pupils. Shutter speed synchronization is the same as for Front–curtain sync.

Hint: This mode causes an inordinate delay in the shutter's operation by which time the critical moment has generally passed and you have missed the shot! Personally, I never use this feature.

[slow] Slow Sync
This mode is only available with P and A exposure modes. The flash fires as soon as the shutter has fully opened, at all shutter speeds between 30 seconds and 1/250 second. It is useful for recording low-level ambient light, as well as those areas of the scene or subject illuminated by flash.

[slow] Slow Sync with Red-eye Reduction
This is the same as Slow-sync mode, except the Red-eye reduction lamp is switched on for approximately one second, before the shutter opens for the reason stated above under Red-eye reduction.

Hint: The same advice applies—avoid this mode!

[rear] Rear-Curtain Sync
In S and M exposure modes, the flash fires just before the shutter closes at all shutter speeds between 30 seconds and 1/250th second. Any image of a moving subject recorded by the ambient light exposure will appear to be behind the parts of the subject illuminated by the flash output.

[slow rear] Slow Rear-Curtain Sync
In P and A exposure modes, the flash fires just before the shutter closes at all shutter speeds between 30 seconds and 1/250th second. Any image of a moving subject recorded by ambient the ambient light exposure will appear to be behind the parts of the subject illuminated by the flash output.

◁ *The pillars in the foreground were lit by Slow sync flash, while the buildings in the background were recorded by the long ambient light exposure.*

Why Use Slow Synchronization Flash?

Attaching a Speedlight to the camera's accessory shoe, or with a dedicated TTL cord (SC-17 or SC-28), when the camera is in either Program (P) or Aperture-Priority (A) exposure mode and turning on the flash, will cause the camera to set a shutter speed in the range of 1/60 to 1/250 second. The speed that is selected depends on the level of ambient light—the brighter the conditions, the shorter the shutter speed that is chosen within this range.

The restriction imposed on the range of available of shutter speeds when using flash in P and A modes, can have a significant affect on the overall exposure. For example, in situations when you photograph a subject outside at night, or in a dark interior, any area of the scene that will be illuminated by ambient light alone is lit dimly, compared with those areas that will be illuminated by the flash. It is more than likely that the level of ambient light will not be sufficient for a proper exposure within this restricted range of shutter speeds and consequently, these areas of the scene will be underexposed. A typical photograph taken under these conditions has a well-exposed subject set against a very dark, featureless background.

To prevent this, select Slow synchronization flash mode (abbreviated to Slow sync), which enables the camera to use all shutter speeds from 1/60 second to the longest shutter speed available on the camera, 30 seconds. The camera will select an appropriate shutter speed for the low level ambient light, so the correct exposure can be achieved for the background. Remember, the flash output will have little, if any, effect in this region, because the intensity of light from the flash will diminish according to the Inverse Square Law. The flash output will be controlled for a proper exposure of the subject and foreground.

Other Flash Features and Functions

Flash Exposure Compensation

Flash exposure compensation can be set on the D200 by pressing and holding the **⚡±** button, while turning the sub-command dial. Compensation can be set in increments of 1/3, 1/2 or 1EV, subject to settings in custom setting b3 (EV Step) over a range of +1 to −3EV (stops).

Tip: If you use the default i-TTL Automatic Balanced Fill-flash mode, it will automatically set a flash compensation, based on scene brightness, contrast, focus distance, and a variety of other factors. The level of automatic adjustment applied by the D200 will often cancel out any compensation factor entered manually by the user. Since there is no way to know what the camera is doing, you will never have control of the flash exposure. To regain control set the flash mode to Standard i-TTL by selecting spot metering.

Flash Value (FV) Lock

Flash Value (FV) Lock allows you to use the camera and Speedlight to estimate the required flash output for a subject and retain this value temporarily, before making the main exposure. This is a very useful feature when you want the main subject located toward the edge of the frame area, particularly if the background is very bright or dark. Under these circumstances, using the normal i-TTL flash modes, there is a risk that the camera may calculate an incorrect level of flash output, and cause the main subject to be either under, or over exposed.

On the D200 the FV lock feature must first be activated via the custom setting f4: select FV Lock, or FV Lock/Lens Data. Raise the built-in flash by pressing the **⚡** button. Now, compose the picture, initially with the main subject in the center of the viewfinder area, then acquire focus by half-depressing the shutter release, before pressing the FUNC button on the camera. This causes the pre-flash pulses to be emitted by the Speedlight, which are used to assess the required amount of flash output. The output value of the

flash is remembered by the camera and the FV Lock icons
⚡LOCK and **⚡L** appear in the control panel and
viewfinder, as a reminder that the function is active.

Now you can recompose the picture and make the exposure by fully depressing the shutter release button. The flash
will fire at the predetermined level. If you alter the focal
length of a zoom lens, or adjust the lens aperture, the FV
function will compensate the flash output automatically.

Note: FV Lock is available on the D200 in the following flash
modes: i-TTL or Commander Mode, set via custom setting e3.
When using the SB-800, FV Lock can also function in Auto
Aperture (AA) and non-TTL (A) automatic flash modes.

Note: The camera-to-subject distance must remain unaltered
during the use of the FV lock function; otherwise, the flash
exposure may be inaccurate.

Flash Color Information Communication
Used with D200, the built-in Speedlight and external SB-800
and SB-600 Speedlights automatically transmit information
about the color temperature of the light they emit to the
camera. If the camera is set to Automatic white balance control it will then use this information to adjust its final white
balance setting in an attempt to match the color temperature
of the flash output.

Note: This function only operates when Auto white balance
has been selected and set on the camera.

Auto FP High-Speed Sync
Available with the SB-800, SB-600, and the built-in Speedlight, this feature is set on the D200 using custom setting
e1 - 1/250s (Auto FP).

One of the limitations of using daylight fill-flash is the
maximum flash sync speed of the camera, which is limited
to 1/250 second; working in bright lighting conditions, it is
often not possible to open the lens aperture very far, due to

the restriction of the maximum shutter speed imposed by the use of flash. The Auto FP High-Speed sync function allows you to use the full range of high shutter speeds available on camera while adjusting the flash output automatically, which makes using fill-flash far more flexible. To achieve this, the flash emits a very rapid series of pulses, instead of a single continuous pulse. The downside is that, at shutter speeds above the normal maximum sync speed, flash output is reduced significantly, which reduces the operational range of the Speedlight.

Wide-Area AF-Assist Illuminator

The purpose of the AF-assist lamp built-in to the SB-600 and SB-800 is to facilitate auto-focus in low light situations. The benefit delivered by these two units is the much wider area that the illumination from the lamp covers, compared with previous Speedlights. This is particularly useful with cameras, such as the D200, with is array of eleven AF-sensor areas, which covers a significant proportion of the frame area.

The effective range of the wide-area AF-assist lamp varies according to the focal length of the lens in use, and the location within the viewfinder area of the selected AF sensor. For example, using a 50mm lens and AF sensor areas in the central portion of the viewfinder area, the effective range of the lamp is between 3.3 ft (1 m) and 33 ft (10 m), but this is reduced at shorter focal lengths. When shooting with a 50mm lens and AF sensor areas at the periphery of the viewfinder area the effective range is reduced to between 3.3 ft (1 m) and 23 ft (7 m), but, again, this is reduced at shorter focal lengths.

Note: Wide-Area AF-Assist Illuminator feature requires an AF lens to be mounted and the camera to be set to Single-servo AF with focus priority selected.

Note: The AF-assist function can be used in isolation on the SB-800 by selecting "Cancel" for the flash "FIRE" option in the custom setting on the Speedlight.

Flash Range, Aperture, and Sensitivity (ISO)

The flash shooting range will vary depending on the values set for the lens aperture and sensitivity (ISO).

Aperture at ISO equivalent of													Range	
100	125	160	200	250	320	400	500	640	800	1000	1250	1600	m	ft.
1.4	1.6	1.8	2	2.2	2.5	2.8	3.2	3.5	4	4.5	5	5.6	1.0–7.5	3.3–24.6
2	2.2	2.5	2.8	3.2	3.5	4	4.5	5	5.6	6.3	7.1	8	0.7–5.4	2.3–17.7
2.8	3.2	3.5	4	4.5	5	5.6	6.3	7.1	8	9	10	11	0.6–3.8	2.0–12.5
4	4.5	5	5.6	6.3	7.1	8	9	10	11	13	14	16	0.6–2.7	2.0–8.9
5.6	6.3	7.1	8	9	10	11	13	14	16	18	20	22	0.6–1.9	2.0–6.2
8	9	10	11	13	14	16	18	20	22	25	29	32	0.6–1.4	2.0–4.6
11	13	14	16	18	20	22	25	29	32	—	—	—	0.6–0.9	2.0–2.9
16	18	20	22	25	29	32	—	—	—	—	—	—	0.6–0.7	2.0–2.3

Maximum Aperture Limitation

In Programmed auto (P) exposure mode, the maximum aperture (smallest f/number) is limited according to the sensitivity (ISO).

Maximum aperture at ISO equivalent of:												
100	125	160	200	250	320	400	500	640	800	1000	1250	1600
2.8	3	3.2	3.3	3.5	3.8	4	4.2	4.5	4.8	5	5.3	5.6

Limitations of the Built-In Speedlight

While the built-in Speedlight of the D200 is not as powerful as an external Speedlight, it can still provide a useful level of illumination at short ranges, especially for the purpose of fill-flash, since it supports flash output level compensation. However, if you want to use the built-in Speedlight as the main light source, you should be aware of the following:

• The proximity of the flash head of the built-in Speedlight is much closer to the central lens axis than with an external flash; so, the likelihood of red-eye occurring is increased significantly.

• The proximity of the built-in Speedlight to the central lens axis often means that the lens obscures the output of the flash, especially if you are using a lens hood. When the camera is held in a horizontal position, the obstruction of the light from the flash will cause a shadow to appear on the bottom edge of the picture.

• The angle of coverage achieved by the built-in Speedlight is limited and only covers the field of view of a 18mm lens. If you are using of a shorter focal length, the flash will not be able to illuminate the corners of the frame and these areas will appear underexposed. Even at the widest limit of coverage it is not uncommon to see a slight fall off of illumination in the extreme corners of the full frame.

Note: Any flash unit places a high demand on batteries; the built-in Speedlights draw their power from the camera's battery, so extended use will exhaust these batteries quite quickly.

Lens Compatibility

Due to the proximity of the built-in Speedlight to the central lens axis, when lenses (mentioned in the table below) are used at the given focal lengths and shooting ranges, there is a possibility that they will obscure some of the light from the flash and cause uneven exposure.

Lens	Zoom position	Minimum Range
AF SDXED12 24mmf/4G	18mm 20mm	1.5m/4ft. 11in. 1.0m/3ft. 3in.
AF S ED 17 35 mm f/2.8D	24mm	1.0m/3ft. 3in.
AF S DX IF ED 17 55 mm f/2.8G	24mm	1.0m/3ft. 3in.
AF ED 18 35 mmf/3.5 4.5D	18mm	1.5m/4ft. 11in.
AF S DXVR ED 18 200 mm f/3.5 5.6G	18mm	1.0m/3ft. 3in.
AF 20 35 mm f/2.8D	20mm 28mm	1.0m/3ft 3in. 1.5m/4ft. 11in.
AF S ED 28 70 mm f/2.8D	35mm	1.0m/3ft3in.

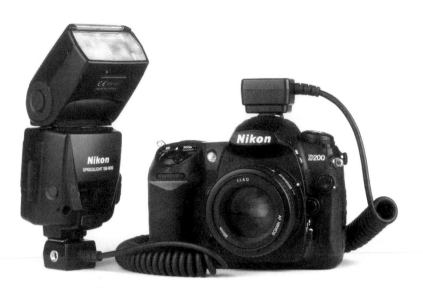

Taking the flash off camera can dramatically improve the quality of your flash photography. Here, an SC-28 dedicated cord is used to connect an off-camera SB-800 with the D200.

Using a Speedlight Off-Camera with a TTL Cord

When you work with a single external Speedlight, it is often desirable to take the flash off the camera. Nikon produce a number of dedicated cords for this purpose: the SC-17, SC-28, and SC-29. All three cords are 4.9 feet (1.5m) long; up to three, SC-17, or SC-28 cords can be connected together to extend the operating range away from the camera.

The benefits of taking a Speedlight off camera include:

- Increasing the angle between the central axis of the lens and the line between the flash head and a subject's eyes will reduce, significantly, the risk of the red-eye effect with humans, or eye-shine with other animals.

254

- In situations when it is not practicable to use bounce flash, moving the flash off camera will usually improve the quality of the lighting, especially the degree of modeling it provides. (Modeling is the representation of depth or form in photography.)

- By taking the flash off camera and directing the light from the Speedlight, it is often possible to control the position of shadows, so that they become less obvious or distracting.

- When using fill-flash, it is often desirable to direct light to a specific part of the scene to help reduce the level of contrast locally.

Hint: Whenever you take a Speedlight off camera and use any flash mode that incorporates focus distance information in the flash output computations, take care as to where you position the flash. If the Speedlight is moved closer to the subject, or farther away than the camera is, the accuracy of the flash output may be compromised, because the TTL flash control system works on the assumption that the flash is located at the same distance from the subject as the camera.

Note: Compatible with either the SB-800, or SB-600 Speedlights, the SC-29 has an AF-assist lamp built into its terminal block that attaches to the camera accessory shoe; positioning an AF-assist lamp immediately above the central axis of the lens. This can help improve the accuracy of autofocus, compared with using the AF-assist lamp built in to these Speedlights, when they are used off the camera. This is because the light emitted by the lamp on the flash unit may not be reflected with sufficient strength, if it strikes the subject at an oblique angle.

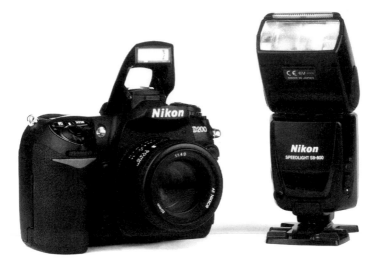

The D200's built-in Speedlight is a fully functioning member of the Creative Lighting System. It can be used in Commander mode to control an off camera SB-600 or SB-800.

Note: A Speedlight connected to the camera via one of Nikon's dedicated TTL cords can be used as the master flash to control multiple Speedlights off camera, using the Advanced Wireless Lighting system (see below).

Using the Built-In Speedlight in Commander Mode

In addition to its own output for flash photography the built-in Speedlight of the D200 camera can be set to control one or more remote Speedlights, wirelessly, in P, A, S, and M exposure modes; this feature is compatible with the SB-800, SB-600, and SB-R200. The remote Speedlights can be controlled a variety of flash modes: TTL, Auto Aperture (for use with remote SB-800 Speedlights only), or Manual. Control is limited to two groups: group A and B, using any one of four channels (1 to 4).

To use the Commander mode, which sets the built-in Speed-light of the Nikon D200 camera to act as a master flash:

1. Open the Custom Setting menu and navigate to Custom Setting-e3 (*Built-in flash mode*).

2. Highlight the *Commander Mode* option and Multi Select right to open a sub-menu of flash mode, flash output level, and control channel options.

3. Highlight *Built-in / Mode* to set the required flash mode and use the Multi Selector to select *TTl*, *M*, or - - *(Flash cancelled)*. If *TTL* or *M* is selected, Multi Select right to highlight *Comp* (flash output level compensation) and use the Multi Selector to select the required value. Multi Select right to set and confirm the value, and highlight *Group A / Mode*.

Hint: Use the -- *(Flash cancelled)* option to set the built-in Speedlight to control remote flash units only, so that it does not contribute light to the flash exposure.

4. Set the required flash mode for group A by using the Multi Selector to select *TTL*, *AA (SB-800 only)*, *M*, or - - *(Flash cancelled)*. If *TTL*, *AA*, or *M* is selected, and you want to set a flash output compensation level, repeat the procedure from Step 3; otherwise, press the multi-selector switch to the right to highlight *Group B / Mode*. Repeat Steps 3 and 4 to set flash mode and flash expo-sure compensation.

5. Highlight *Channel* and use the up and down buttons on the multi selector switch to select the required channel number.

6. Then, press the ENTER button on the back of the camera to confirm and lock the settings made in Steps 3 – 5 above.

7. Once the remote Speedlight(s) are set to operate in the remote flash mode, and the ready light is lit, the system is ready to be used.

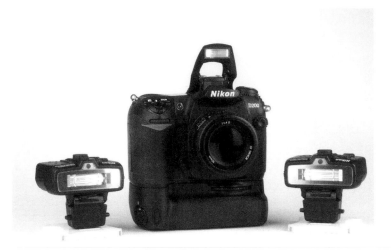

Here the D200's built in Speedlight is controlling two SB-R200 flash units for close-up photography.

Effective Range of
the Advanced Wireless Lighting System

When the following units are used as the master flash or commander unit for wireless control of compatible remote Speedlights (SB-800, SB-600, and SB-R200), the effective range of operation is as follows:

- **SB-800** – When the SB-800 is used as a master flash, Nikon states that the maximum effective operating range between it and the remote Speedlights is 33 ft (10 m), along the central axis of the lens, and 16 ft (5 m) to 23 ft (7 m) within 30° of the central axis of the lens.

- **SU-800** – The SU-800 is a dedicated IR transmitter. Unlike the SB-800 and built-in Speedlights that emit the control signals as part of a full spectrum emission, when used as a master flash, the SU-800 only emits IR light. Thus, it is a more powerful master flash unit than other Speedlights used in this role. Nikon states that it is capable of controlling remote SB-800 and SB-600 Speedlights up to a maximum range of 66 ft (20 m).

- **SU-800/SB-R200** – When the SU-800 is used as the commander unit, Nikon states that the maximum effective operating range between it and remote SB-R200 Speedlights is 13 ft (4 m) along the central axis of the lens, and 9.8 ft (3 m) within 30° of the central axis of the lens.

- **D200 Built-in Speedlight** – The built-in Speedlight of the D200 camera used as the master flash, can control remote Speedlights placed within 30° of the central axis of the lens up to a maximum range of 33 ft (10 m), between 30° and 60° from the central axis of the lens the maximum range is 16 ft (5 m).

Note: I have found Nikon's quoted maximum operating ranges for the components of the Advanced Wireless Lighting system to be very conservative. For example, I have used SB-800 Speedlights as master and remote units at ranges outdoors of 100 ft (30 m) or more. This is especially applicable in situations where there have been reflective surfaces such as walls and foliage close by; this is three times greater than Nikon's suggested maximum range. However, in bright sunlight, which contains a high level of naturally occurring IR light, you may find the practical limit of the operating range is reduced.

Note: Nikon states that communication between the master and remote flash units cannot be performed properly if there is an obstruction between them. In practice I have used remote flash units very successfully without line-of-sight between the master flash and the sensor on the remote Speedlight(s). However, every shooting situation is different, so my advice is to set up the lighting system to your requirements and always take test shots to ensure it works as you intended. If not, adjust the location of the remote Speedlights.

Note: For full details of Nikon's flash system, see my book, Magic Lantern Guides: Nikon AF Speedlight System, published by Lark Books.

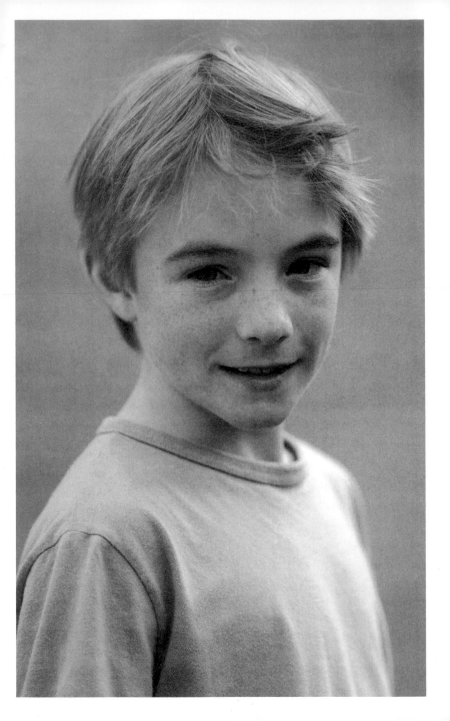

Nikon Lenses and Accessories

Nikon's legendary "F" mount on its Nikkor lenses has been virtually unchanged since the introduction of the original Nikon F camera in 1959. As a result, the majority of the lenses produced by Nikon throughout more than four decades can be mounted on the D200 and used with many of the camera's flash and ambient light exposure control functions.

The DX-Format Sensor

All Nikon digital SLR cameras to date have the same size sensor, which Nikon calls the DX-format (also referred to as APS-C). At 15.6 x 23.7 mm it is smaller than a 35mm film frame. This reduces the field-of-view seen by the D200 by about 1.5x compared with 35mm film cameras.

The circle represents the total area covered by the image circle projected from a 35mm format lens. The pale grey rectangle is the image area for a 35mm film frame (24 x 36 mm), and the dark grey rectangle represents the area covered by the DX-format (15.6 x 23.7 mm) sensor used in the D200. (Diagram not shown to scale)

Short telephotos make great portrait lenses. On a 35mm camera, the 85mm to 105mm focal-length range is a top choice of professionals. Due to the smaller size of the D200's sensor, focal lengths of 55mm to 75mm are ideal for portraits such as this.

However, marketing people do not like to talk in terms of negative aspects; they much prefer positives! Hence, advertisement copyrighters' hype such as "it's like getting a free 1.4x teleconverter" or "the 1.5x magnification of focal length," has instilled an impression that the focal length of a 35mm format lens increases by 1.5x in some way, as if by magic, when attached to a DX-format camera like the D200. This is not correct—a 300mm lens on a Nikon 35mm film camera is still a 300mm lens on the D200—no ifs, no buts! Furthermore, a teleconverter generally reduces image sharpness and contrast. However, since no extra glass is required to achieve the magnified image recorded by the D200, these issues are irrelevant.

What actually changes is the field-of-view, which is decreased; that's that negative aspect! In other words, the view seen through the camera with a DX-format sized sensor becomes narrower. Consequently, a 35mm lens on the D200 "sees" a field-of-view equivalent to a focal length about 1.5x greater (the actual factor is closer to 1.52x). If you were to shoot two pictures—one with a D200 and the other with a Nikon 35mm film camera, mounted side-by-side pointing at exactly the same scene with the same focal length lens, and then cropped the film image to the same area as the sensor in the D200—you would end up with identical pictures.

The following table gives the approximate effective focal length equivalent for a lens used with a 35mm format camera when the same focal length is used with the D200:

Focal length with 35mm format	12	14	17	18	20	24	28	35	50	60
Effective focal length – DX-format	18	21	25.5	27	30	36	42	52.5	75	90

Focal length with 35mm format	70	85	105	135	180	200	300	400	500	600
Effective focal length – DX-format	105	127.5	157.5	202.5	270	300	450	600	750	900

Choosing a Lens

There is a beneficial side effect of this reduced angle-of-view. Since the sensor of the D200 is only using the central portion of the total image projected by those lenses designed for 35mm format film cameras, the effects of optical aberrations and defects are kept to a minimum, as these are generally more prevalent toward the edge of the image circle. When using many of the Nikkor lenses designed for 35mm film cameras, you will find that some, or all, of the following will be reduced significantly, if not eliminated altogether:

- Reduced light fall-off toward the edge and corners of the image area
- Reduced chromatic aberration
- Linear distortion – both barrel and pin-cushion
- Flat field focus
- Vignetting with filters or lens hoods

Wide-angle lenses offer a large field-of-view. Typically they are associated with the sweeping vistas of landscape photography, but wide-angles are great for many subjects. Their close focusing ability, extended depth-of-field, and angle-of-view can be combined to create dynamic compositions when the subject is placed close to the lens, so that it dominates the foreground and is set against an expansive backdrop.

Telephoto lenses provide a narrower angle-of-view that magnifies a subject, making these lenses a good choice for sports, action, and wildlife photography. The optical effects of a telephoto can be used in many other areas of photography, such a portrait and landscape, because they can help

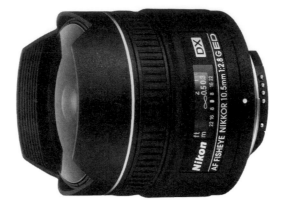

If you want to go wide, Nikon's AF DX Fisheye 10.5mm f/2.8 G ED provides a field of view on the D200 that is similar to a 16mm wide-angle lens on a 35mm SLR.

isolate a subject from its background due to their limited depth-of-field, particularly at large apertures.

Zoom lenses allow you to adjust the focal length, the range of which can be exclusively wide-angle, telephoto, or span both. Technically, most modern lenses described as zooms are actually vari-focal lenses; a true zoom lens maintains focus as the focal length is altered, which cannot be said of many lenses produced currently. Zoom lenses are extremely versatile, as you have several focal lengths available in one lens, which reduces the amount of lenses you need and the time spent changing lenses. However, convenience comes at a price; many zoom lenses have smaller maximum apertures (large f/ number), often two-stops less than fixed focal length types, which can be an issue when shooting in low light. Zoom lenses with large maximum apertures (small f/ numbers) tend to be expensive due to the complexity of their optical engineering. For general photography with the D200, one or several lenses that offer focal lengths between say 18mm and 200mm will cover most shooting situations. For the highest level of compatibility and functionality you should use either D- or G-type Nikkor lenses.

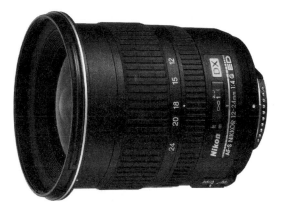

The AF-S DX 12-24mm f/4G IF-ED was the first lens in Nikon's DX lens line-up, which is designed specifically for use on its digital SLR cameras.

Features of Nikon Lenses

The descriptions of Nikkor lenses are peppered with initials. Here is an explanation of what these designate:

- **D-type** – these lenses have a conventional aperture ring and an electronic chip (CPU) that communicates information about lens aperture and focus distance between the lens and the camera body. A "D" appears on the lens barrel.

- **G-type** – these lenses have no aperture ring and are only compatible with Nikon cameras that allow the aperture value to be set from the camera. They have an electronic chip (CPU) that communicates information about lens aperture and focus distance between the lens and the camera body, similar to the D-type lenses. A "G" appears on the lens barrel.

- **AF-type** – these lenses are the predecessors to D and G-type lenses. The have a conventional aperture ring and do not communicate focus distance information to the camera.

- **DX** – these lenses have been especially designed for use on Nikon digital SLR cameras. They project a smaller image circle compared with lenses designed for the 35mm format cameras, and the light exiting their rear element is collimated (accurately parallel) to improve the efficiency of the photo sites (pixels) on the camera's sensor.

- **Non-CPU** – Nikon uses the term "non-CPU" to describe any Nikkor lens that lacks the electrical connections and components that communicate information about some lens settings to the camera. (With the exception of the 85mm PC-Micro lens and Ai-P type Nikkor lenses, all manual focus Nikkor lenses are non-CPU types).

- **AF-S** – this denotes that the lens has a silent-wave motor (SWM) for focusing; alternating magnetic fields drive the motor that moves lenses elements to change focus. This system offers the fastest auto focusing of all AF Nikkor lenses. Most AF-S lenses have an additional feature that allows the photographer to switch between autofocus and manual focus, without adjusting any camera controls, by turning the focus ring.

- **AF-I** – predecessor to the AF-S type lenses. These lenses also have an internal focusing motor.

- **ED** – to reduce the effect of chromatic aberration Nikon developed a special type of glass to bring various wavelengths of light to a common point of focus.

- **IF** – to speed up focusing, particularly with long focal length lenses, Nikon developed their internal focusing (IF) system. This moves a group of elements within the lens so that it does not alter length during focusing, and prevents the front filter mount from rotating, which facilitates use of filters such as a polarizer.

- **VR** – Vibration Reduction is Nikon's name for a sophisticated technology that enables a lens to counter the effects of camera shake or other vibration. VR lenses use a set of built-in motion sensors, which activate micro-motors to shift certain lens elements to improve the sharpness of pictures.

Using Non-CPU Lenses

Nikon divides all of its lenses in to two broad groups: CPU and non-CPU lenses. CPU is a reference to the electronics in the lens, which allows them to be controlled from a compatible camera body. All autofocus Nikkor lenses have CPUs. However, earlier lenses are, generally, non-CPU types, including most manual focus lenses. (The exceptions are the Ai-P type and PC-Micro 85mm f/2.8D lens.) I have several older manual focus Nikkor lenses that I treasure for their optical quality! The sophisticated electronics of the D200 permits me to use them, even though their operation is fully manual and mechanical.

By inputting the focal length of the lens and its maximum aperture (smallest f/number) into the D200 many of the features and functions of the CPU-type lenses are available with non-CPU lenses. When lens data is registered in the camera the following operations can be performed with a non-CPU lens:

• The aperture value is displayed in the control panel and viewfinder.
• Flash output is adjusted automatically for changes to the aperture value.
• The aperture value is listed in image file information.
• The automatic zoom-head function of the SB-800 and SB-600 Speedlights will function.
• The lens focal length is listed in image file information.
• Color Matrix metering is available (although it may be necessary to use center-weighted or spot metering with some lenses, such as Reflex-Nikkor types).
• The precision of center-weighted metering, spot metering, and i-TTL flash exposure control is improved.

Specifying Lens Data

By specifying the lens focal length and maximum aperture value, it is possible to use many of the D200's features with a compatible non-CPU type lens. The information about a non-CPU type lens can be entered using the *Non-CPU Lens Data* option in the Shooting menu, or by pressing the FUNC button on the front of the camera and rotating the command dials (the main command dial is used to enter lens focal length and the sub command dial to input the maximum aperture value).

Highlight the Non-CPU Lens Data option and Multi Select to the right to open a page that displays two options: *Focal length* (mm) and *Maximum Aperture*. Highlight *Focal Length* and Multi Select right to open a page that displays a list of focal length ranges. Highlight the appropriate range for the focal length you wish to input and Multi Select right to open a page that displays a list of specific focal lengths. Highlight the focal length of your lens and Multi Select right to confirm your selection.

Entering the maximum aperture value using the *Non-CPU Lens Data* option is a similar process. Highlight the *Non-CPU Lens Data* option and Multi Select right Highlight *Maximum Aperture* and Multi Select right to open a page that displays a list of aperture values. Highlight the appropriate aperture value you wish to input and Multi Select right to confirm your selection.

The quickest method is to use the FUNC button and command dials to enter the lens data. This is particularly helpful if you change between different Non-CPU type lenses in one shooting session.

First, select the *FV Lock/Lens Data* option from the items listed at Custom Setting f4. To enter the lens focal length, press the FUNC button and rotate the main command dial, until the appropriate focal length value is displayed in the control panel. Then release the FUNC button. To enter the lens maximum aperture value using this route, select the

FV Lock/Lens Data option from the items listed at Custom Setting f4; if you have not already done so to enter a focal length value, press the FUNC and rotate the sub-command dial until the appropriate maximum aperture value is displayed in the control panel. Then release the FUNC button.

Note: The D200 only retains the last values for focal length and maximum aperture that were input to the camera. If you want to use a different lens, input the focal length and maximum aperture value accordingly. This is the reason that I recommend using the FUNC button/command dial method for registering lens data.

Note: If you attach a non-CPU type zoom lens, the lens data is not adjusted automatically as the focal length/maximum aperture value changes while operating the zoom function; if these values change, input the new focal length and maximum aperture value accordingly.

Exposure Modes with Non-CPU Lenses
Non-CPU type lenses can only be used in either Aperture-Priority (A) or Manual (M) exposure modes, and the lens aperture must be set using the aperture ring on the lens. If the maximum aperture is not specified via the shooting menu, the aperture value displayed on the D200 will not be correct. It will be the difference between the maximum aperture of the lens and the aperture set on the aperture ring, but it is displayed as a whole number next to *ΔF* . For example, if a lens with a maximum aperture of f/2.8 is used and the aperture ring is set to f/5.6, the display in the viewfinder and control panel LCD will show *ΔF* 2.

If you attempt to select either Program (P) or Shutter-Priority (S) exposure mode, the D200 will set Aperture-Priority (A) mode automatically, and the exposure mode icon in the control panel LCD will blink, while A is displayed in the viewfinder.

Note: If the relevant lens data for a non-CPU type lens is not specified, the D200 does not perform color Matrix metering if Matrix metering is set on the camera; center-weighted metering will be used.

Lens Compatibility

Nikon makes a huge range of Nikkor lenses. The following table provides the compatibility of Nikkor lenses with the D200:

Camera setting / Lens/accessory	Focus		Mode			Metering		
	AF	M (with electronic range finder)	M	P S	A M	3D	Color	
CPU lenses[1] Type G or D AF Nikkor[2]; AF-S, AF-I Nikkor	●	●	●	●	●	●	—	●[3]
PC-Micro Nikkor 85 mm f/2.8D[4]	—	●[5]	●	—	●[6]	●	—	●[3]
AF-S/AF-I Teleconverter[7]	●[8]	●[8]	●	●	●	●	—	●[3]
Other AF Nikkor (except lenses for F3AF)	●[9]	●[9]	●	●	●	—	●	●[3]
AI-P Nikkor	—	●[10]	●	●	●	—	●	●[3]
Non-CPU lenses[11] AI-modified, AI-, AI-S, or Series E Nikkor[12]	—	●[10]	●	—	●[13]	—	●[14]	●[15]
Medical Nikkor 120 mm f/4	—	●	●	—	●[16]	—	—	—
Reflex Nikkor	—	—	●	—	●[13]	—	—	●[15]
PC-Nikkor	—	●[5]	●	●	●[17]	—	—	●
AI-type Teleconverter[18]	—	●[8]	●	—	●[13]	—	●[14]	●[15]
TC-16A AF Teleconverter	—	●[8]	●	—	●[13]	—	●[14]	●[15]
PB-6 Bellows Focusing Attachment[19]	—	●[8]	●	—	●[20]	—	—	●
Auto extension rings (PK-series 11-A, 12, or 13; PN-11)	—	●[8]	●	—	●[13]	—	—	●

1. *IX Nikkor lenses cannot be used.*
2. *Vibration Reduction (Vt) supported with VR lenses.*
3. *Spot metering meters selected focus area.*
4. *The cameras exposure metering and flash control systems do not work properly when shifting and/or tilting the lens, or when an aperture other than the maximum aperture is used.*
5. *Electronic range finder can not be used with shifting or tilting.*
6. *Manual exposure mode only.*
7. *Compatible with AF I Nikkor lenses and with all AF S lenses exept AF S DX VR ED 18-200 mm f/3.5-5.6G; AF S DX ED 12-24 mm f/4G,*
  17-55 mm f/2.8G, 18-55 mm f/3.5-5.6G, 18-70 mm f/3.5-4.5G, and 55-200 mm f/4-5.6G; AF 5 VR ED 24-120 mm f/3.5-5.66; and AF S ED 17-35 mm f/2.8D, 24-85 mm f/3.5-4.5G, and 28-70 mm f/2.8D.
8. *With maximum effective aperture of f/5.6 or faster.*
9. *If AF 80-200 mm f/2.8-5, AF 35-70 mm f/2.8-5, new model AF 28-85 mm f/3.5-4.55, or AF 28-85 mm f/3.5-4.5S is zoomed in while focusing at minimum range, image on matte screen in viewfinder may not be in focus when in focus indicator is displayed. Focus manually using image in viewfinder as guide.*

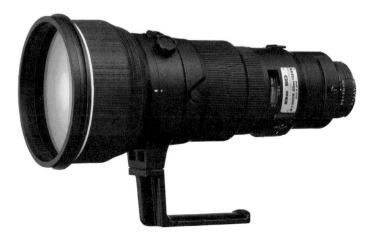

The AF-S 400mm f/2.8D IF-ED II Nikkor is a great choice for use with the D200. It is lightweight and, because of the D200's DX sensor, this lens provides a field of view that is similar to a 600mm lens on a 35mm camera. That's a lot of power for bird and wildlife photography!

10. With maximum aperture of f/5.6 or faster.

11. Some lenses cannot be used (see following page).

12. Range of rotation for Ai 80 200 mm f/2.85 ED tripod mount limited by camera body. Filters cannot be exchanged while Ai 200 400 mm f/45 ED is mounted on camera.

13. If maximum aperture is specified using Non-CPU Lens Data option in shooting menu, aperture value will be displayed in viewfinder and control panel.

14. Can be used only if lens focal length and maximum aperture are specified using Non CPU Lens Data option in shooting menu. Use spot or center-weighted metering if desired results are not achieved.

15. For improved precision, specify lens focal length and maximum aperture using Non CPU Lens Data option in shooting menu.

16. Can be used at in manual exposure modes at shutter speeds slower than 1/125s. If maximum aperture is specified using Non CPU Lens Data option in shooting menu, aperture value will be displayed in viewfinder and control panel.

17. Exposure determined by presetting lens aperture. In aperture-priority auto exposure mode, preset aperture using lens aperture ring before performing AE lock or shifting lens. In manual exposure mode, preset aperture using lens aperture ring and determine exposure before shifting lens.

18. Exposure compensation required when used with AI 28-85 mm f/3.5-4.55, AI 35-105 mm f/3.5-4.5S, AI 35-135 mm f/3.5-4.5S, or AF S 80-200 mm f/2.8D.
See teleconverter manual for details.

19. Requires PR 12 OF Pr 13 dull) extension ring.

20. Use preset aperture. In exposure mode A, set aperture using focusing attachment before determining exposure and taking photograph.

* PF-4 Reprocopy Outfit requires PA 4 Camera Holder.

Incompatible Lenses and Accessories

The following accessories and lenses are not compatible with the D200. Warning: using them may damage your equipment:

- K2 extension rings
- All pre Ai-type Nikkor lenses (Ai-types introduced from 1977 onwards)
- Lenses that require the AU-1 focusing unit (400mm f4.5, 600mm f/5.6, 800mm f/8, 1200mm f/11)
- Fisheye-Nikkor (6mm f/5.6, 8mm f/8, OP 10mm f/5.6)
- 21mm f/4 (first type with protruding rear element)
- 180-600mm f/8ED (serial numbers 174041 – 1744127)
- 200-600m f/9.5 (serial numbers 280001 – 300490)
- AF 80mm f/2.8, AF200mm f/3.5, TC-16 teleconverter (for F3AF camera)
- PC 28mm f/4 (serial numbers 180900 or earlier)
- PC 35mm f/2.8 (serial numbers 851001 – 906200)
- PC 35mm f/3.5 (early type)
- Reflex 1000mm f/11 (serial numbers 142361 – 143000)
- Reflex 2000mm f/11 (serial numbers 200111 – 200310)

Filters

In most shooting situations, the D200's white balance control eliminates the need to use the color correction or color compensating filters that were necessary with film. Nevertheless, filters should be part of any digital photographer's equipment, because there are a few filter effects that you cannot replicate using a computer. I recommend that you start with these filters:

Polarizing Filters

The most useful, and probably best-known, filter is a polarizer. Often associated with the ability to shoot through glass or deepen the color of a blue sky, a polarizer has many other uses. The unique effects of this filter make it essential for film or digital photography. For example, the polarizer is a favorite with landscape photographers because removes reflections from non-metallic surfaces including water. A polarizer can also help reduce the glare caused by the reflection of the sky from foliage, thereby intensifying its color. This effect makes a polarizer a "must have" for photographing autumn leaves.

Hint: The automatic focusing and TTL metering systems of the D200 will not function properly, if you use a "linear-type" polarizing filter, so make sure you purchase a circular-polarizer, such as the Nikon Circular Polarizer II.

Neutral Density Filters

Even at the base sensitivity of ISO 100 available on the D200, it is often not possible to set a lens aperture, or shutter speed that will achieve the desired results when shooting in very bright light. Continuous tone neutral density filters reduce the overall exposure by lowering the amount of light that reaches the camera's sensor. They allow you to use longer shutter speeds and/or wider apertures in bright conditions. Nikon no longer produces continuous neutral density filters but many independent companies do.

Graduated Neutral Density Filters

Coping with the excessive contrast is one of the challenges of digital photography. For example, the sky is often much brighter than the land, which can make shooting landscapes tricky. If you set the exposure to record the darker portion of the scene, the sky is often too bright to be recorded properly and ends up being overexposed, lacking color or detail.

Graduated neutral density filters that are clear on one end and become progressively denser toward the other are the ideal solution. They come in a variety of strengths and rates of change. If you use a slot-in type filter system, is easy to align these graduated filters so their dense area darkens the sky leaving the clear portion over the foreground area unaffected. Nikon does not produce graduated neutral density filter, but many independent companies do.

Another way to solve this exposure problem is to make two exposures of the same scene (one for the shadow areas and the other for the highlight areas) and then combine the two shots in to one using software and a computer. But sometimes an element in the scene can move between making the two exposures, and the technique is revealed! I always advocate trying to get "it right" in the camera, so you spend less time in front of a computer and more time taking pictures.

Hint: Nikon states that the 3D Color Matrix and Matrix metering of the D200 is not recommended when using for any filter with a filter factor over 1x. The filter factor is the amount of exposure compensation you need to apply to compensate for the reduction in light transmission caused by the filter. For example a filter factor of 2x is equivalent to one-stop, a factor of 8x is equivalent to three-stops. Because this rule applies to polarizing and neutral density filters, switch to center-weighted or spot metering. The TTL metering system of the D200 will account, automatically, for any exposure compensation required when a filter is fitted to the lens.

General Nikon Accessories

- **BF-1A**—Body cap that helps prevent dust from entering the camera. Keep it in place at all times when a lens is not mounted on the camera.

  Note: The earlier BF-1 type body cap cannot be used, because it may damage the lens mount of the D200

- **DG-2**—Viewfinder eyepiece magnifier. This provides about 2x magnification of the central area of the viewfinder field. (Note: It requires the Eyepiece Adapter to be fitted. See below.)

- **DK-5**—Viewfinder eyepiece cover. This is required when using the camera remotely in auto exposure modes to prevent light from entering the viewfinder and affecting exposure measurement.

- **DK-3**—Circular rubber eyecup for the Nikon FM3A. It can be attached via the square-to-circular viewfinder accessory Eyepiece Adapter; it also requires a viewfinder eyepiece filter for the FM3A camera to hold it in place. The circular eyecup provides a better light seal when held to the photographer's eye than the DK-21 square eyecup that is standard with the D200.

- **DK-21**—Standard square rubber eyecup supplied with the D200.

- **DK-21M**—Replaces standard DK-21 eyecup and provides 1.2x magnification of the viewfinder.

- **DR-6**—Right angle viewer that attaches to the square frame of the D200's viewfinder eyepiece. It is useful when the camera is at a low shooting position.

- **EC-AD1**—Adapter that accepts Type I CompactFlash memory cards for connection to PCMCIA card slot.

- **Eyepiece adapter**—This accessory has no specific designation and is only identified by its Nikon product code: No. 2370. It allows round format viewfinder accessories, such as the DG-2, to be mounted on the square viewfinder eyepiece of the D200

- **EH-6**—Multi-voltage AC adapter for powering the D200.

- **EN-EL3e**—Lithium-ion rechargeable battery for the D200 (also compatible with D100, D70-series, and D50 cameras).

- **MB-D200**—Battery pack for the D200. It accepts up to two EN-EL3e batteries, or six AA-size batteries in the MS-D200 battery holder.

- **MC-21**—9.75 ft (3 m) extension cord for 10-pin accessories that connects to 10-pin terminal on D200.

- **MC-23**—15 inch (0.4 m) cord for connecting two compatible cameras for near simultaneous shutter release. It plugs into the 10-pin terminal on D200.

- **MC-30**—30 inch (0.8 m) standard remote shutter release cord. It plugs into the 10-pin terminal on D200.

- **MC-35**—Cord for attaching a GPS device to the D200.

- **MC-36**—33 inch (0.85 m) remote shutter release, which has an intervalometer for time-lapse photography. It plugs into the 10-pin terminal on D200.

- **MH-18a**—Multi-voltage AC charger for a single EN-EL3e battery.

- **MH-19**—Multiple battery charger. It can charge two EN-EL3e batteries, and supports either a multi-voltage AC supply or 12V DC motor vehicle supply.

- **ML-3 Remote Control**—An infrared remote release for the D200. It connects to the camera's ten-pin remote terminal. The transmitter unit requires 2, AAA-size batteries. The receiver unit is powered by the camera.

- **MS-D200**—A battery holder for six AA-sized batteries. It can be used as an alternative power supply for the D200 when fitted with the MB-D200 battery pack.

- **SC-28**—TTL flash cord. It maintains full functionality of compatible external Speedlight with the D200.

- **SC-29**—TTL flash cord with built-in AF-assist lamp. It maintains full functionality of compatible external Speedlight with the D200.

- **WT-3 / WT3A**—Wireless transmitter for D200.

Nikon Software

- **PictureProject**—The image files from the D200 require version 1.6.1 or later of this very basic image transfer and editing application. A copy is supplied with the camera.

- **Nikon View**—Nikon's long established browser application is recommended over PictureProject. Image files from the D200 require version 6.2.7 or later.

- **Nikon View Pro**—Successor to Nikon View, this new application has been developed to speed up image transfer, editing, and management, and is particularly useful if you shoot large quantities of images.

- **Nikon Capture**—The D200 requires version 4.4.0 or higher. Software application with two components: Nikon Capture – Editor for image adjustment and editing, supports D200 NEF raw files, and Nikon Capture – camera Control that offers remote camera control via USB cord connection.

- **Nikon Capture NX**—The latest iteration of the Capture application. It is an entirely new application dedicated to image editing, and incorporates the unique U-point technology for making complex selections within an image area with ease.

- **Nikon Camera Control Pro**—Successor to the Camera Control element of Nikon Capture. It is a standalone application for photographers who wish to be able to control a D200 camera remotely from a computer.

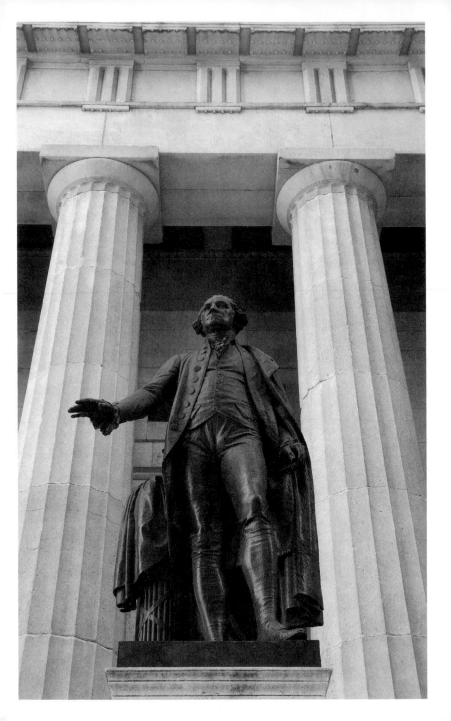

Working Digitally

You may be surprised to learn that apart from image data, the picture files generated by the D200 contain a wealth of other information that includes the shooting parameters and instructions about printing pictures, among other things. This information is "tagged" to the image file using a number of common standards depending on the sort of information to be saved with the image file.

Supported standards:

DCF (v 2.0): Design Rule for Camera File System (DCF) is a standard used widely in the digital imaging industry to ensure compatibility across different makes of cameras.

DPOF: Digital Print Order Format (DPOF) is a standard used widely to enable pictures to be printed from a created print order and saved on a memory card.

EXIF (v 2.21): The D200 supports Exchangeable Image File Format for Digital Still cameras (EXIF). This standard allows information stored with image files to be read by software, and used for ensuring image quality when printed on an EXIF-compliant printer.

PictBridge: A standard that permits an image file stored on a memory card to be output directly to a printer without the need to first connect the camera to a computer or download the image file from a memory card to a computer.

☞ *Becoming familiar with the file standards and software programs supported by the D200 is an important step towards streamlining your digital workflow.*

Exchangeable Image File Format (EXIF)

The D200 uses the EXIF (2.21) standard to tag additional information to each image file it records. This information is sometimes referred to as metadata, which is a more generic term. Most popular digital imaging software is able to read and interpret the EXIF tags so the information can be displayed, but other software is not as capable, in which case some or all of the EXIF data values may not be available. The information recorded includes:

- Nikon (the name of the camera manufacturer)
- D200 (the model number)
- Camera firmware version number
- Exposure information (including shutter speed, aperture, exposure mode, ISO, EV value, date/time, exposure compensation, flash mode, and focal length)
- Thumbnail of the main image

Examining EXIF data by either viewing the image information pages on the camera's monitor screen or by accessing the shooting data in appropriate software is a great teaching aid. You can see exactly what the camera settings were for each shot. By comparing pictures and the shooting data, you can quickly learn about the technical aspects of exposure, focusing, metering, and flash exposure control.

International Press Telecommunications Council (IPTC)

Other information, or metadata, that can be tagged to an image file includes the use of a standard developed by the International Press Telecommunications Council (IPTC). Known as Digital Newsphoto Parameter Record (DNPR), it can append image information including details of the origin, authorship, copyright, caption details, and key words for searching purposes. Any application that is DNPR compliant will show this information and allow you to edit it. If you are considering submitting any pictures you shoot with the D200 for publication you should make use of DNPR

(IPTC) metadata, as most publishing organizations require it
to be present before accepting a submission.

Note: DNPR data is often erroneously referred to as "IPTC data."

Camera Connections

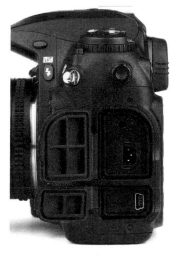

*The D200 has several ports
located under covers on the left
side of the camera.*

Connecting to a Television

The D200 can be connected to a television set or VCR for
playback or recording of images. In many countries, the
camera is supplied with the EG-D100 video cable for this
purpose. First, select the appropriate video standard:

Open the Setup menu ⚐ and use the Multi Selector to
navigate to the *Video Mode* item. Multi Select right, and
Multi Select up or down to highlight the required option:
NTSC or *PAL.*

Note: NTSC is the video standard used in the US, Canada,
and Japan. PAL is used in most European countries.

Before connecting the camera to the video cord, make sure the camera power is switched off. Open the large rubber cover on the left end of the camera body to reveal the ports for Video out (top) and DC-in (bottom). Connect the narrow jack-pin of the EG-D100 to the camera and the other end to the TV/VCR. Tune the TV to the video channel, and turn on the camera. The image that would normally be displayed on the LCD monitor will be shown on the television screen or can be recorded to videotape.

Note: The LCD monitor will remain blank but all other camera operations will function normally. So, you can take pictures with the camera connected to a TV set and carry out review/playback functions as you would on the monitor screen.

Note: If you intend to use the camera for an extended period for image playback via a TV or VCR it is probably best to use the EH-6 AC adapter to power the camera.

Connecting to a Computer

The D200 can be connected directly to a computer via the supplied UC-E4 USB cable. The camera supports the high-speed USB (2.0) interface that offers a maximum transfer rate of 480Mbps. You can download images from the camera using the supplied Nikon PictureProject software, or Nikon View, which is available separately. Alternatively, the D200 can be controlled from a computer using the optional Nikon Capture (v 4.4.0, or later), or Nikon Camera Control Pro software.

Hint: If you use the D200 tethered to a computer for any function, ensure that the EN-EL3e battery is fully charged. Preferably, use the EH-6 mains AC adapter to prevent interruptions to data transfer by loss of power.

Before connecting the D200 to a computer appropriate Nikon software must be installed, and the camera must be configured for one of the two USB connection options, via the Setup menu.

Open the ⓨ menu and navigate to the *USB* item. Multi Select right to display the two options: *M Mass Storage* and *P PTP*. Highlight the required option (see descriptions below) and press Multi Select right to select it.

- **Mass Storage:** In this configuration, the D200 acts like a card reader and the computer sees the memory card in the camera as an external storage device; it only allows the computer to read the data on the memory card. Use this option if computer is running Windows (98SE, Me, or 2000 Pro). This is the default option.

- **Picture Transfer Protocol (PTP):** In this configuration the D200 acts like another device on a computer network and the computer can communicate and control camera operations. Use this option if the computer is running Windows XP (Home or Pro), or Macintosh OS X.

Note: If you use the *Mass Storage* option, ensure the camera is un-mounted from the computer system in accordance with the correct procedure for the operating system in use, before the camera is switched off and disconnected from the USB cord.

Note: You must select PTP to the camera control feature in Nikon Capture 4, or Nikon Camera Control Pro software.

Note: *Mass Storage* can also be selected with Windows XP (Home or Pro), or Macintosh OS X.

Card Readers

Although the D200 can be tethered directly to a computer via a USB cord for transferring image data, there are several reasons why you should consider using a dedicated memory card reader as an alternative:

- If you use the tethered camera method, you will its drain battery power with a risk that data could be lost or corrupted if the power fails.

- Using a card reader allows you to run software to recover lost or corrupted image files as well as diagnose problems with the memory card.
- You can leave a card reader permanently attached to your computer, which further reduces the risk of losing or corrupting files as a result of a poor connection due to the wear and tear caused by constantly connecting the camera.

Approved Memory Cards

There are a plethora of memory cards on the market but Nikon have only tested and approved those listed in the table below for use with the D200.

CompactFlash cards and Microdrive technology is well established, so although Nikon will not guarantee operation with other makes of card, you should not experience any problems.

Nikon Approved Memory Cards For D200

Manufacturer	Card Type / Series	Capacity
SanDisk	SDCFB	128MB, 256MB, 512MB 1GB, 2GB, and 4GB
SanDisk	SDCFB (Type II)	300MB
SanDisk	SDCF2B (Type II) series	256MB
SanDisk	SDCFH (Ultra II)	256MB, 512MB, 1GB, 2GB, 4GB, and 8GB
SanDisk	SDCFX (Extreme III)	1GB, 2GB, and 4GB
Lexar Media	Red label series	128MB, 256MB, and 512MB
Lexar Media	High Speed 40x WA* (Platinum)	256MB, 512MB, and 1GB
Lexar Media	Professional 40x WA*	8GB
Lexar Media	Professional 80x WA*	512MB, 1GB, 2GB, and 4GB
Lexar Media	Professional 80x WA* with LockTight technology	512MB and 2GB
Various	Microdrives	1GB, 2GB, 4GB, and 6GB

*   *The D200 does not support Lexar's Write Acceleration (WA) technologies.*

Nikon states that, while other brands and capacities of cards may work, operation cannot be guaranteed. If you intend to use a memory card not listed in the table above, it is important to check with the manufacturer in respect to its compatibility. Should you experience any problems related to the memory card, use one of the approved cards for the purposes of trouble-shooting.

Memory Card Capacity

The table below provides information on the approximate number of images that can be stored on a 1GB memory card at the various image quality, and size settings available on the D200. All memory cards use a small proportion of their memory capacity to store data required for the card to operate, therefore the amount of memory available for storing image files will be slightly less than the quoted maximum capacity of the card.

Quality	Size	File Size [1]	No. Images [1]	Buffer Capacity [1,2]
NEF (RAW)	—	15.8	60	22
NEF (RAW) + JPEG Fine [3,4,5,6]	L	20.7	44	19
	M	18.6	49	19
	S	17.1	55	19
NEF (RAW) + JPEG Normal [3,4,5,6]	L	18.3	50	19
	M	17.2	54	19
	S	16.5	57	19
NEF (RAW) + JPEG Basic [3,4,5,6]	L	17.1	55	19
	M	16.5	57	19
	S	16.2	58	19
JPEG Fine 5	L	4.8	167	37
	M	2.7	294	56
	S	1.2	650	74
JPEG Normal 5	L	2.4	332	54
	M	1.4	578	74
	S	0.63	1200	76
JPEG Basic 5	L	1.2	650	57
	M	0.7	1100	75
	S	0.33	2200	76

1. *File size will vary according to the scene photographed, and the make of memory card used. Therefore, all figures are approximate.*

2. *This is the maximum number of image files that can be stored in the buffer memory, when sensitivity equivalent is set to ISO 100. Capacity will be reduced if noise reduction is active.*
3. *Combined total for NEF (RAW) and JEPG image files.*
4. *Quoted figures based on use of uncompressed NEF (RAW) files. Selecting compression for NEF (RAW) will reduce file size by approximately 40 – 50%. The number of image files that can be recorded increases, although camera display remains unchanged.*
5. *Quoted figures assume that the JPEG Compression feature in the Shooting menu is set to Size Priority. Selecting Optimal Quality from the JPEG Compression feature will increase file size by up to 80%. Therefore, the number of images that can be recorded and the capacity of the buffer memory will be reduced accordingly.*
6. *Image size applies to JPEG image files only. Size of NEF (RAW) files is fixed.*

Direct Printing

As mentioned above, the D200 supports a number of standards that, among other features, allow the user to print pictures directly from the camera, via a USB connection, without the aid of a computer. It is possible to select an individual image or a group of images. Regardless, this feature is only compatible with JPEG format image files, and a printer that supports the PictBridge standard.

Note: Direct printing from the D200 is only supported for JPEG files. Nikon recommends images destined for direct printing should be recorded in the sRGB color space.

Linking the D200 with a Printer
The D200 can be connected to a PictBridge compatible printer to print pictures direct from the camera.

First, set the *USB* option in the 🏠 menu to PTP. Next, ensure the camera is switched off, turn the printer on, and connect the printer to the camera via the supplied UC-E4 USB lead.

Note: Printing cannot be performed with the default *USB* option of *Mass Storage*.

286

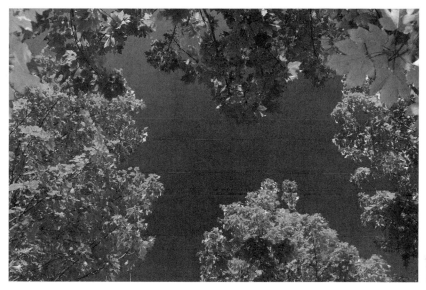

You can use the D200 to print directly from camera to printer without a computer.

Note: It is essential that you make sure the camera battery is fully charged before commencing direct printing from the camera. Preferably use the EH-6 mains AC adapter.

Note: Nikon does not recommend connecting via a USB hub.

Turn the camera on, and a welcome message will be shown followed by the PictBridge playback display on the camera's monitor screen. To scroll through the images saved on the memory card use the Multi Selector. To access an enlarged view of the displayed image press and hold 🔘 button. To view up to six images at a time, press 🔘 and rotate the main command dial. Highlight individual pictures, press 🔘 , and rotate the main command dial to display the selected image full frame.

There are two options for printing pictures: one-by-one, or in multiples.

Printing Pictures One at a Time

To print the image selected in the PictBridge playback display, press and release the ● button. The PictBridge printing menu will be displayed. Use Multi Select up or down to select the required option.

Option	Description
Start Printing	Select to print the image highlighted in the PictBridge display. To cancel function press ● button.
Page Size	Select the appropriate paper size from *Default Printer* item: 3.5 x 5-inch, 5 x 7-inch, Hagaki, 100 x 150 mm, 4 x 6-inch, 8 x 10-inch, Letter, A3, or A4. Then press Multi Select right to select and return to the print menu.
Number of Copies	Use Multi Select up or down to select the number of copies of the highlighted image to be printed (maximum 99). Then Multi-Select right to return to the print menu.
Border	Multi Select up or down to select *Printer Default* (uses default setting of current printer), *Print with Border* (white border), or *No Border*. Multi Select right to return to the print menu.
Time Stamp	Multi Select up or down to select *Printer Default* (uses default setting of current printer), *Print Time Stamp* (date and time images was recorded are printed), or *No Time Stamp*.
Cropping	Multi Select up or down to select *Crop* (picture can be cropped in-camera), or *No Crop* (printed full frame). Multi Select right to select and return to the print menu.

To crop image, rotate main command dial to determine size of crop and use the Multi Selector to position the crop frame. Press ● to return to the print menu. |

Printing Multiple Images via PictBridge

To print multiple images, or an index print (contact sheet), connect the camera to a compatible printer as described above. Once the PictBridge display is open press ▭▭▭ and a menu with three options will be displayed:

Option	Description
Print Select	The selected images are printed
Print (DPOF)	The current DPOF print order set is printed (DPOF date and information options are not supported)
Index Print	Creates and index print of all images saved in the JPEG format. If the memory card contains more than 256 JPEG images only 265 will be printed. Press ⊕ button to display a sub-menu with three further options: *Page Size, Border, Time Stamp.* These have the same options as described in the table above for single image printing.

Choose *Print Select* from the *PictBridge* menu. Six thumbnail images will be displayed on the monitor screen. Scroll through the images and press ⊕ to see the highlighted image full frame.

To select the image highlighted currently press Multi Select up. The number of copies to be printed is set to one. To specify the number of copies of each image selected for printing Multi Select up to raise the number and down to lower the number. Repeat this process in respect of each image required to be printed. Display the print options and set page size, border type, and time stamp options as required according to the instructions above. To print selected images, highlight *Start Printing* and Multi Select right.

Note: Images saved in the NEF (RAW) format will be displayed in the *Print Selected* menu but it is not possible to select them for printing.

Digital Print Order Format (DPOF)

The D200 supports the Digital Print Order Format (DPOF) standard that embeds an instruction set in the appropriate EXIF data fields of an image file. This allows you to insert the memory card into any DPOF compatible home printer or commercial mini-lab printer, and automatically get a set of prints of your chosen images. Apart from the fact you do not have to tether the camera to a compatible printer as described above, this feature can be particularly useful if, for example, you are away from home, say on vacation. You can still produce prints from your digital files, even if you do not have access to your own printer, since prints can be made on any DPOF compatible printer.

To select images for printing, highlight *Print Set* from the Playback menu. The *Select/Set* option will be highlighted; Multi Select right to select it. The camera will display a thumbnail of all the images stored on the inserted memory card, in groups of up to six thumbnails. Scroll through the images; a yellow frame bounds the highlighted image. To view the highlighted image full frame, press and hold the ⊕ button.

To select the highlighted image for printing, press the center of the Multi Selector and a small icon of a printer and a number will appear in the upper right corner of the thumbnail image. This designates the image to be printed and the number of copies to be produced. To change the number of prints for the highlighted image, press and hold the ⊙ button while scrolling up or down using Multi Select.

Once all images to be printed have been selected, press the ⊛ button to save the selected group of images. To imprint shooting data on the image, highlight *Data Imprint* and select *OK*. To print the date/time the image was recorded on the image, highlight *Imprint Date* and select *OK*. Finally, to finish, save the *Print Set* order, highlight *Done* and Multi Select right.

To remove images from the *Print Set*, repeat steps for selecting images, and when the image to be removed from the Print Set is highlighted, press the center of the Multi Selector. Save changes to the *Print Set* by pressing ⊙ .

To deselect an entire print set, select *Print Set* from ▶ menu. Multi Select right, and Multi Select up or down to highlight *Deselect All*. Highlight the required option *Yes* or *No* and Multi Select right to confirm the selection.

Note: *Print Set* selections can only be made from JPEG format images stored on the memory card. If an image was shot using a NEF+JPEG option, only the JPEG image can be selected for printing.

Note: There are subtle differences in the functionality between the two direct printing routes. For example, direct printing with the D200 connected to a PictBridge compatible printer allows you to perform cropping of the image before printing, whereas printing from the memory card using a print set created from the DPOF standard images can only be printed full frame.

Nikon Software

It is beyond the scope of this book to fully describe the features and functions of Nikon's dedicated software. Details can be obtained from the technical support sections of the Web sites maintained by Nikon. The following is intended to provide a brief overview.

The D200 comes with a copy of Nikon PictureProject 1.6.1, Nikon's browser application 'intended' to replace the stalwart Nikon View. I say 'intended' because, despite statements made in mid-2003 suggesting that Nikon View would be taken no further than version 6.0, the current version is at 6.2.7, which was introduced during late 2005 to offer support to the D200.

Nikon has continued to update View to ensure compatibility with the many of the recent upgrades to Nikon Capture, although it does not support all of its tools from Capture version 4.3 and higher when working with NEF (RAW) files. At the time of writing, Nikon has stated their intention to further upgrade Nikon View to a version that will be known as Nikon View Pro. That is the good news. The bad news is that the release of View Pro has been delayed until "late 2006," and it will no longer be available for free download but will have to be purchased.

I believe the continued support and development of Nikon View is a clear indication of the limitations of Picture-Project, particularly in respect of support for NEF (RAW) files, something that leaves PictureProject wanting. If you have not tried Nikon View 6.2.7, I would strongly recommend that you do – after all it is free!

Note: For information about Nikon software and to download updates to existing applications updates, I recommend you visit the various technical support Web sites maintained by Nikon, which can be accessed via: http://www.nikon.com.

PictureProject

As mentioned above, the D200 comes supplied with a copy of Nikon PictureProject 1.6.1. It and Nikon View are designed to facilitate the transfer of images from a memory card to a computer, either directly from a camera or via a card reader. PictureProject and View also allow for a number of preferences to be set, including file naming and numbering. Both applications provide an image browsing capability to display, review, sort, and edit images to help the user manage their image file collection.

As soon as the transfer is complete and images have been placed in the appropriate folder, the browser window will auto-launch and the last set of images to be imported will be displayed as a series of thumbnail pictures. Shooting data can be viewed in Nikon PictureProject by opening the View menu and selecting Display > List, or alternatively click on the List button in the bottom right corner of the main pane, and the information for each image shown in the main pane will be displayed beside it. In Nikon View, click on the Shooting Data tab. The information for the highlighted image is then shown in a box that opens beneath the menu bar. Both applications allow you to search for other images in the directory tree shown to the left side of the main browser window.

PictureProject permits you to perform very basic editing. Clicking on the Edit button displays buttons to crop, rotate, and zoom the image, as well as a red-eye reduction tool. Opening the Photo Enhance menu reveals some further options, including tools for controlling Brightness, D-Lighting, Color Booster, Photo Effects, Sharpening, and Straightening.

Nikon View
By comparison, Nikon View contains a restricted version of Nikon Editor, as found in Nikon Capture. It allows you to use a limited number of tools and controls, including brightness, contrast, image size, sharpening (with no parameters—just Off, Low, Medium, and High), and red-eye reduction (only available for JPEG files). Nikon View benefits from having further controls that permit exposure compensation of +/- 2EV, and modification of the white balance value (within the available presets) for NEF (RAW) files can be adjusted at any time. Plus NEF (RAW) files can be saved as either 8-bit or16-bit TIFF files, as well as in the JPEG format.

Note: It is not possible to rescue grossly overexposed images using exposure compensation, as areas with burnt out highlights will have no data for the application to work with.

Note: In practical terms, the range of exposure compensation for NEF files using Nikon Editor within Nikon View software is closer to − 1.5EV to +1EV. Changes beyond these limits can introduce unwanted artifacts.

Nikon View Pro
Once it is available Nikon View Pro will include the following features:

- Fast image display – quick display of JPEG, TIFF, and NEF (RAW) images.
- Action key – a single key with up to five assigned individual actions (selected and combined by user)
- Digital Newsphoto Parameter Record (DNPR) data editing – allows DNPR data saved to the IPTC standard to be edited and copied from one image to another.
- Five display modes – make it fast, easy, and convenient to select images and check details
- Single image display mode – offers a choice between 100% and 50% scale
- Multi image display modes (vertical and horizontal) – make image comparisons easy, with one window to be fixed and the other to be replaced
- Full-screen display mode – maximizes display size with a frameless window option
- Marking – adds various possible operations (including sorting, moving, copying, and organizing) to marked images
- FTP data transfer – supports File Transfer Protocol (FTP) for transferring selected images

Nikon Capture
Nikon Capture (use only version 4.4.0 or newer with the D200) is a far more sophisticated application compared to Nikon PictureProject or Nikon View; it permits a much greater level of image control and the ability to operate compatible cameras remotely. It is available as an optional extra, and has two distinct components: Nikon Editor and Nikon Camera Control. Nikon Editor is used to assist processing and enhancing of NEF (RAW) and JPEG files, with the option of converting them to other formats or opening them directly into another image-processing application, such as Adobe Photoshop. Nikon Camera Control allows full remote control of a D200 while the camera is connected to a computer via the supplied UC-E4 USB cable. It also allows

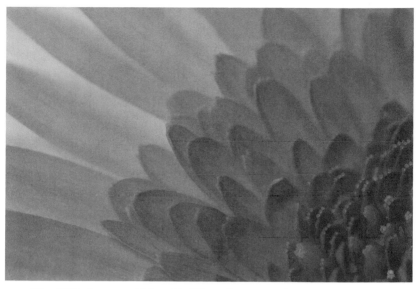

The D200 is compatible with Nikon Capture software, version 4.4.0 or newer.

the direct transfer of images from the camera to a computer, effectively turning the computer hard drive in to a large volume memory card.

Nikon Capture Editor offers many features, including:

- Advanced white balance control with the ability to select a specific color temperature or sample from a gray point.
- Advanced NEF file control that permits attributes such as exposure compensation, sharpening, contrast, color mode, saturation, and hue to be modified after the exposure has been made, without affecting the original image data.
- The Image Dust Off feature, which compares an NEF file with a reference image taken with the same camera to help reduce the effects of any dust particles on the low-pass filter.

- The D-Lighting tool, which emulates the dodge & burn techniques of traditional photographic printing to control highlight and shadow areas to produce a more balanced exposure.
- A Color Noise Reduction tool, which minimizes the effect of random electronic noise that can occur, especially at high sensitivity (ISO) settings.
- An Edge Noise Reduction tool that accentuates the boundary between areas of the image to make them more distinct.
- The Color Moiré Reduction feature helps to remove the effects of moiré, which can occur when an image contains areas with a very fine repeating pattern.
- LCH Editor allows for control of Luminosity (overall lightness), Chroma (color saturation), and Hue in separate channels.
- Fisheye Lens tool converts images taken with the AF Fisheye-Nikkor DX 10.5mm f/2.8G lens so they appear as though they were taken using a conventional rectilinear lens with a diagonal angle-of-view equivalent to approximately 120°.

Nikon Capture NX

The next iteration of Nikon Capture is also due to be released during the second half of 2006. At the time of writing I have only had access to a beta version of this exciting new application but it looks very impressive, and is significantly quicker, especially when handling NEF (RAW) files, compared with Nikon Capture 4.4.0. Capture NX represents a complete re-write of the application by nik Software, a wholly independent software company, and incorporates their unique U-point technology that permits complex selections of an area within an image to be made with accuracy and speed that is far greater than using current digital imaging software. The user has an extensive toolbox available to enhance and modify any image file, regardless of whether it was saved in the NEF (RAW), TIFF, or JPEG format.

Digital Workflow

Using film for photography is familiar to most people: load the camera, take the pictures, and have someone else do the processing and printing for you. Shooting digitally, however, brings many new aspects to your photography and provides a far greater level of control. Therefore, it is essential to develop a routine to make sure that you work in an efficient and effective way. You may wish to consider the following 7-point workflow as a general guide to establishing your own.

Preparation
- Familiarize yourself with the camera. The more intuitive you become with your equipment, the more time you can spend concentrating on the scene/subject being photographed.
- Make sure the camera battery is charged and always carry a spare.
- Rather than save all your pictures to a single high capacity memory card, reduce the chance of a catastrophic loss due to card failure/loss by spreading the risk over several memory cards.
- Always clean the low-pass filter array in front of the sensor to reduce the level of post-processing work.
- Always format the memory card in the camera in which it will be used each time you insert a card.

Shooting
- Adjust camera settings to match the requirements of your shoot; choose an appropriate image quality, size, ISO, color space, and white balance.
- Set other camera controls such as metering and auto focus according to the shooting conditions.
- Use the *Image Comment* feature (see pages 188-189) to assign a note about the authorship/copyright of the images you shoot.
- Review images and make any adjustments you deem necessary. The histogram display is extremely useful for checking on exposure values.

- Do not be in too much of a hurry to delete pictures unless they are obvious failures. It is often better to edit after shooting rather than "on the fly."

Transfer
- Before transferring images to your computer, designate a specific folder or folders in which the images will be stored.
- Use a card reader rather than connecting the camera directly to the computer. It is much faster, more reliable, and reduces wear and tear on the camera.
- If your browser application permits you to assign general information to the image files during transfer (e.g. DNPR (IPTC) metadata) make sure you complete appropriate fields for image authorship and copyright.
- Consider renaming files and assigning further information and key words to facilitate searching for images at a later date.

Edit and File
- Use a browsing application to sort through your pictures. Do not be in too much of a hurry to edit out pictures. It is often best to take a second look at images a few days or even weeks after they were shot, as your opinions about images will change.
- Print a contact sheet of thumbnail images to help you decide which images to retain.

Processing
- Make copies of RAW files and save them to a working file format such as TIFF or PSD (Adobe Photoshop).
- Do not use the JPEG format for processing.
- Make adjustments in an orderly and logical sequence, starting with overall brightness, contrast, and color. Then make more local adjustments to correct problems or enhance the image.
- Save your adjusted file as a master copy to which you can then apply a crop, resizing, un-sharp mask, and any other finishing touches appropriate to your output requirements.

Archive

- Data can become lost or corrupted at any time for a variety of reasons so always make multiple back-up copies of your original files and the edited master copies.
- CDs have a limited capacity. Consider DVDs, or an external hard disk drive. No electronic storage media is guaranteed 100% safe, nor does it have an infinite lifespan, so always check your back-up copies regularly and repeat the back-up process as required.

Display

- We all shoot pictures for others to see and enjoy. Digital technology has expanded the possibilities of image display considerably; we can e-mail pictures to family, friends, colleagues, and clients, prepare digital "slideshows," or post images to a web site for pleasure or profit.
- Home printing in full color is now reliable, cost effective, and above all achievable. Spend some time to set up your system properly and work methodically; calibrate your monitor and printer, use an appropriate resolution for the print size you require, and choose paper type and finish accordingly.
- Once you have a high-quality print, ensure you present it in a manner befitting its status; frame it or mount it securely. This will also help to protect it from the effects of light and atmospheric pollutants.

Caring for Your D200

Obviously keeping your camera and accessory equipment in a clean, dry environment is very important. But regardless of how scrupulous you are about this, dust and dirt will eventually accumulate on or inside your equipment.

Since prevention is better than a cure, always keep the camera body and lens caps in place when you are not using the equipment. Always switch the D200 off before attaching or detaching a lens to prevent particles being attracted to the low-pass filter by the electrical charge of the sensor. Remember, gravity is your friend! When you change lenses, get in to the habit of holding the camera body with the lens mount facing down. For the same reason, do not carry or store your D200 on its back, as particles already inside the camera will settle on the low-pass filter. Periodically vacuum-clean the interior of your camera bag/case; it is amazing how much debris can collect there. Sealing you camera body in a clear plastic bag, which you then keep within your camera case will add another valuable layer of protection in very dusty or damp conditions. In the latter situation, keep some sachets of silica gel inside the bag to absorb any moisture.

Putting together a basic cleaning kit is straightforward. Consider the following:

- a 1/2-inch (12 mm) artist's paint brush with soft sable hair for general cleaning
- a micro-fiber lens cloth for cleaning lens elements
- a micro-fiber towel (available form any good outdoors store) for absorbing moisture when working in damp conditions (I find these towels invaluable in all sorts of conditions, and they are soft enough to use for cleaning lenses and filters)
- rubber bulb blower, either from a traditional blower brush, or a purpose made blower for use in cleaning lenses and the low-pass filter

Always brush or blow as much material off the equipment before wiping it with a cloth. For lens elements and filters, use a micro-fiber cloth and wipe surfaces in short strokes, not a sweeping circular motion. Turn the cloth frequently to prevent depositing the dirt you have just removed back on the same surface. For any residue that cannot be removed with a dry cloth, you will need to resort to a lens cleaning fluid suitable for photographic lenses. Apply the fluid, sparingly, to the cloth not directly to the lens, as it may seep inside and cause damage. Wipe the residue away and then buff the glass with a dry area of the cloth. Any lens cloth should be washed on a regular basis to keep it clean.

Caution: Clean the camera at your own risk. If you are unsure of whether to clean the camera yourself, or your camera needs extensive internal cleaning, take it to an authorized service center.

Cleaning the Low-Pass Filter

Dust and any other material that settles on the low-pass filter array in front of the CCD sensor will often appear as dark spots in your pictures, because they cast a shadow on the CCD sensor that is located behind the filter array. The exact nature of their appearance will depend on their size and the lens aperture you use. At very large apertures (f/1.4) it is likely that most very small dust specks will not be visible. However, at small apertures (f/22) they will probably show up as well defined black spots.

Nikon expressly recommends that you should have the low-pass filter cleaned by an authorized service center. However, recognizing that this is likely to be impractical for a variety of reasons, Nikon has provided the D200 with a facility to lock up the reflex mirror to access the low-pass filter array for cleaning.

Caution: Nikon states that under no circumstances should you touch or wipe the filter array.

To inspect and/or clean the low-pass filter, access the mirror lock-up feature via the 🔧 menu. Open the menu and scroll to *Mirror Lock-up*, then Multi Select right to display *Start – OK*. Multi Select right again. A dialog box will appear with the following instruction: *When shutter button is pressed, mirror lifts and shutter opens. To lower mirror, turn camera off.*

Once the shutter is pressed, the mirror will lift and remain in its raised position. The control panel display will show a series of dashes that flash, and all other information will disappear. Keep the camera facing down so any debris falls away from the filter. Look up into the lens mount to inspect the low-pass filter surface (it is probably helpful to shine a light on to it) but remember the photo-sites on the CCD of the D200 are just 5.9-microns square (one micron = one thousandth of a millimeter), so offending particles are often very, very small, and it is unlikely you will be able to resolve them by eye.

Note: If the battery level of the camera drops to 🔋 or below, or the camera is powered using 'AA' size batteries in the MS-D200 with the MB-D200 battery pack, you will not be able to access the *Mirror Lock-up* option in the 🔧 menu.

Note: If the mirror is locked up for cleaning and the battery power drains too low, the camera emits an audible warning and the AF-assist lamp will begin to flash, indicating that the mirror will be automatically lowered in approximately two minutes.

To clean the low-pass filter yourself, keep the camera facing down, and use a rubber bulb blower to gently 'puff' air towards the filter array surface. Take care that you do not enter any part of the blower into the camera. Never use an ordinary brush or compressed air canister to clean the filter array; they can easily leave a residue or damage its surface. Once you have finished cleaning, switch the camera OFF to return the mirror to its down-position. If the blower bulb method fails to remove any stubborn material, I recommend you have the sensor cleaned professionally.

For users with plenty of confidence, there are is range of proprietary sensor cleaning materials available from photographic suppliers (see the list of resources on pages 310-311) that can be used to clean the filter array. It must be stressed that you do this entirely at your own risk, and it is essential that the camera's battery be fully charged before you attempt any of these procedures (preferably, use the EH-6 mains AC adapter to ensure a continuous power supply). If the power supply fails during the cleaning process the shutter will close and the mirror will return to its down-position, with potentially dire consequences if you have any cleaning utensils in the camera!

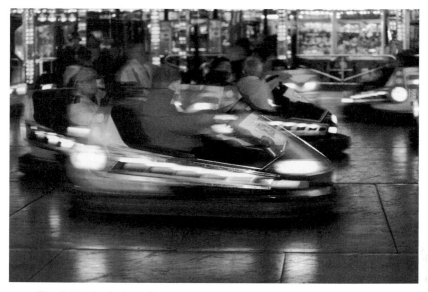

The D200 is designed to take great pictures in all sorts of shooting conditions, but you may occasionally need to refer to this book's troubleshooting guide if the camera is not operating as expected.

Finally, if you have Nikon Capture software, you can use the *Dust Off Ref* Photo feature with NEF (RAW) files to remove the effects of dust particles on the low-pass filter by masking their shadows electronically. This feature is reasonably effective, but since the dust particles can be dislodged and shift between shots, there is no guarantee that this technique will be successful if you save only one reference file during the course of a shoot.

Troubleshooting

On occasion, the D200 may not operate as you expect. This may be due to an alternative setting that has been made (often inadvertently), or for some other reason. Many of the reasons for these problems are common and the solutions are set out in the table below:

Problem	Solution
Camera takes longer than expected to power on	Delete files / folders
Viewfinder appears out of focus	• Adjust viewfinder focus • Use diopter adjustment lens
Viewfinder display is dark	• Battery not inserted • Battery exhausted
Displays turn off unexpectedly	Set longer delay for monitor off / meter off
Displays in LCD panels appear slow to react and are dimmed	Affect of high or low temperature
Fine lines appear in vicinity of active focus area on focusing screen	Normal – this is not a fault
Viewfinder display appears red	Normal – this is not a fault
Playback menu cannot be accessed	No memory card inserted
Image size cannot be altered	NEF (RAW) selected for image quality
Shutter release will not operate	• Aperture not set to minimum value • Memory card not installed or is full • Flash charging • Focus not acquired • bu L b selected in S exposure mode
Unable to select focus area	• Unlock focus area selector • Monitor is on; camera in Playback mode
AF-assist lamp does not light	• Camera in C focus mode • Center focus area or focus area group not selected • Closest priority is selected for group dynamic-area AF • *OFF* selected at Custom Setting a9
	• Lamp has shut down automatically to cool
Range of shutter speeds is limited	Flash in use – sync speed imposed

Problem	Solution
Focus does not lock when shutter release is depressed halfway	Camera in C focus mode: use AF-L/AE-L button
Final picture shows more than viewfinder	Viewfinder coverage is limited to approx. 95% of full frame area
Pictures out of focus	• Select S or C focus mode • AF unable to operate; use manual focus
Recording time is unusually long	Noise reduction in operation
Random bright pixels appear in image	• Use lower ISO setting • Use High ISO noise reduction
	• Shutter speed exceeds 8 seconds; use long exposure noise reduction
Dark spots / blotches appear in pictures	• Dirt on lens • Dirt on low-pass filter
Colors appear unnatural	• Inappropriate WB set • Adjust *Optimize Image* settings
C shooting modes unavailable	Close the built-in flash unit
Unable to obtain WB measurement in Preset WB	Illumination of test target too dark or too bright
Source image cannot be selected for setting WB	Image not created with D200
WB bracketing not available	NEF (RAW) or NEF (RAW) + JPEG selected for image quality
Results with Optimize Image vary from image to image	Avoid *Auto* for *Sharpening*, *Tone Compensation*, and *Saturation* options
Metering value cannot be altered	Auto-exposure lock is active
Exposure compensation cannot be used	Select P, A, or S exposure modes
Pictures shots in upright orientation (tall) displayed in horizontal (wide) orientation	• Select *ON* for *Rotate Tall* • *OFF* selected for *Auto Image Rotation* • Camera orientation was altered while shooting in continuous mode • Camera was pointed up/down when shooting

Problem	Solution
Unable to delete image	Image protection set; remove protection
Not all images displayed in Playback mode	Select *All* for *Playback Folder*
No images displayed in Playback mode	Select *All* for *Playback Folder*
Cannot change print order	Memory card is full; delete images
Unable to print direct from camera via USB connection	Set *USB* to *PTP*
Unable to select image for direct printing	Image saved as NEF (RAW) file
Unable to display image on TV	Select correct video mode
Unable to transfer images to computer	Select correct *USB* option
Unable to use Camera Control with Nikon Capture	Set *USB* to *PTP*
Date of recording image is incorrect	Set camera clock accordingly

Error Messages and Displays

The D200 is a sophisticated electronic device capable of reporting a range malfunctions and problems by way of indicators and error messages that appear in the displays of the viewfinder, control panel, and monitor screen. The following table will assist you in finding a solution should one of these indicators or messages be displayed.

Electro-Static Interference

Operation of the D200 is totally dependent on electrical power. Occasionally, the camera may stop functioning properly or display unusual characters or unexpected messages in the viewfinder and LCD displays. Such behavior is generally due to the effects of a strong external electro-static charge. If this occurs, try switching the camera off, disconnecting it from its power supply (remove the EN-EL3e battery, or unplug the EH-6 mains AC adapter), then reconnecting the power, and turning the camera on again. If the symptoms persist, the camera will require inspection by an authorized technician.

Indicator		Problem	Solution
Control panel	**View-finder**		
FEE (blinks)		Lens aperture ring is not locked at minimum aperture.	Lock ring at minimum aperture (largest f/-number).
◁▬◢	◁▬◢	Low battery.	Ready fully-charged spare battery.
◁▬◢ (blinks)	◁▬◢ (blinks)	• Battery exhausted. • Battery information not available.	• Recharge or exchange with fully-charged spare battery. • Battery can not be used in camera.
CLOCK (blinks)		Camera clock is not set.	Set camera clock.
⊿F		No lens attached, or non-CPU lens attached without specifying maximum aperture. Aperture shown in stops from maximum aperture.	Aperture value will be displayed if maximum aperture is specified.
	● (blinks)	Camera unable to focus using autofocus.	Focus manually.

H i		Subject too bright; photo will be overexposed.	• Choose lower sensitivity.
			• Use optional Neutral Density (ND) filter
			• In exposure mode:
			  S Increase shutter speed
			  A Choose smaller aperture (larger f/-number)

Lo		Subject too dark; photo will be underexposed.	• Choose a higher sensitivity (ISO equivalency)
			• Use optional Speedlight
			• In exposure mode:
			  S Lower shutter speed
			  A Choose a larger aperture (smaller f/-number)

bulb (blinks)		bulb selected in mode **M** and mode dial rotated to **S**.	Change shutter speed or select mode **M**.
⚡ (blinks)	⚡ (blinks)	Speedlight that does not support i-TTL flash control attached and set to TTL.	Change flash mode setting on optional Speedlight.
📷 / 0 (blinks)	ⵑd (blinks)	Memory insufficient to record further photos at current settings, or camera has run out of file or folder numbers.	• Reduce quality or size. • Delete photographs. • Insert new memory card.
(-E-)	📷 (blinks) (-E-)	No memory card.	Insert memory card.
Err (blinks)		Camera malfunction.	Release shutter. If error persists or appears frequently, consult with Nikon-authorized service representative.

Indicator				
Monitor	Control panel	View-finder	Problem	Solution
NO CARD PRESENT	(- E -)	🔲 (blinks) (- E -)	Camera cannot detect memory card.	Turn camera off and confirm that card is correctly inserted.
THIS CARD CAN NOT BE USED	(C H R) (blinks)		• Error accessing memory card. • Unable to create new folder.	• Use Nikon-approved card. • Check that contacts are clean. If card is damaged, contact retailer or Nikon representative. • Delete files or insert new memory card.
CARD IS NOT FORMATTED (displayed when 🔘 button is pressed)	(F o r) (blinks)		Memory card has not been formatted for use in D200.	Format memory card.
FOLDER CONTAINS NO IMAGES			• Memory card contains no images. • Current folder is empty.	• Insert another card. • Set **Playback Folder** to **All**.
ALL IMAGES HIDDEN			All photos in current folder are hidden.	Set **Playback Folder** to **All** or use **Hide Image** to reveal hidden photos.
FILE DOES NOT CONTAIN IMAGE DATA			File has been created or modified using a computer or different make of camera, or file is corrupt.	Delete file or reformat memory card.

Using a Global Positioning System (GPS) Device

It is possible to use the D200 camera in conjunction with a Global Positioning System (GPS) device to record additional data about the camera's location with each image file at the time of exposure. Nikon has confirmed that the camera is compatible with GPS devices from the Garmin eTrex and Magellan SporTrak series (it is possible that the D200 will support other makes/types of GPS devices).

To work with the D200, a GPS device must conform to version 2.01, or later, of the National Marine Electronics Association NMEA0183 protocol. It is connected to the camera's ten-pin remote terminal using the Nikon MC-35 cord, which is available as an extra accessory.

As soon as the camera confirms communication with a connected GPS device, **GPS** will be displayed in the control panel. The information recorded when an exposure is made with **GPS** displayed includes current latitude, longitude, altitude, and time using the Universal Time Co-ordinated (UTC) standard. The time provided by the GPS device and recorded by the camera is independent of the camera's internal clock.

Note: The camera's exposure meter will not turn off automatically while a GPS device is connected and active (i.e. **GPS** is displayed in the control panel).

Note: If no data is received from the GPS device for two seconds, the camera will cease to record GPS information and **GPS** will disappear from the control panel display. If **GPS** blinks, the GPS device is searching for a signal. The camera cannot record GPS information while it is in this state.

Web Support

Nikon maintains product support, and provides further information on-line at the following sites:

http://www.nikon.com/ – global gateway to Nikon Corporation

http://www.nikonusa.com/ – for continental North America

http://www..europe-nikon.com/support – for most European countries

http://www.nikon-asia.com/ – for Asia, Oceania, Middle East, and Africa

Resources

A number of other manufacturers and suppliers provide equipment to compliment and enhance the performance of the cameras and flash accessories produced by Nikon. The following is a list of some of them:

Gitzo – Manufacturers of tripods, monopods, and general camera support accessories.

http://www.gitzo.com/

Kirk Enterprises – Manufacturers of camera and flash accessories, including flash brackets.

http://www.kirkphoto.com/

Lastolite – Manufacturers of lighting accessories for portable flash units, and a wide range of reflectors, diffusers and other light modifying devices.

http://www.lastolite.com/

Lee Filters – Manufacturers of both lens and lighting filters, including graduated filter types.

http://www.leefilters.com/

Lexar Media – Manufacturers of flash memory cards, including CompactFlash cards compatible with the D200.

http://www.lexar.com/

Manfrotto – Manufacturers of tripods, lighting stands and flash support accessories.

http://www.manfrotto.com

Really Right Stuff – Manufacturers of an extensive range of camera, flash, close-up, and panoramic photography accessories.

http://www.reallyrightstuff.com/

SanDisk – Manufacturers of flash memory cards, including CompactFlash cards compatible with the D200.

http://www.sandisk.com/

Singh-Ray – Manufacturers of camera lens filters, including graduated filter types.

http://www.singh-ray.com/

Glossary

angle of view
The area seen by a lens, usually measured in degrees across the diagonal of the film frame.

aperture
The opening in the lens that allows light to enter the camera. Aperture is usually described as an f/number. The higher the f/number, the smaller the aperture; the lower the f/number, the larger the aperture.

Aperture-Priority mode (A)
A type of automatic exposure in which you manually select the aperture and the camera automatically selects the shutter speed.

artifact
Information that is not part of the scene but appears in the image due to technology. Artifacts can occur in film or digital images and include increased grain, flare, static marks, color flaws, etc.

automatic exposure (AE)
When the camera measures light and makes the adjustments necessary to create proper image density on sensitized medium.

automatic focus (AF)
When the camera automatically adjusts the lens elements to sharply render the subject.

available light
The amount of illumination at a given location that applies to natural and artificial light sources but not those supplied specifically for photography. It is also called existing light or ambient light.

backlight
Light that projects toward the camera from behind the subject.

backup
A copy of a file or program made to ensure that, if the original is lost or damaged, the necessary information is still intact.

bit
Binary digit. This is the basic unit of binary computation. See also, byte.

bit depth
The number of bits per pixel that determines the number of colors the image can display. Eight bits per pixel is the minimum requirement for a photo-quality color image.

buffer
Temporarily stores data so that other programs, on the camera or the computer, can continue to run while data is in transition.

bulb
A camera setting that allows the shutter to stay open as long as the shutter release is depressed.

byte
A single group of eight bits that is processed as one unit. See also, bit.

card reader
Device that connects to your computer and enables quick and easy download of images from memory card to computer.

CCD
Charge Coupled Device. This is a digital camera sensor that is sensitized by applying an electrical charge to the sensor prior to its exposure to light. It converts light energy into an electrical pulse.

CLS
Creative Lighting System. This is a flash control system that Nikon introduced with its SB-800 and SB-600 Speedlights, See also, Speedlight.

color space
A mapped relationship between colors and computer data about the colors.

compression
Method of reducing file size through removal of redundant data, as with the JPEG file format.

CPU
Central Processing Unit. This is the "brains" of a computer or a lens that perform principle computational functions.

critical focus
The most sharply focused plane within an image.

depth of field
The image space in front of and behind the plane of focus that appears acceptable sharp in the photograph.

diopter
A measurement of the refractive power of a lens. Also, it may be a supplementary lens that is defined by its focal length and power of magnification.

dpi
Dots per inch. Used to define the resolution of a printer, this term refers to the number of dots of ink that a printer can lay down in an inch.

DPOF
Digital Print Order Format. A feature that enables the camera to supply data about the printing order of image files and the supplementary data contained within them. This feature can only be used in conjunction with a DPOF compatible printer.

electronic flash
A device with a glass or plastic tube filled with gas that, when electrified, creates an intense flash of light. Also called a strobe. Unlike a flash bulb, it is reusable.

EV
Exposure Value. A number that quantifies the amount of light within a scene, allowing you to determine the relative combinations of aperture and shutter speed to accurately reproduce the light levels of that exposure.

EXIF
Exchangeable Image File Format. This format is used for storing an image file's interchange information.

exposure
When light enters the camera and reacts with the sensitized medium. The term can also refer to the amount of light that strikes the light sensitive medium.

FAT
File Allocation Table. This is a method used be computer operating systems to keep track of files stored on the hard drive.

file format
The form in which digital images are stored and recorded, e.g., JPEG, RAW, TIFF, etc.

fill-flash
The technique to help reduce the overall contrast in a scene, or subject by mixing light from a flash unit to the main continuous ambient light source.

FireWire
A high speed data transfer standard that allows outlying accessories to be plugged and unplugged from the computer while it is turned on. Some digital cameras and card readers use FireWire to connect to the computer. FireWire transfers data faster than USB. See also, Mbps.

firmware
Software that is permanently incorporated into a hardware chip. All computer-based equipment, including digital cameras, use firmware of some kind.

focal length
When the lens is focused on infinity, it is the distance from the optical center of the lens to the focal plane.

focal plane
The plane on which a lens forms a sharp image. Also, it may be the film plane or sensor plane.

focus
An optimum sharpness or image clarity that occurs when a lens creates a sharp image by converging light rays to specific points at the focal plane. The word also refers to the act of adjusting the lens to achieve optimal image sharpness.

FP high-speed sync
Focal Plane high-speed sync. Some digital cameras emulate high shutter speeds be switching the camera sensor on and off rather than moving the shutter blades or curtains that cover it. This allows flash units to be synchronized at shutter speeds higher than the standard sync speed. In this flash mode, the level of flash output is reduced and, consequently, the shooting range is reduced.

f/stop
The size of the aperture or diaphragm opening of a lens, also referred to as f/number or stop. The term stands for the ratio of the focal length (f) of the lens to the width of its aperture opening. (f/1.4 = wide opening and f/22 = narrow opening.) Each stop up (lower f/number) doubles the amount of light reaching the sensitized medium. Each stop down (higher f/number) halves the amount of light reaching the sensitized medium.

FV (Flash Value) Lock
A feature for Nikon cameras compatible with the CLS that allows the user to lock a particular flash output value even if the aperture, composition, or focal length is altered.

gigabyte (GB)
Just over one billion bytes.

gray card
A card used to take accurate exposure readings. It typically has a white side that reflects 90% of the light and a gray side that reflects 18%.

grayscale
A successive series of tones ranging between black and white, which have no color.

Guide Number (GN)
A number used to quantify the output of a flash unit. It is derived by using this formula: GN = aperture x distance. Guide numbers are expressed for a given ISO film speed in either feet or meters.

hard drive
A contained storage unit made up of magnetically sensitive disks.

histogram
A graphic representation of image tones.

hot shoe
An electronically connected flash mount on the camera body. It enables direct communication between the camera and an external flash, and synchronizes the shutter release with the firing of the flash.

image-processing program
Software that allows for image alteration and enhancement.

infinity ∞
In photographic terms, the theoretical most distant point of focus.

interpolation
Process used to increase image resolution by creating new pixels based on existing pixels. The software intelligently looks at existing pixels and creates new pixels to fill the gaps and achieve a higher resolution.

Inverse Square Law
In terms of the output from a Speedlight it defines the amount of light fall-off, and is equal to the reciprocal of the square of the distance between the flash and the subject.

IS
Image Stabilization. This is a technology that reduces camera shake and vibration. It is used in lenses, binoculars, camcorders, etc.

i-TTL
A Nikon TTL flash control system that has a refined monitor pre-flash sequence and offers improved flash exposure control. See also, TTL.

JPEG
Joint Photographic Experts Group. This is a lossy compression file format that works with any computer and photo software. JPEG examines an image for redundant information and then removes it. It is a variable compression format because the amount of left-over data depends on the detail in the photo and the amount of compression. At low compression/high quality, the loss of data has a negligible effect on the photo. However, JPEG should not be used as a working format – the file should be reopened and saved in a format such as TIFF, which does not compress the image.

LCD
Liquid Crystal Display, which is a flat screen with two clear polarizing sheets on either side of a liquid crystal solution. When activated by an electric current, the LCD causes the crystals to either pass through or block light in order to create a colored image display.

lossless
Image compression in which no data is lost.

lossy
Image compression in which data is lost and, thereby, image quality is lessened. This means that the greater the compression, the lesser the image quality.

low-pass filter
A filter designed to remove elements of an image that correspond to high-frequency data, such as sharp edges and fine detail, to reduce the effect of moiré. See also, moiré.

macro lens
A lens designed to be at top sharpness over a flat field when focused at close distances and reproduction ratios up to 1:1.

Manual Exposure mode (M)
A camera operating mode that requires the user to determine and set both the aperture and shutter speed. This is the opposite of automatic exposure.

Mbps
Megabits per second. This unit is used to describe the rate of data transfer. See also, megabit.

megabit
One million bits of data. See also, bit.

megabyte (MB)
Just over one million bytes.

megapixel
A million pixels.

memory card
A solid state removable storage medium used in digital devices. They can store still images, moving images, or sound, as well as related file data. There are several different types, including CompactFlash, SmartMedia, and xD, or Sony's proprietary Memory Stick, to name a few. Individual card capacity is limited by available storage as well as by the size of the recorded data (determined by factors such as image resolution and file format). See also, CompactFlash (CF) card, file format.

microdrive
A removable storage medium with moving parts. They are miniature hard drives based on the dimensions of a CompactFlash Type II card. Microdrives are more susceptible to the effects of impact, high altitude, and low temperature than solid-state cards are. See also, memory card.

middle gray
Halfway between black and white, it is an average gray tone with 18% reflectance. See also, gray card.

midtone
The tone that appears as medium brightness, or medium gray tone, in a photographic print.

MOSFET
Metal Oxide Semiconductor Field Effect Transistor, which is used as an amplifier in digital cameras.

NEF
Nikon Electronic File. This is Nikon's proprietary RAW file format, used by Nikon digital cameras. In order to process and view NEF files in your computer, you will need Nikon View (version 6.1 or newer) and Nikon Capture (version 4.1 or newer).

noise
The digital equivalent of grain. It is often caused by a number of different factors, such as a high ISO setting, heat, sensor design, etc. Though usually undesirable, it may be added for creative effect using an image-processing program.

operating system (OS)
The system software that provides the environment within which all other software operates.

overexposed
When too much light is recorded with the image, causing the photo to be too light in tone.

pan
Moving the camera to follow a moving subject. When a slow shutter speed is used, this creates an image in which the subject appears sharp and the background is blurred.

perspective
The effect of the distance between the camera and image elements upon the perceived size of objects in an image. It is also an expression of this three-dimensional relationship in two dimensions.

pixel
Derived fro picture element. A pixel is the base component of a digital image. Every individual pixel can have a distinct color and tone.

Program mode (P)
In Program exposure mode, the camera selects a combination of shutter speed and aperture automatically.

RAM
Stands for Random Access Memory, which is a computer's memory capacity, directly accessible from the central processing unit.

RAW
An image file format that has little or no internal processing applied by the camera. It contains 12-bit color information, a wider range of data than 8-bit formats such as JPEG.

RAW+JPEG
An image file format that records two files per capture; one RAW file and one JPEG file.

Rear-curtain sync
A feature that causes the flash unit to fire just prior to the shutter closing. It is used for creative effect when mixing flash and ambient light.

resolution
The amount of data available for an image as applied to image size. It is expressed in pixels or megapixels, or sometimes as lines per inch on a monitor or dots per inch on a printed image.

RGB mode
Red, Green, and Blue. This is the color model most commonly used to display color images on video systems, film recorders, and computer monitors. It displays all visible colors as combinations of red, green, and blue. RGB mode is the most common color mode for viewing and working with digital files onscreen.

saturation
The intensity or richness of a hue or color.

shutter
The apparatus that controls the amount of time during which light is allowed to reach the sensitized medium.

Shutter-Priority mode (S)
An automatic exposure mode in which you manually select the shutter speed and the camera automatically selects the aperture.

slow sync
A flash mode in which a slow shutter speed is used in order to allow low-level ambient light to be recorded be the sensitized medium.

SLR
Single-lens reflex. A camera with a mirror that reflects the image entering the lens through a pentaprism or pentamirror onto the viewfinder screen. When you take the picture, the mirror reflexes out of the way, the focal plane shutter opens, and the image is recorded.

stop down
To reduce the size of the diaphragm opening by using a higher f/number.

stop up
To increase the size of the diaphragm opening by using a lower f/number.

synchronize
Causing a flash unit to fire simultaneously with the complete opening of the camera's shutter.

thumbnail
A miniaturized representation of an image file.

TIFF
Tagged Image File Format. This popular digital format uses lossless compression.

TTL
Through-the-Lens, i.e. TTL metering.

USB
Universal Serial Bus. This interface standard allows outlying accessories to be plugged and unplugged from the computer while it is turned on. USB 2.0 enables high-speed data transfer.

viewfinder screen
The ground glass surface on which you view your image.

VR
Vibration Reduction. This technology is used in such photographic accessories as a VR lens.

wide-angle lens
A lens that produces a greater angle of view than you would see with your eyes, often causing the image to appear stretched. See also, short lens.

Wi-Fi
Wireless Fidelity, a technology that allows for wireless networking between one Wi-Fi compatible product and another.

Wireless Lighting System
A communication method used to control remote Speedlights by sending signals in the form of light pulses from a master flash, or commander unit.

zoom lens
A lens that can be adjusted to cover a wide range of focal lengths.

Index